MASTERING
THE
TRADER
WITHIN

Mastering The Trader Within: A Mindset For Success

Published by Gatekeeper Press
7853 Gunn Hwy., Suite 209
Tampa, FL 33626
www.GatekeeperPress.com

Library of Congress Control Number: 2025937051

ISBN (hardcover): 9781662963896
ISBN (paperback): 9781662963902
eISBN: 9781662963919

MASTERING THE TRADER WITHIN

A MINDSET FOR SUCCESS

ANMOL SINGH

gatekeeper press™

Tampa, Florida

CONTENTS

———◆———

PREFACE   vii

INTRODUCTION   ix

1. YOUR BRAIN CHEMISTRY   1

2. THE FOUNDATION OF TRADING PSYCHOLOGY   5

3. UNDERSTANDING EMOTIONS IN TRADING   15

4. DEVELOPING A PROFESSIONAL TRADER'S MINDSET   27

5. PRACTICAL TECHNIQUES FOR MASTERING
   TRADING PSYCHOLOGY   38

6. OVERCOMING COMMON PSYCHOLOGICAL PITFALLS   57

7. CREATING YOUR PERSONAL TRADING PLAN   68

8. MOVING FORWARD: BECOMING A MASTER TRADER   81

9. ADVANCED TRADING PSYCHOLOGY CONCEPTS   106

10. BUILDING A SUPPORT SYSTEM FOR TRADERS   126

11. THE INTERSECTION OF PHYSICAL HEALTH AND
    TRADING PSYCHOLOGY   140

12. MARKET VOLATILITY AND UNCERTAINITY   153

13. SUSTAINING LONG-TERM PERFORMANCE AND LIFELONG LEARNING.   168

14. THE POWER OF TRADING AS A CAREER   180

15. BUILDING SUCCESSFUL TRADING HABITS   192

CONCLUSION   206

ABOUT THE AUTHOR   210

PRACTICAL EXERCISES & ACTION ITEMS   212

APPENDIX I: LEARNING TO BREATHE   237

PREFACE

My path to becoming a profitable trader spanned several rough years, filled with account drawdowns and emotional turmoil. You might recognize these moments - staring at screens for hours, questioning every trade, and feeling the crushing weight of losses. The technical analysis seemed straightforward enough. The candlestick patterns, support and resistance levels, and trend lines all made perfect sense on paper. Yet something kept sabotaging my results.

Trading had consumed my life during those early days. I spent countless hours studying charts, reading books, and attending seminars. My family worried as they watched me pour more money and time into what seemed a lost cause. The breaking point came after a particularly devastating loss when I risked far too much on a single trade. That trade went against me, wiping out months of careful gains in mere minutes. The pain of that moment remains vivid years later.

The real transformation began when I shifted focus from obsessing over technical indicators to examining my own psychology. A mentor helped me see how my impatience and need for constant action pushed me into poor trades. My fear of missing opportunities led to overtrading, while my ego prevented me from admitting mistakes quickly. These realizations changed everything. By working on my mental game first, the technical aspects fell into place naturally.

Each small improvement in my mindset showed up in my trading results. Learning to sit patiently and wait for ideal setups, rather than forcing trades out of boredom. Accepting losses as a normal part of the business, instead of emotional failures. Treating trading as a probability game where individual outcomes matter less than following my proven process. These mental shifts compounded over time into consistent profitability.

Today, after coaching hundreds of traders, these same patterns emerge repeatedly: talented traders who understand markets but sabotage themselves through poor psychology. My own prior struggles help me connect with their challenges. I know the frustration of having knowledge but still making emotional mistakes. This shared experience drives my passion for helping others master the mental side of trading.

INTRODUCTION

The methods and insights in this book come from both personal experience and years of observing which psychological techniques actually work in real trading. You'll find practical strategies for managing fear, overcoming analysis paralysis, and maintaining discipline through market volatility. More importantly, you'll develop awareness of your own mental patterns and learn tools to rewire them for success.

My goal extends beyond just sharing information - I want to guide you through the same transformation that revolutionized my own trading. The journey requires honesty, patience and commitment to change. But the results - consistent profitability and emotional peace - make it worthwhile. Your technical skills combined with rock-solid psychology will create an unstoppable combination in the markets.

Consider this book your roadmap for developing the mindset of a successful trader, without all the chaos that overthinking and emotional interference can sometimes bring. Each chapter builds on core psychological principles while providing actionable techniques you can implement immediately. You may see yourself in some of the case studies of both struggles and breakthroughs, and you'll gain perspective on your own trading journey. Most importantly, you'll develop the mental tools needed for long-term success in the markets.

Your presence here shows you recognize the importance of trading psychology. That awareness already puts you ahead of many traders who focus solely on technical analysis. The material we'll cover together will help you align your mindset—the way you think about making trades—with your market knowledge. When those elements work in harmony, consistent profitability becomes natural rather than forced.

The trading psychology breakthroughs that turned my career around remain just as relevant today. Markets change, but human nature stays remarkably consistent. By mastering your mental game, you gain an edge that transcends any particular strategy or market condition. Let's explore the psychological principles and practical techniques that can transform your trading results.

What You'll Learn

Each chapter builds upon practical experiences from successful traders. The opening chapters establish fundamental psychological principles through actual trading scenarios. You'll see how emotions impact decision-making and learn specific techniques to maintain objectivity under pressure.

The middle sections provide hands-on tools for psychological improvement. Daily mindfulness practices, specific journaling prompts, and concrete decision-making frameworks help you develop robust trading habits. These tools come directly from trading floor experiences and have helped hundreds of traders improve their results.

Advanced chapters tackle sophisticated psychological challenges. Through detailed case studies, you'll examine how successful traders handle complex scenarios. From managing large positions to dealing with drawdowns, each study provides actionable insights for your own trading.

Maria struggled with revenge trading after losses. The techniques in Chapter 5 helped her develop a "reset routine" - a specific set of steps to regain emotional balance before placing new trades. Her win rate improved by 25% after implementing this routine.

Physical wellbeing impacts trading performance significantly. The final chapters explore practical ways to optimize your physical state for better trading decisions. Simple adjustments to sleep, exercise, and nutrition can dramatically improve your mental clarity during market hours.

The book includes specific exercises after each concept. You'll find journaling prompts, reflection questions, and practical drills to reinforce key ideas. These exercises come from real trading experiences and provide measurable ways to track your psychological development.

Every concept connects to actual market scenarios. Rather than abstract theories, you'll work with concrete examples from live trading. This practical approach helps you apply psychological principles directly to your trading decisions.

The included trading plan template integrates both technical and psychological elements. You'll develop specific rules for managing emotions during trades, along with clear guidelines for maintaining discipline under pressure. This comprehensive approach sets you up for consistent execution.

Support proves crucial for lasting improvement. The later chapters show you how to build effective support networks while maintaining decisional independence. You'll learn specific ways to leverage relationships with other traders while developing your own style.

Through dedicated practice of these principles, you'll develop the psychological resilience needed for consistent profitability. The book provides clear metrics to track your progress and specific milestones to guide your development as a trader.

CHAPTER 1

YOUR BRAIN CHEMISTRY

———◆———

Your trading screen shows a perfect setup. The indicators align, and your analysis suggests a profitable trade. Yet you hesitate. Minutes pass, and the opportunity slips away. Hours later, you watch as the market moves exactly as you predicted, leaving you with regret instead of profits.

Sam, a trader from Chicago, faced this scenario daily. His technical analysis proved correct 70% of the time, but his account balance told a different story. The problem? His psychology sabotaged his execution.

Michael, another trader, consistently cut his profits short while letting losses run.

Sarah, a brilliant technical trader, lost her entire account in a week during volatile market conditions. Her strategy remained solid - but fear and panic led her to abandon her proven system at precisely the wrong moment. The markets revealed a gap between her technical knowledge and emotional control.

Market psychology drives every price movement. The same psychological forces - fear, greed, uncertainty - affect your individual trading decisions.

Emotions shape every decision in the markets. Through my years training traders, I've watched countless skilled analysts fail because their emotions hijacked their judgment.

The brain processes financial gains and losses in the same region that handles physical threats. When a trade moves against you, your body responds with the same stress chemicals as if facing actual danger. Your heart rate increases, muscles tense, and rational thinking decreases. Mike, an experienced day trader, discovered this when tracking his physiological responses during trading. His blood pressure spiked significantly during drawdowns, affecting his ability to follow his trading rules.

Greed operates through your brain's reward pathways, releasing dopamine that creates a euphoric high during winning streaks. This chemical rush can override logical analysis. —After several profitable months, you may feel unstoppable, ignoring risk management as you increase your position sizes dramatically. The inevitable market reversal, however, can wipe out gains and more. This is what happens when the brain's reward system overrides trading discipline.

Your mind follows predictable patterns in processing market information.

- **Confirmation bias** leads you to notice data supporting your existing views while filtering out contradictory signals.

- **Loss aversion** makes the pain of losses feel twice as intense as the pleasure of equivalent gains.

Understanding these cognitive biases helps explain why smart traders make seemingly irrational decisions under pressure.

The stress of trading triggers measurable changes in brain chemistry and function. Extended periods of high stress impair memory, decrease impulse control, and reduce analytical capabilities - the exact mental skills traders need most. Regular breaks, proper sleep, and stress management techniques become crucial tools for maintaining peak mental performance in the markets.

Trading success requires rewiring deeply ingrained mental patterns. Your brain adapts and creates new neural pathways through consistent practice and repetition. For impulsive traders, practicing mindfulness meditation and following strict trading rules will, over time, literally restructure your brain, making disciplined trading your default response rather than an ongoing struggle.

Market movements trigger powerful emotional responses, but you can learn to process these feelings without acting on them. Develop a system of logging your emotional state before each trade. By tracking patterns between your feelings and trading results, you can identify specific emotional triggers that predict poor decision-making. This awareness will allow you to step back when those triggers appear.

The most successful traders maintain consistent performance by managing their mental state. They understand that emotional control matters more than market analysis. Track your sleep quality, exercise, and stress levels alongside your trading metrics, and adjust your trading size based on your mental readiness, recognizing that psychology drives results more than strategy.

Your trading results reflect your psychological development more than your technical skills. Your trading strategy can stay exactly the same, but your results will dramatically improve after addressing underlying emotional patterns. Often, childhood money beliefs affect trading decisions. Resolving these issues will lead to more objective market analysis.

Market mastery comes through psychological growth and development. Every trader faces internal battles between emotion and logic, impulse and discipline. By understanding the brain science behind trading psychology, you can develop practical tools for managing your mental state. This psychological edge often determines who succeeds and who struggles in the markets.

CHAPTER 2

THE FOUNDATION OF TRADING PSYCHOLOGY

Trading as a Mirror of Our Mindset

Your trading results reveal much more than market knowledge - they expose your core beliefs, emotions, and habits. When you place a trade, your deepest thoughts and feelings surface through your actions. The charts tell one story, while your response to market movements tells another.

A trader with solid market analysis may repeatedly exit profitable trades early due to past experiences of losing money. Another trader might hold losing positions too long because they struggle to accept small setbacks. These behaviors stem from their mindset rather than market conditions.

Trading amplifies your existing traits and tendencies. If you feel anxious about financial decisions, that anxiety will appear in hesitant entries and premature exits. When you crave validation, you might overtrade to prove yourself. The market becomes a reflection, showing you exactly who you are under pressure.

Professional traders understand this dynamic. They monitor their emotional state as carefully as they watch price action. By paying attention to their responses during trades, they gain valuable insights into their decision-making process. This awareness allows them to adjust their approach and maintain consistency.

Your trading results provide feedback about your psychological readiness. Consistent profits often indicate emotional stability and disciplined execution. Erratic performance points to underlying mental challenges that need attention. The numbers tell the truth about your current mindset.

The path to trading success requires both technical skills and psychological development. When you view difficult market periods as opportunities to strengthen your mindset, you accelerate your growth. Each trading session gives you a chance to observe yourself and make productive changes.

Many traders focus exclusively on market analysis while ignoring the psychological aspects of trading. They study charts endlessly but pay minimal attention to their emotional responses. This imbalanced approach limits their progress and prevents sustainable success.

Your trading decisions emerge from the interaction between market conditions and your psychological state. During volatile periods, an unstable mindset leads to impulsive actions and preventable losses. A balanced psychology allows you to execute your strategy regardless of market behavior.

The most valuable insights often come from examining your trades through a psychological lens. When you review your trading journal, look beyond the technical aspects. Notice the emotional factors that influenced your decisions and the resulting gain or loss. This deeper analysis reveals areas for improvement.

Every market movement presents a chance to practice emotional regulation and disciplined execution. Rather than reacting automatically to price changes, pause to observe your initial response. This brief moment of awareness helps you make conscious, mindful trading decisions aligned with your strategy.

Building a strong trading mindset requires dedication and consistent effort. Pay attention to how your psychology affects your trading results. Use this feedback to develop greater self-awareness and emotional stability. With time and practice, your trading will reflect a mature, disciplined approach to the markets.

Early Struggles and Lessons Learned

My first year of trading taught me more about myself than any other experience in my life. Each morning, I sat at my desk armed with technical analysis books, chart patterns, and trading strategies. The markets opened, and despite all my preparation, my emotions took control. My hands shook as I placed trades, and my heart raced with every price movement.

One trade stands out vividly in my memory. I had analyzed a stock for hours, identified the perfect entry point, and executed the trade according to my plan. The position moved in my favor, showing a modest profit. Instead of sticking to my target, anxiety crept in. Thoughts of previous losses flooded my mind. I clicked the sell button, taking a small gain.

Minutes later, the stock soared to my original target price - and beyond. That single moment revealed a crucial truth: my technical knowledge meant little without emotional control. I had all the right tools but lacked the psychological foundation to use them effectively. This pattern repeated itself countless times in different forms.

On other occasions, I held onto losing trades far too long. The stock would move against my position, but I refused to accept the small loss. Pride and stubbornness kept me in the trade. I made excuses, telling myself the market would turn around. These emotional decisions cost me dearly, both financially and mentally.

The turning point came when I shifted my focus from acquiring more technical knowledge to understanding my psychological responses. I started keeping a detailed journal of my emotional states during trades. Patterns emerged. Fear dominated my profitable trades, while pride controlled my losing positions. This awareness became the foundation for real improvement.

Through this process, I discovered that successful trading requires a balance of technical skill and emotional control. The best strategy proves useless when emotions override your decision-making. Market analysis helps you find opportunities, but psychology determines how well you execute your plans and manage your positions.

My early struggles revealed that trading magnifies your existing emotional patterns. If you struggle with patience in daily life, the markets will expose this trait. If you have difficulty admitting mistakes, holding onto losing trades becomes a costly habit. These realizations shifted my entire approach to trading education.

The transformation in my trading results came from accepting and working with my emotions rather than fighting them. I developed specific protocols for different emotional states. When I felt fear rising, I reviewed my original analysis. If pride prevented me from exiting losing trades, I implemented strict stop-loss orders that executed automatically.

Personal development became as important as market analysis in my daily routine. Meditation helped me stay centered during market volatility. Regular exercise reduced stress and improved decision-making. These practices strengthened my psychological foundation and enhanced my trading performance.

Looking back at those early experiences, every mistake provided valuable insights about myself and the markets. Technical analysis gave me the tools to identify opportunities, but understanding and managing my emotions enabled me to capitalize on them. This combination of knowledge and psychological awareness made consistent profitability possible.

My journey from struggling trader to consistent performer emphasized that success requires more than information - it demands transformation. Each trading session tests your emotional discipline and psychological preparation. When you embrace these challenges as opportunities for growth, both your trading and personal development accelerate.

Comparing Two Traders: James vs. Delia

James and Delia both trade the same market with identical strategies. They use the same indicators, follow the same rules, and receive the same market alerts. Yet their trading results tell completely different stories. The distinction between them lies purely in their psychological approach to the markets.

James maintains unwavering focus during market hours. When his strategy signals a buy, he executes without hesitation. His position sizing stays consistent regardless of previous trades. During drawdowns, he follows his stop-loss rules precisely. His calm demeanor allows him to stick to his trading plan through both winning and losing streaks.

Watching Delia trade reveals a stark contrast. She second-guesses every signal from her system. After a losing trade, she reduces her position size drastically. When she sees a profit, she exits early, afraid of giving back gains. Her trading decisions stem from emotional reactions rather than systematic execution of her strategy.

The morning routine of each trader sets the tone for their day. James reviews his trading plan, checks his emotional state, and prepares his watchlist methodically. He treats each trading day as an opportunity to execute his strategy. His preparation focuses on maintaining his disciplined approach rather than predicting market moves.

Delia rushes into each trading session, eager to make up for previous losses or catch the next big move. She scrolls through social media for trading ideas, changing her approach based on other traders' opinions. Her emotional state fluctuates with each market tick, leading to impulsive decisions and frequent strategy changes.

During a sharp market decline, the difference between their approaches becomes evident. James follows his risk management rules, taking small losses where necessary. He understands market volatility as a regular occurrence. His equity curve shows steady progress despite temporary setbacks.

Delia panics during the same market decline. She overrides her stop-losses, hoping prices will recover. When they fall further, she doubles her position, attempting to average down. These emotional decisions lead to larger losses and increased stress, affecting her judgment in subsequent trades.

The monthly results reflect their contrasting approaches. James maintains consistent returns through disciplined execution. His winning percentage stays stable, and his risk management prevents large drawdowns. His systematic approach produces reliable results over time.

Delia's performance chart shows wild swings. Some months yield exceptional returns when her emotional trades work in her favor. Other months show devastating losses when her lack of discipline leads to poor decisions. The inconsistency makes it impossible to build sustainable trading capital.

Through market ups and downs, James demonstrates the power of psychological stability. His success comes from executing a proven strategy with emotional control. He understands that consistent profits require consistent behavior, regardless of market conditions.

The contrast between James and Delia proves that trading success depends more on psychological factors than technical analysis. While both traders possess the same technical tools and knowledge, their mindsets determine their results. James's disciplined approach creates sustainable success, while Delia's emotional trading leads to inconsistent performance.

Technical vs. Mental Game

Your trading performance depends on two equally important factors: technical knowledge and psychological readiness. In equal measure, they will affect your results, whether negative or positive.

Many traders spend countless hours perfecting their technical analysis while overlooking the mental aspects of trading. The most sophisticated trading strategy becomes ineffective when emotions interfere with its execution.

Market analysis provides the foundation for trading decisions. Charts, indicators, and price patterns help identify potential opportunities. Yet these tools require clear thinking and emotional balance to be used effectively. During market volatility, your ability to maintain composure determines whether you follow your strategy or abandon it under pressure, and your results will reflect how you handle every trade.

Take a moment to examine your own trading behavior. Write down specific instances when emotions affected your trading decisions. Are you seeing a pattern? Consider times when you stuck to your strategy despite market pressure, and moments when feelings overrode your trading rules. This self-assessment reveals areas where psychological factors influence your results.

Trading psychology manifests in various ways:

Some traders exit profitable positions too early due to past experiences of losing money. Others hold losing trades too long because they struggle to accept small setbacks. These behaviors stem from emotional responses rather than rational analysis of market conditions.

The relationship between technical and mental aspects becomes clear during challenging market periods. A trader might have excellent entry signals but fail to act due to fear. Another trader may identify perfect exit points but hold positions too long due to greed. The technical analysis works, but the execution falters due to psychological factors.

Strong emotions can override the best-planned strategies. When fear takes control, you might miss valid trading signals. During periods of overconfidence, you could ignore risk management rules. These emotional responses happen quickly, often before you realize their influence on your decisions.

Building psychological strength requires regular practice. Monitor your emotional state throughout the trading day. Pay attention to how different market conditions affect your mindset. Record these observations alongside your technical analysis. This combined approach helps you understand both aspects of your trading.

Successful traders develop specific protocols for different emotional states. They create rules for managing fear, greed, and other powerful feelings. These psychological guidelines complement their technical trading rules. Together, they form a complete framework for consistent performance.

The integration of technical and mental skills happens gradually. Each trading session provides opportunities to practice both aspects simultaneously. As you execute trades, observe your emotional responses. Notice how your psychological state affects your ability to follow your strategy.

Your trading results improve when technical and mental aspects align. Maintaining emotional balance allows you to execute your strategy as planned. This consistency leads to better performance over time. The combination of solid analysis and psychological stability creates sustainable trading success.

Understanding this relationship changes how you approach trader development. Technical skills and psychological preparation receive equal attention. This balanced focus helps you build a strong foundation for long-term trading success.

Emotions shape every decision in the markets. Through my years training traders, I've watched countless skilled analysts fail because their emotions hijacked their judgment.

CHAPTER 3

UNDERSTANDING EMOTIONS IN TRADING

The True Cost of Emotions

Fear and greed create the biggest impact on your trading results. These powerful emotions override logic, sabotage well-planned strategies, and drain your trading account. Through the experiences of two traders, Ethan and Rebecca, you will see how these emotions manifest in real trading situations.

Ethan developed his fear of market drawdowns after losing 30% of his account in his first month of trading. His hands trembled every time he placed a trade. The moment prices moved against his position, his stomach churned. He exited trades at the smallest sign of a pullback, missing out on significant profits when the market continued in his predicted direction.

The psychological toll affected Ethan beyond his trading desk. He checked his phone constantly, worried about missing market moves. His sleep suffered as he obsessed over potential losses. The stress impacted his personal relationships. His fear transformed trading from an opportunity for growth into a source of constant anxiety.

Rebecca's story reveals the opposite emotional extreme. After a string of profitable trades, she became overconfident. She pushed her profit targets higher, refusing to exit positions when they reached her original goals. The market eventually reversed, erasing her gains and cutting deep into her trading capital.

Greed clouded Rebecca's judgment completely. She ignored her risk management rules, increased her position sizes, and traded without proper analysis. The dopamine rush from winning trades convinced her she could predict market moves perfectly. This emotional high led to a devastating series of losses.

Your trading account reflects these emotional battles daily. Fear causes missed opportunities and minimized profits. Greed leads to oversized positions and ignored stop-losses. Both emotions result in inconsistent performance and psychological strain. The financial consequences compound over time.

A detailed examination of trading records reveals clear patterns.

Emotional decisions cluster around certain market conditions. High-volatility periods trigger fear responses. Strong upward moves activate greed. Understanding these patterns helps you recognize emotional influences on your trading decisions.

However, just because we recognize patterns and want to make changes, it's often difficult to do so in the heat of the moment. When we are in the grip of some emotion, it's almost impossible to take a step back and correct ourselves. So, what should we do?

Understanding the Subconscious Mind

Our experiences teach us how to behave. What we've been taught becomes our world view, and this is how we approach every situation. If you were raised with a lack mentality, you might be fearful of loss. If you have a few successes but there I no apparent reason for them, such as following a plan, you might attribute it to luck or your own genius.

The subconscious mind holds on to an experience and assumes every interaction after that will have the same result; this is what it expects and this is what controls your thinking. The only way to break free from previous thoughts and events is to see them from a different perspective or substitute a positive result for a previously negative one. This takes time and effort. Over time, with repeated effort, your subconscious will assume your new input really happened because it does not know the difference between what has happened and what we tell it has happened.

Reprogramming the subconscious is a solution that requires a structured approach to emotional awareness. Keep a trading journal documenting your feelings before, during, and after each trade. Track how emotions affect your execution. This data provides insights into your psychological triggers and trading behavior.

Then, when you are ready to sit quietly and input new data into the subconscious, you will know specifically what you want to change.

Physical symptoms often signal emotional trading. Sweaty palms, rapid heartbeat, and shallow breathing indicate fear taking control. Excitement, euphoria, and restlessness suggest greed influencing decisions. Recognizing these signs early allows you to pause and reassess your actions. When you begin to experience these physical symptoms, stop, breath, and assess.

Prevention works better than correction in emotional trading. Establish firm rules for position sizing, stop-losses, and profit targets before market hours. Write these rules down and keep them visible. Look at this as your mission and values statement. These rules will be your anchor, a boundary you cannot cross regardless of what your emotions are telling you.

Think about it this way: if you had the capacity to stop an emotion while you're in the grip of that emotion, you probably would not be feeling that emotion to begin with. When emotions surge, these guidelines provide an objective framework for decisions, something you should always fall back on to keep you grounded and clear.

The path to emotional control requires dedication and practice. Each trading day presents opportunities to strengthen your psychological discipline. Small improvements compound over time, leading to more consistent and profitable trading results.

Fear-Based vs. Confidence-Based Trading

Your emotional state during trading creates two distinct approaches to the markets. Fear-based trading leads to hesitation, premature exits, and missed opportunities. Confidence-based trading enables calm analysis and systematic execution. The difference between these approaches determines your long-term success in the markets.

Brandon's experience illustrates this contrast perfectly. When he started trading, every price movement triggered an emotional response. His hands shook while placing orders. He exited profitable trades at the first sign of a pullback. His fear of losing money prevented him from following his trading plan effectively.

The physical symptoms of fear-based trading affected Brandon's entire routine. His heart raced before market open. Shallow breathing and sweaty palms accompanied each trade entry. He spent hours second-guessing his analysis instead of focusing on market opportunities. These stress responses degraded his decision-making abilities throughout the trading day.

Through dedicated practice, Brandon developed a confidence-based approach. He created specific rules for entries, exits, and position sizing. Each morning, he reviewed his trading plan calmly. When setup conditions appeared, he executed his strategy methodically. His emotional control improved with each successful application of his system. He also kept a journal he could refer back to in order to track his progress.

The transformation showed in Brandon's trading results. His equity curve became steadier as he eliminated emotional decisions. Position sizing stayed consistent regardless of previous outcomes. He maintained his risk parameters even during volatile market conditions. His newfound confidence stemmed from trusting his analysis and following his rules.

Fear-based traders react to market movements emotionally. They cut winners short due to anxiety about giving back profits. They hesitate to enter valid setups because of past losses. Their trading decisions reflect internal fears rather than market analysis. This reactive approach creates inconsistent results and psychological strain.

Confidence-based traders follow their strategies systematically. They enter positions when their criteria align, regardless of recent outcomes. They maintain their stops and targets as planned. Their trading decisions flow from analysis and preparation rather than emotional impulses. This methodical approach produces more reliable results over time.

The distinction appears clearly during market volatility. Fear-based traders freeze or make panic decisions when prices move quickly. Confidence-based traders stick to their plans and manage risk effectively. Their emotional stability allows them to capitalize on opportunities that fear-based traders miss.

Your trading journal reveals which approach dominates your decisions. Review your trades for signs of emotional versus systematic execution. Look for patterns in your behavior during different market conditions. This analysis helps you identify areas where fear affects your trading performance.

Building confidence requires consistent application of proven methods. Focus on following your trading rules exactly. Track your adherence to your plan. Celebrate instances of proper execution regardless of outcomes. These small victories accumulate into lasting trading confidence.

Moving from fear-based to confidence-based trading happens gradually. Each day presents opportunities to strengthen your systematic approach. Maintain your focus on proper execution rather than results. Your trading psychology improves with each confident decision you make.

Neuroplasticity and Emotional Hardwiring

In the previous section, we discussed how the subconscious mind works. Your brain changes with every trade you make. Each market decision strengthens specific neural pathways, creating automatic responses to price movements. These brain patterns influence how you react to trading situations, often without your awareness. Understanding this process helps you develop more effective trading habits.

The science of neuroplasticity reveals how your brain adapts to repeated experiences. When you check your phone during market hours, your brain creates a connection between trading and anxiety. Each time you exit a trade early due to fear, you reinforce the link between market movements and emotional reactions.

Maria discovered this pattern in her trading. She noticed herself reaching for her phone whenever the market opened. Her heart rate increased as she scrolled through price charts. These physical responses occurred automatically, triggered by trading-related activities. The behavior had become hardwired through repetition.

Breaking these patterns requires conscious effort and consistent practice.

Maria started her rewiring process with morning meditation. She focused on her breathing before market open, creating new associations between trading and calmness. Her brain gradually formed different neural pathways, linking market activities with centered awareness instead of anxiety.

Interactive Exercise

- Set aside a few minutes each morning or evening to meditate and clear your head.

- Think about how you want your day to go, or how it went.

- Imagine your next trading day as a clear path, without emotional input disrupting your planned strategy.

Your trading environment plays a crucial role in this rewiring process. A clean, organized trading space sends different signals to your brain than a cluttered desk with multiple distractions. The physical setup influences your mental state and affects how your brain processes market information.

Positive self-talk creates new neural pathways. Replace phrases like "I always lose money" with "I execute my strategy effectively." Your brain responds to these affirmations by building new connections. Regular repetition of constructive thoughts rewires your automatic responses to market situations.

Following trading rules consistently helps establish healthy neural patterns. Each time you maintain your stop-loss, you strengthen the connection between market discipline and successful trading. Your brain learns to associate systematic execution with positive outcomes, reducing emotional interference.

Physical exercise supports neuroplasticity in trading. Regular workouts increase blood flow to your brain, enhancing its ability to form new neural connections. Traders who incorporate exercise into their routines often report improved focus and emotional control during market hours.

Adequate sleep allows your brain to consolidate new trading patterns. During deep sleep, your brain processes the day's experiences and strengthens beneficial neural pathways. Quality rest improves your ability to maintain emotional balance and make clear trading decisions.

The transformation of trading habits through neuroplasticity requires patience. Your brain needs time to build new neural networks and weaken old patterns. Consistent practice of positive trading behaviors gradually creates more effective automatic responses to market situations.

Your trading success depends on developing supportive neural pathways. Pay attention to your automatic responses during market hours. Practice behaviors that promote clear thinking and emotional balance. These efforts reshape your brain's approach to trading, leading to improved performance.

Practical Techniques to Manage Emotions

Your emotional state dictates trading success more than any technical indicator. Through simple yet powerful practices, you can develop stronger emotional control during market hours. These techniques build your psychological resilience and improve trading performance.

The morning breath practice sets your mental foundation for trading. Sit comfortably at your desk five minutes before market open. Breathe deeply through your nose for a count of four. Hold for two counts. Release through your mouth for six counts. This practice activates your parasympathetic nervous system, reducing stress and improving focus.

Professional trader Sarah credits her turnaround to emotional logging. She documents her feelings before each trade: "Anxious about previous loss, hesitant to enter." During trades: "Stomach tight, wanting to exit early." After trades: "Relief when closed, regardless of outcome." This detailed record revealed patterns in her emotional responses.

Trading psychology improves through gradual position sizing adjustments. Monica started with minimal amounts until she could follow her rules consistently. She increased size only after demonstrating emotional control at each level. This methodical approach built her confidence while protecting her capital during the learning process.

Physical symptoms provide early warning signs of emotional trading. Marcus noticed his shoulders tensing before impulsive trades. By recognizing this signal, he learned to pause and reassess his decisions. Small physical awareness prevented many emotional trading mistakes.

Your trading environment affects your emotional state. Create a dedicated space free from distractions. Keep your desk organized. Display your trading rules prominently. These environmental factors support clear thinking and reduce emotional interference during market hours.

The emotional reset button works wonders during trading sessions. When you feel overwhelmed, stand up and stretch. Walk around for two minutes. This physical movement breaks the cycle of emotional escalation and helps you return to trading with renewed focus.

Trading journals gain power through emotional context. Record market conditions alongside your feelings. Note specific triggers that prompt fear or greed. Include physical symptoms and thought patterns. This comprehensive approach reveals connections between market situations and emotional responses.

Time away from screens serves as emotional recovery. Schedule regular breaks during trading hours. Use these moments for brief meditation or gentle movement. This practice prevents emotional fatigue and maintains your psychological stamina throughout the day.

Supporting practices enhance emotional management. Regular exercise reduces overall stress levels. Proper sleep improves emotional regulation. Healthy nutrition supports clear thinking. These lifestyle factors contribute to better trading psychology.

Your development as a trader depends on emotional mastery. Practice these techniques consistently. Track your progress through detailed journaling. Celebrate improvements in emotional control. These efforts compound over time, creating lasting positive changes in your trading psychology.

CHAPTER 4

DEVELOPING A PROFESSIONAL TRADER'S MINDSET

---◆---

Developing a Professional Trader's Mindset

Your trading success stems from unwavering discipline and rock-solid accountability. The market puts you through rigorous tests every day, pushing against your established rules. Most traders falter here - they know what to do but struggle to follow through. A professional mindset makes the difference between consistent profits and regular drawdowns.

Gabriel broke his trading rules repeatedly, despite eight years of market experience. His account balance swung wildly as emotions drove his decisions. Everything changed when he started keeping a detailed accountability journal.

"Writing down my mistakes made them real," he explained. "I could see patterns I wasn't even aware of and, frankly, I was amazed at how many times I'd made the same mistakes over and over." His daily logs forced him to confront each deviation from his trading plan.

Watching your actions transforms how you trade. Gabriel documented everything - position sizes, entry points, exit decisions. More importantly, he recorded why he made each choice. This simple habit revealed surprising patterns. He overtraded during market volatility, moved stop-losses when trades went against him, and sized up positions after winning streaks.

Trade execution demands absolute clarity. Your rules work as guardrails, keeping you safe on the right path and in the right direction when emotions run hot and threaten to lead you astray. Every aspect needs clear guidelines - from position sizing to exit criteria. Gabriel created specific checkpoints throughout his trading day. Before entering a trade, he verified it against his predetermined criteria. After closing positions, he assessed his adherence to the plan.

Trading generates intense emotional pressure. Without strict routines, impulse decisions creep in and undermine results. Successful traders maintain rigid schedules - preparation time, trading windows, and performance reviews. This structure eliminates emotional decision-making. It creates space between market movements and your responses.

Documentation reveals hidden weaknesses in your trading approach. Beyond prices and positions, record your emotional state and market conditions. This detailed record highlights triggers that lead to poor choices. Gabriel's journal showed how overconfidence after winning streaks led him to take excessive risks. By spotting this pattern, he implemented strict position sizing limits.

The market rewards consistent execution above all else. Professional traders understand this truth deeply. They focus on following their system rather than chasing quick profits. Each trade presents an opportunity to demonstrate commitment to proven rules. This mindset shift transforms trading from gambling into a business.

Concrete consequences reinforce good habits. When Gabriel broke his rules twice in one day, he stopped trading until the next session. This forced reset prevented emotional spirals and compounding mistakes. He measured his progress through objective metrics - win rates, average gains versus losses, and plan adherence percentages.

Trading partnerships provide valuable accountability. Share your trading plan and goals with other serious traders. Regular check-ins motivate consistent discipline. Both traders must commit to honest feedback and support. These relationships work best when focused on process improvement rather than results.

Monthly reviews cement your progress. Set aside dedicated time to analyze your trading journal. Look for subtle patterns and recurring challenges. Create specific action steps to address weak points. Small adjustments compound into major improvements over time. Keep your standards high and your commitment unwavering.

Building professional trading habits takes sustained effort. Your daily choices accumulate into your long-term results. Through methodical documentation, regular assessment, and steadfast discipline, you develop the mindset required for lasting success. Each market session offers fresh opportunities to strengthen these crucial skills.

Consistency Over Perfection

The pursuit of perfect trades keeps many traders stuck in analysis paralysis. Mike, a veteran trader with fifteen years of experience, discovered this truth through thousands of market hours. He spent years searching for the perfect setup, only to miss countless opportunities while waiting for ideal conditions.

Trading works through probabilities and statistics. A trader who wins 55% of their trades can build substantial profits through proper position sizing and risk management. Mike tracked his results meticulously, discovering his simple trend-following strategy won 53% of the time. By accepting these odds and executing consistently, his account grew steadily month after month.

Statistical edges appear in various forms. Some traders spot reversals at key price levels. Others trade breakouts from consolidation patterns. The specific method matters less than your ability to execute it repeatedly. Sarah specialized in trading gaps at market open. Her strategy worked 48% of the time, but her winners averaged twice the size of her losses, creating profitability through consistent application.

Psychological barriers often prevent traders from maintaining consistency. The fear of losing causes hesitation on valid setups. Greed pushes traders to hold positions beyond their planned exit points. Tom struggled with these emotions until he automated his execution process. His trading platform automatically entered positions when his criteria aligned, removing emotional interference from his decisions.

Market conditions change constantly, affecting any strategy's effectiveness. Accepting this reality frees you to focus on execution rather than prediction. Maria adjusted her position sizes based on market volatility but maintained strict adherence to her entry and exit rules. This flexibility within structure allowed her strategy to adapt while preserving its statistical edge.

Documentation strengthens consistency. Record every trade, including the setup, position size, and outcome. Review these records weekly to spot patterns in your execution. Carlos noticed his win rate dropped significantly during afternoon trading hours. By limiting his trading to morning sessions, his performance improved dramatically. Small adjustments based on real data compound into meaningful improvements.

Trading requires mechanical precision in execution. Your strategy provides the framework, but only consistent application turns that framework into profits.

David compared his trading to running a business - each trade represented a single transaction in a much larger operation. This perspective helped him maintain emotional distance from individual results.

Physical routines support mental consistency. Regular sleep schedules, exercise, and proper nutrition create stability in your decision-making process. Linda established a morning ritual of exercise and meditation before markets opened. These habits cleared her mind and prepared her for focused execution of her strategy.

Market participation demands sustained attention. Distractions erode consistency and lead to missed opportunities or poor execution. Robert created a dedicated trading space free from external interruptions. His environment supported his ability to concentrate on price action and maintain disciplined execution of his strategy.

Professional traders build their success on repeatable processes. They execute the same actions under similar conditions, regardless of recent results or emotional states. Jennifer developed specific checklists for her trading routine. These tools ensured she maintained consistency even during stressful market periods.

Building Discipline & Self-Responsibility

Trading demands exceptional self-control. You make every decision independently, without supervision or external accountability. This freedom presents unique challenges. Many traders struggle with maintaining discipline when nobody watches over their shoulder. Your success depends entirely on your ability to enforce your own rules and take responsibility for your actions.

Daniel faced this challenge head-on during his early trading days. He compulsively entered trades whenever markets showed slight movement. His overtrading led to substantial losses and emotional exhaustion. The breaking point came after a particularly rough month where he executed over 200 trades, most resulting in losses.

He realized something had to change.

The solution emerged through strict self-imposed limits. Daniel established a firm rule: three trades maximum per day. This simple boundary transformed his approach to market opportunities. He became selective, waiting for setups that matched his criteria perfectly. Each trade carried more significance, forcing him to consider his decisions carefully.

Self-enforcement requires concrete mechanisms. Daniel implemented a trade logging system, tracking every action in real-time. His spreadsheet included entry points, position sizes, and detailed notes about his decision-making process. This documentation created accountability - he could review his performance objectively and identify areas for improvement.

Trading success stems from personal responsibility. Blaming market conditions, other traders, or external factors undermines growth. Sarah learned this lesson after six months of inconsistent results. She recorded her emotional state alongside her trades, revealing how her mindset affected her decisions. This awareness led to better self-regulation and improved performance.

Professional traders maintain strict routines. They prepare thoroughly before market open, execute trades according to predetermined criteria, and review their performance afterward. Mark developed a morning checklist covering market analysis, risk assessment, and mental preparation. These structured habits reinforced his discipline throughout trading sessions.

Your trading rules must have teeth. Create specific consequences for breaking them. Alex established a "cooling off" period - if he exceeded his daily trade limit, he stopped trading for 48 hours. This penalty made him think twice before violating his guidelines. The temporary restriction prevented emotional revenge trading and preserved his capital.

Trading partners strengthen accountability. Regular check-ins with fellow traders help maintain discipline. Rachel and Michael reviewed their trades weekly, discussing adherence to their respective plans. This mutual support system caught potential issues before they became problematic habits. They celebrated disciplined execution rather than profitable outcomes.

Physical environment affects trading discipline. Create a dedicated space for market analysis and execution. Lisa removed distractions from her trading area - phone notifications, social media, unnecessary browser tabs. This focused setup helped her maintain concentration and follow her trading rules consistently.

Self-responsibility extends beyond individual trades. Professional traders manage their entire trading business independently. They handle record-keeping, performance analysis, and strategy refinement. Kevin treated his trading operation with the same seriousness as a traditional business, maintaining detailed records and regular performance reviews.

Spotting Cognitive Biases

Your brain plays tricks on you while trading. These mental shortcuts, called cognitive biases, affect your decisions in subtle yet powerful ways. Marcus discovered this after reviewing his trading journal. During winning streaks, he doubled his position sizes, convinced of his superior skill. This overconfidence bias led to devastating losses when market conditions changed.

Confirmation bias appears when traders search exclusively for information supporting their existing positions. Rachel held onto a losing trade in tech stocks, reading only bullish articles and ignoring clear technical breakdown signals. Her selective attention to confirming evidence cost her significant capital. She learned to actively seek opposing viewpoints before making trading decisions.

The recency bias causes traders to overweight recent events. After three profitable trades, Sofia expected the fourth trade to succeed automatically. This assumption made her overlook crucial risk factors. By documenting her thought process, she identified this pattern and developed a checklist to evaluate each trade independently, regardless of previous outcomes.

Anchoring bias occurs when traders fixate on specific price points. Tom refused to exit a losing position because he anchored to his entry price, waiting for the market to return to break-even. This mental attachment prevented rational decision-making. He overcame this by focusing on current market conditions rather than historical price points.

The sunk cost fallacy keeps traders in losing positions too long. Michael added to losing trades, trying to average down his cost basis. He believed his previous investment justified holding on despite deteriorating conditions. Through mentorship, he learned to evaluate positions based on present circumstances, ignoring already spent capital.

Attribution bias affects how traders explain their results. Karen attributed her winning trades to skill while blaming losses on bad luck or market manipulation. This prevented objective analysis of her trading performance. By treating both wins and losses as learning opportunities, she improved her strategic decision-making.

The gambler's fallacy influences trading frequency. After several losses, Peter believed he was "due" for a win. This false probability assumption led to overtrading. He implemented mandatory break periods between trades to reset his thinking and maintain objectivity.

Availability bias causes traders to overemphasize easily remembered information. After a prominent market crash, James became overly defensive, missing profitable opportunities due to vivid memories of past losses. He developed a systematic trading approach to counter emotional decision-making based on dramatic market events.

The bandwagon effect pushes traders to follow crowds. Sarah bought meme stocks at peak prices because everyone else seemed profitable. This herd mentality resulted in substantial losses. She learned to rely on her own analysis rather than following popular market sentiment.

Self-awareness helps combat cognitive biases. Professional traders review their decisions regularly, identifying patterns in their thinking. David recorded his emotional state and market assumptions for each trade. This practice revealed his susceptibility to specific biases, allowing him to implement preventive measures. Through continuous self-monitoring and adjustment, he developed more objective trading practices.

CHAPTER 5

PRACTICAL TECHNIQUES FOR MASTERING TRADING PSYCHOLOGY

———◆———

Trading psychology turns theoretical knowledge into practical success. Your mind controls every decision you make in the markets, from entry points to exit strategies. Through specific mental techniques, you can maintain composure during market volatility and make clear-headed choices that align with your strategy.

Brain science shows that staying calm while trading activates your prefrontal cortex - the rational decision-making part of your brain. When stress kicks in, your emotional centers take over, leading to impulsive choices that override practical thinking. You enter survival mode. By practicing mindfulness techniques, you keep your thinking brain engaged even when markets get wild.

Mindfulness grounds you in the present moment rather than getting caught up in market noise. A simple breathing exercise before executing trades can prevent emotional reactions. Watch your thoughts and feelings without judgment, maintaining objectivity about market movements.

Kiana, a day trader, struggled with impulsive decisions until she started doing quick mindful check-ins throughout her trading day. She takes three deep breaths before every trade entry, bringing her focus back to her strategy rather than reacting to market volatility. This small habit has dramatically improved her trading consistency. (See Appendix I: Learning to Breathe)

Beyond mindfulness, visualization preps your mind for various market scenarios.

Interactive Exercise:

- Find a quiet area in your home to practice visualization.

- Close your eyes and see yourself calmly handling both wins and losses.

- Create movement in your vision. This should not be a static picture. See yourself in your work environment doing all the things you would normally do, but you're doing it calmly and strategically.

Mental rehearsal builds the neural pathways for composed trading when real money hits the line.

- Daily journaling also reinforces good habits by tracking your psychological state alongside trade outcomes.

- Physical techniques complement mental ones. Regular exercise releases tension that can cloud judgment.

- Proper sleep gives your brain the rest needed for sharp decision-making.

- Even your trading environment matters - a clean, organized workspace promotes mental clarity and reduces stress.

Customize these techniques to match your trading style and personality. Some traders thrive with morning meditation, while others prefer mid-day breathing breaks. The key lies in consistency - small daily practices compound into major psychological improvements over time.

Start with one technique and master it before adding others. Track how different practices affect your trading performance. Pay attention to which methods most effectively keep you centered during market volatility. Your psychological toolkit should evolve with your trading experience.

Research proves that managing emotions through mindfulness leads to better decisions under pressure. Emotional intelligence is about what's happening right now, how you react on the spot. When you stay calm, you access your full cognitive abilities rather than defaulting to fight-or-flight responses. This translates directly to more profitable trading through clearer analysis and disciplined execution.

Studies show that traders who practice emotional regulation techniques have more consistent results than those who trade purely on technical analysis. By combining solid strategy with strong psychology, you create a complete approach to successful trading.

The intensity and duration of debilitative emotions such as fear and anger play a role in how draining an emotion will become, and in the case of trading, how much damage they can do.

Take a step back:

- What is your belief regarding what's going on?

- Is your reaction based on what you believe is going to happen?

- Is your reaction based on a negative bias?

Changing ingrained mental patterns takes dedicated practice. Set aside specific times for psychological exercises, treating them as essential as market analysis. Review your progress regularly, adjusting techniques that feel stale or ineffective.

Track both your psychological state and trading results to identify connections. Notice how your mental preparation affects trade outcomes. Use this data to refine your approach, building an increasingly effective psychological framework for trading success.

Many traders start strong with psychological practices but struggle to maintain them during busy market periods. Schedule your mental exercises at specific times, making them non-negotiable parts of your trading routine. When markets get hectic, these habits become even more crucial for maintaining composure.

Address resistance to psychological practices by remembering their impact on your bottom line. Every minute spent on mental preparation pays dividends through better trading decisions. View these techniques as essential tools for protecting and growing your capital.

As your psychological awareness grows, you can spot subtle emotional shifts before they affect your trading. This early warning system prevents reactive decisions and keeps you aligned with your strategy. Advanced practitioners often develop personalized combinations of techniques that work synergistically.

Integrate psychological practices with your technical analysis. Use mindfulness to maintain objectivity when reviewing charts. Apply visualization to prepare for high-stakes trading situations. Your mental game should complement and enhance your analytical approach.

Cognitive Reframing

Your internal dialogue shapes your trading decisions more than any technical indicator. When you catch yourself thinking "This market always moves against me," you create a self-fulfilling prophecy. By changing these thought patterns, you transform your trading performance. Many successful traders credit their achievements to mastering their internal dialogue.

Mike, a Forex trader, used to tell himself "I mess up every breakout trade." This belief made him hesitate on valid setups, missing profitable opportunities. Through dedicated practice, he changed this thought to "Each trade provides valuable data." His win rate improved by 30% over three months simply by adjusting his mindset.

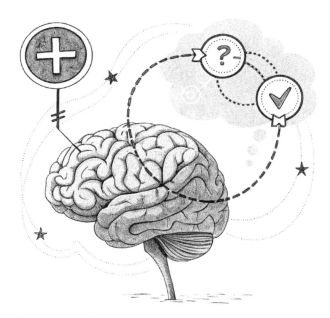

During intense market periods, your brain generates automatic thoughts. These pop up without invitation and can trigger emotional responses. A sudden price drop might spark the thought "I will lose everything." This creates anxiety, leading to premature exits. By identifying and rewriting these thoughts, you regain control of your trading decisions.

Trading Psychology in Practice

Sarah dealt with persistent thoughts of "I should have known better" after losses. She learned to reframe this into "Every outcome teaches me something valuable." This shift helped her analyze trades objectively instead of beating herself up. Her new perspective led to better risk management and more strategic position sizing.

The process requires patience and consistency. Keep a thought journal beside your trading station. Write down recurring negative thoughts as they appear. Then write an alternative perspective that serves you better. "The market is too risky" becomes "I manage risk effectively through proper position sizing." This builds new neural pathways over time.

Your brain responds to repetition. Professional traders make cognitive reframing a daily practice. Before market open, review your most common negative thoughts and their empowering alternatives. This mental preparation proves especially valuable during challenging market conditions. Many traders post their reframed thoughts near their monitors as constant reminders.

Psychological resilience develops through regular cognitive reframing. Tom struggled with the thought "One loss will wipe out my gains." He reframed it to "My risk management protects my capital." This mental shift allowed him to trade with confidence, knowing each position followed his proven system. His account grew steadily as fear subsided.

The impact extends beyond individual trades. Maria noticed her thought "Other traders know more than me" held her back from developing her own style. She reframed it to "My unique perspective gives me an edge." This empowered her to trust her analysis and create a profitable trading approach aligned with her strengths.

Remember: your subconscious does not know the difference between what has happened and what you tell it has happened!

Your trading environment influences your thoughts.

- Create a workspace that reinforces positive thinking.

- Post your reframed statements where you can see them.

- Some traders keep a "victory journal" highlighting successful trades and effective thought patterns. This builds a foundation of confidence based on real experiences.

- Monitor your progress through measurable metrics.

- Track how reframed thoughts affect your trading decisions.

- Keep records to reinforce your commitment to mental mastery.

Many traders notice improved hold times on winning trades and quicker exits from losing positions. The data proves that cognitive reframing directly impacts trading performance.

Don't forget: Your physical state also affects mental patterns. Regular exercise, proper sleep, and healthy nutrition support clear thinking. Add deep breathing exercises when negative thoughts arise. This combination of physical and mental techniques creates lasting change. Your mind functions best when your body maintains peak condition.

Advanced traders use cognitive reframing proactively. They anticipate challenging scenarios and prepare empowering responses. Before earnings announcements or economic reports, they review potential thoughts and their reframed alternatives. This mental preparation allows calm execution during high-pressure moments.

Visualization for Peak Performance

Your brain creates success patterns through mental practice. Elite traders, like athletes, spend dedicated time visualizing perfect trade executions. This mental conditioning builds neural pathways that activate during actual trading. Through consistent visualization, you program your mind for peak performance under pressure.

Marisol transformed her trading through visualization. She struggled with exiting profitable trades too early, driven by fear. Once she recognized this pattern, she began to spend five minutes each morning visualizing herself holding positions through normal market fluctuations. Within weeks, her average profit per trade doubled as she learned to stay calm during price swings.

Professional athletes use visualization to prepare for competition, and successful traders apply these same principles to market activities.

Trading often demands split-second choices under pressure. Through visualization, you prepare your mind to react appropriately when real money moves. Many traders report that challenging market situations feel familiar because they've mentally practiced their responses. They've "been there before." Like any performer, the way you perform in rehearsal is the way you'll perform on stage. This preparation reduces anxiety and promotes clear thinking, and highlights the power of the subconscious.

Interactive Element

Your brain responds to vivid mental practice

Make a short list of possible market scenarios and rehearse your reactions to them. By rehearsing or visualizing them, you will build muscle memory for proper trade execution, creating pathways for composed decision-making.

The visualization technique works best with specific detail.

- See yourself checking your indicators, confirming your setup criteria, and placing orders with confidence.

- Feel the emotional control as prices move.

- Experience the satisfaction of following your plan regardless of outcome.

Be sure to add movement to your vision. A static picture is just that: a picture. Your mind responds to what it believes to be a real event, your rehearsal. These mental rehearsals create a blueprint for actual trading behavior.

Physical comfort enhances visualization effectiveness. Find a quiet space before market open. Sit comfortably with your eyes closed. Take several deep diaphragmatic breaths to center yourself. (See Appendix I: Learning to Breathe). Then walk through your ideal trading sequence. Include all sensory details - the screens, the clicking of your mouse, the steady rhythm of your breathing as you maintain composure.

Carlos used visualization to overcome analysis paralysis. He would freeze when perfect setups appeared, missing opportunities through hesitation. By visualizing smooth, decisive action during his setup conditions, he developed the confidence to execute trades promptly. His visualization practice focused on rapid pattern recognition and immediate action.

Visualization addresses specific trading challenges. If you struggle with holding winners, visualize yourself staying calm as profits grow. For issues with stop losses, practice seeing yourself exit losing trades promptly without emotion. The key lies in regular repetition - your brain strengthens these positive patterns through consistent practice.

Track your visualization practice alongside trading results. Many traders notice improved performance in scenarios they've mentally rehearsed. Keep notes on challenging situations and incorporate them into your visualization routine. This targeted practice builds confidence in previously difficult areas.

Your trading environment impacts visualization quality. Create a calm, organized workspace that matches your mental practice. Some traders post reminder notes about their visualization goals near their monitors. This alignment between mental rehearsal and physical setup reinforces positive trading behaviors.

Advanced traders combine visualization with breathing exercises and affirmations. This multi-layered approach creates powerful psychological preparation. The mental, emotional, and physical elements work together, producing heightened trading performance. Regular practice integrates these components into automatic responses.

Professional trading requires sustained mental stamina. Visualization builds psychological endurance for long trading sessions. By mentally practicing focus and calm through extended periods, you develop greater resilience. This preparation proves especially valuable during volatile market conditions.

Stress Management & Decision-Making

Market volatility triggers stress hormones in your body. The fight or flight response at the core of our brain is a survival mechanism. The liver and pancreas dump enormous amounts of sugar and insulin into the bloodstream as a response to what feels like an emergency. Cortisol floods the system, compromising your ability to think clearly. Your brain shifts from rational analysis to emotional reactions.

Worry is a stress, telling your body to get ready for "fight or flight." We project what may happen in te future and assess whether or not we have the resources needed to cope. Not only will this affect your emotional state, but it does chronic harm to your body. Understanding these biological responses helps you manage them effectively during trading sessions.

- **<u>Box breathing</u>** provides immediate stress relief during market turbulence. The technique involves breathing in through the nose for 4 counts, holding for 4 counts, exhaling slowly through the mouth for 4 counts, and maintaining the bottom of the "box" for 4 counts.

This pattern signals your brain and regulates your nervous system, bringing you back to a state of calm analysis. Many professional traders use this method before important trading decisions.

Marcus, a day trader, faced constant stress during volatile market opens. His heart would race, and his palms would sweat. Through regular box breathing practice, he learned to maintain composure. His execution improved significantly once he gained control of his stress response. His trading journal showed 40% fewer emotional trades after implementing this technique.

- **Physical exercise** plays a crucial role in stress management. Traders who maintain regular workout routines report better focus and emotional control. The endorphins released during exercise counteract stress hormones. A morning workout can set you up for clearer thinking throughout the trading day.

- **Sleep quality** directly impacts your stress tolerance. Well-rested traders handle market pressure more effectively. Poor sleep elevates cortisol levels before trading even begins. Creating a consistent sleep schedule supports optimal decision-making. Many successful traders prioritize sleep as part of their stress management strategy.

- **Your trading environment** affects stress levels. A cluttered desk can increase anxiety subconsciously. Organize your workspace to promote calm focus. Some traders use plants or soft lighting to create a relaxing atmosphere. These environmental factors contribute to better stress management during intense market periods.

Stress often manifests physically before you notice it mentally. Pay attention to tension in your shoulders, changes in breathing, or stomach discomfort. These physical signals warn you of rising stress levels. Early recognition allows you to implement management techniques before stress affects your trading decisions.

Sarah developed a pre-market stress management routine. She combines stretching, box breathing, and brief meditation. This preparation helps her start each trading session in a calm, focused state. Her win rate increased by 25% after establishing this routine. The combination of physical and mental techniques proves particularly effective.

- **Regular breaks** prevent stress accumulation during trading hours. Step away from your screens every hour, even briefly. Use these moments for quick stress relief exercises. Many traders schedule specific break times to maintain consistent stress management throughout the day.

- **Hydration and nutrition** impact your stress response. Stable blood sugar helps maintain emotional equilibrium. Keep water and healthy snacks nearby during trading sessions. This physical support enhances your mental resilience when markets become challenging.

Advanced traders develop personalized stress management systems. They identify their unique stress triggers and create specific response plans. This targeted approach allows for rapid stress reduction during crucial trading moments. Your stress management strategy should evolve with your trading experience.

Monitor your stress levels alongside your trading performance. Notice patterns between elevated stress and trading mistakes. This awareness helps refine your management techniques. Many traders keep stress scores in their trading journals, tracking the relationship between stress and trading outcomes.

Building a Routine

Strong trading habits emerge from consistent daily practices. A structured routine separates professional traders from amateurs. Your morning preparation sets the tone for the entire trading day, while evening review strengthens your skills for tomorrow.

Lisa developed her morning routine through careful testing. She arrives at her desk 45 minutes before market open. The first 15 minutes go to market analysis - checking futures, reading key news, and updating her watchlist. She spends the next 15 minutes in quiet meditation, clearing her mind of outside distractions. The final 15 minutes focus on reviewing her trading plan and setting specific targets for the day.

The pre-market routine matters more than most traders realize. James learned this lesson the hard way after a series of impulsive trades cost him significant money. He rushed into trading without preparation, reacting emotionally to market moves. After implementing a strict morning routine, his trading improved dramatically. His new process includes physical exercise, market research, and strategy review.

Mental preparation creates the foundation for successful trading. Your brain needs time to shift into trading mode. Many traders use breathing exercises or light stretching to enhance mental clarity. Some read their trading rules aloud, reinforcing their commitment to disciplined execution. These practices align your mind with your trading objectives.

The post-market review proves equally important. Kate dedicates 30 minutes after the close to analyze her trades. She rates her emotional control on each position, noting when fear or greed influenced her decisions. This self-assessment helps her identify patterns and adjust her approach. Her trading journal includes both technical and psychological observations.

Physical organization supports mental clarity. Maria keeps her trading station meticulously arranged. Her monitors display specific information in consistent locations. She prepares her trading tools and references before the market opens. This orderly environment reduces stress and promotes focused decision-making.

Documentation strengthens your routine. Michael tracks every aspect of his trading day in a detailed journal. He records market conditions, trade rationales, and emotional states. Each entry includes a score for routine adherence. This data helps him refine his process and maintain accountability.

Trading requires intense concentration. Regular breaks prevent mental fatigue and maintain peak performance. David schedules five-minute breaks every hour. He steps away from his screens, stretches, and resets his focus. These brief pauses help him stay sharp during long trading sessions.

Your routine should evolve with your trading growth. Alex adjusts his process based on performance data. He noticed better results on days with longer pre-market preparation. This observation led him to start his routine 30 minutes earlier. Small refinements add up to significant improvements over time.

The evening review closes your trading day properly. Rachel examines her trades without emotional attachment. She celebrates disciplined execution rather than focusing solely on profits. Her review includes questions about emotional control, routine adherence, and areas for improvement. This reflection guides her preparation for the next trading day.

Consistency matters more than perfection. Sam follows his routine even on challenging days. He understands that habits build through repetition. Minor adjustments keep his routine fresh and relevant. His commitment to the process supports steady trading improvement.

Your psychological state affects every trading decision. The routine provides structure for maintaining emotional balance. Through consistent practice, these habits become automatic responses. They create a professional framework for approaching the markets systematically.

Building Resilience

Trading resilience means bouncing back from setbacks while maintaining emotional balance. Markets test your psychological strength every day. Through specific practices and mindset shifts, you develop the ability to handle both wins and losses with equanimity.

Maria faced a devastating loss that wiped out three months of profits. Instead of giving up, she used this experience to strengthen her trading approach. She wrote down specific lessons from the loss and created new risk management rules. Within two months, she recovered her losses and developed stronger emotional control.

- **Affirmations** reshape your trading mindset. Carol repeats "Each trade teaches me something valuable" before every market session. This mental programming helps her view outcomes objectively rather than emotionally. Her trading journal shows improved decision-making since implementing daily affirmations.

- **Realistic goals** build sustainable confidence. Robert set an achievable target of 1% account growth per week. This moderate approach reduced pressure and allowed him to trade with clear thinking. His consistency improved dramatically once he stopped chasing unrealistic returns.

- **<u>Support networks</u>** provide crucial perspective during challenging periods. James joined a group of experienced traders who met weekly to discuss psychological challenges. Their shared experiences helped him understand that setbacks affect everyone. The group accountability motivated him to maintain high trading standards.

- **<u>Physical resilience</u>** supports mental toughness. Sarah incorporated regular exercise into her trading routine. The endorphins from morning workouts improved her stress tolerance during market hours. She noticed better emotional control on days when she exercised before trading.

- **<u>Trading journals</u>** track resilience development. Michael records his emotional state alongside technical analysis. He rates his psychological recovery after losses on a 1-10 scale. This data helps him identify effective coping strategies and areas needing improvement.

Advanced traders build resilience through **scenario planning**. They mentally prepare for various market situations, developing specific response strategies. This preparation reduces emotional reactions when challenges arise. Their trading reflects calculated decisions rather than emotional responses.

Market volatility tests trading resilience. Lisa maintains composure during wild price swings by focusing on her **predetermined rules**. She views market movements as neutral events rather than personal threats. This perspective allows clear thinking under pressure.

Personal growth strengthens trading resilience. Alex reads trading psychology books and attends workshops to enhance his mental game. He applies new concepts gradually, testing their effectiveness in real market conditions. His trading shows steady improvement through continuous learning.

Environmental factors influence resilience. David created a **dedicated trading space** that promotes calm focus. He removes distractions and maintains organization. This structured environment supports better decision-making during market stress.

Systematic review builds lasting resilience. Karen examines her trades weekly, identifying both technical and psychological patterns. She celebrates maintained composure as much as profitable trades. This balanced evaluation strengthens her trading foundation.

CHAPTER 6
OVERCOMING COMMON PSYCHOLOGICAL PITFALLS

---◆---

Managing Fear & Greed

Money brings out powerful emotions. The trading floor surfaces these raw feelings, especially fear and greed. These emotions can hijack your decision-making, causing significant trading losses.

Successful traders deal with fear and greed by sticking to proven strategies and following strict protocols. They focus on executing their plan rather than getting caught up in emotional reactions to market moves.

Antonio learned this lesson after several painful experiences with revenge trading. Each loss triggered an urge to make back the money fast. He doubled his position sizes and ignored risk management rules. The stress of these larger positions made him exit trades early when they moved against him. This cycle repeated until his account dwindled by 60%.

Through mentoring, Antonio created clear position sizing rules and pre-defined exit points. He wrote specific criteria for entering trades based on his strategy. Most importantly, he automated his stops and profit targets. This removed the temptation to override them based on emotions. Over six months of following this system, his trading results stabilized.

Greed pushes traders to take outsized risks. The thrill of a big win can override rational decision-making. Many blow up their accounts by betting too much capital on speculative trades. The solution involves calculating position sizes in advance and setting strict loss limits per trade and per day. When you hit your daily loss limit, you stop trading until the next session.

Fear causes missed opportunities and poor exits. Traders exit winning positions too early because they worry about giving back profits. They hesitate to take valid signals after losses. The antidote involves reviewing historical data to build confidence in your strategy. Track your win rate and average reward-to-risk ratio. This shifts focus from individual trades to long-term results.

Emotional discipline separates profitable traders from unprofitable ones. Top traders view the market as a probability game requiring consistent execution. They accept small losses as a normal part of their business. Their trading decisions come from careful analysis rather than knee-jerk reactions. This mindset develops through deliberate practice and self-awareness.

Tracking your emotional state helps identify problematic patterns. Keep a detailed trade journal noting how you felt before, during, and after each trade. Look for situations that trigger impulsive decisions. Common triggers include reaching daily loss limits, having multiple losing trades, or taking heat on a position. Understanding your triggers allows you to prepare mentally.

Developing routines creates emotional stability. Arrive at your trading desk early to review overnight markets calmly. Use a pre-trade checklist confirming your setup meets all criteria. Take regular breaks to maintain mental clarity. End each day reviewing your trades objectively. Simple habits like these build discipline over time.

Success comes from managing your inner game - the thoughts and emotions driving your decisions. Focus on executing your proven strategy rather than trying to predict market direction. Accept that markets move randomly in the short term. Your edge emerges from disciplined trading over many iterations. The process matters more than individual trades.

Building emotional resilience takes time and practice. Work with a mentor or trading group for support and accountability. Study your trading history to identify recurring psychological pitfalls. Create rules and systems to protect yourself during emotional extremes. Most importantly, stay committed to steady improvement rather than seeking instant results.

Dealing with Losses and Setbacks

Trading often involves financial pain. Each loss hits hard, causing emotional wounds that take time to heal. Many traders struggle to process these setbacks constructively. The successful ones view losses as educational expenses - payments necessary to gain market expertise. When you reframe losses this way, they become valuable learning opportunities rather than crushing defeats.

A loss recovery plan provides structure during challenging periods. Maria, a veteran trader, developed her plan after a series of losses shook her confidence. She stepped away from her screens for 30 minutes after each loss. During this time, she wrote detailed notes about the trade setup, her execution, and her emotional state. This practice helped her identify areas for improvement.

Position sizing adjustments form another key component of recovery. After two consecutive losses, Maria reduced her trade size by 50%. This gave her breathing room to rebuild confidence while protecting her capital. Once she strung together three profitable trades at the smaller size, she gradually increased back to her standard positions. The measured approach prevented emotional trading decisions.

Documentation plays a crucial role in bouncing back from setbacks. Your trading journal should capture both technical and psychological factors. Record market conditions, entry and exit prices, position sizes, and profit/loss amounts. Also note your mindset before the trade, how you handled any adversity, and what you learned. This data helps spot harmful patterns.

Money management rules become especially important after losses. Set a maximum daily loss limit and stick to it firmly. Calculate the exact dollar amount you'll risk per trade based on your account size. Track your cumulative losses to stay within weekly and monthly risk parameters. These boundaries prevent small setbacks from becoming major drawdowns.

Mentorship provides valuable perspective during rough patches. Find experienced traders who made it through similar challenges. They can share practical strategies for regaining confidence and returning to profitable trading. Regular check-ins with mentors create accountability and emotional support. Their guidance helps avoid common recovery pitfalls.

Physical activity releases tension after tough trading sessions. A brisk walk or workout shifts focus away from losses. The exercise clears your mind and resets your emotional state. Many traders incorporate movement breaks throughout their day. The physical outlet prevents stress from building up and affecting future trades.

Time management affects recovery success. Schedule regular breaks between trades to process outcomes calmly. Block out hours for market research and trade review. Create space in your day for activities unrelated to trading. A balanced routine maintains perspective when losses occur.

Support from fellow traders speeds up recovery. Join online communities or local trading groups. Share your experiences dealing with setbacks. Learn how others bounced back from similar situations. The camaraderie reminds you that losses affect everyone in this business. Discussing challenges openly reduces their emotional impact.

Tracking improvements motivates continued growth. Keep a spreadsheet of key trading metrics - win rate, profit factor, maximum drawdown. Review these numbers weekly to gauge your progress. Celebrate small wins as you rebuild. The data provides concrete evidence that your recovery plan works.

Building Resilience

Resilience in trading means developing the ability to recover from setbacks and maintain a steady emotional state, regardless of market fluctuations. It's about building mental toughness so you can bounce back and keep moving forward without carrying emotional baggage from previous trades.

Bouncing Back With Purpose

Every trader faces losses, but the difference between successful traders and others lies in how they respond. Losses are not failures; they are opportunities to learn and grow. Instead of dwelling on the outcome, focus on analyzing what you can control—your decisions, your mindset, and your preparation.

Consider affirming this: "Every trade teaches me something valuable." These words act as a reset button, redirecting your energy toward improvement. Resilience allows you to view setbacks as temporary and part of the journey.

The Role of Supportive Peers

Surrounding yourself with like-minded individuals can significantly boost your resilience. A community of traders, mentors, or supportive peers provides perspective and encouragement. They remind you that losses are common and help you see your progress objectively.

Engaging in discussions with others who share your goals also fosters accountability. Sharing your challenges and hearing others' experiences can lighten the emotional load and motivate you to stay consistent in your efforts.

Setting Realistic Goals

Goals that are realistic and measurable lay the groundwork for sustainable progress. When your goals are clear, each step toward them builds confidence and reinforces your resilience. Unrealistic expectations, however, lead to frustration and burnout.

Break your goals into achievable milestones. Celebrate small victories along the way. For example, aim to follow your trading plan for a week without deviation. These smaller accomplishments stack up, creating a foundation of trust in your abilities.

The Power of Affirmations

Affirmations are a powerful tool for reshaping your mindset and building resilience. Repeating statements such as "I trust my analysis" or "Losses are part of the process" helps anchor you in positivity and focus. These reminders act as a buffer against negative self-talk that often follows challenging trading days.

Practice saying these affirmations daily, especially after reviewing your trades. Over time, these affirmations replace self-doubt with a sense of purpose and clarity. (Affirmations should be repeated throughout the day, all day, several times a day).

Practical Exercises for Resilience

Emotional Journaling

After each trading session, write down what you felt during the trades. Identify triggers for frustration, fear, or excitement. Over time, patterns will emerge. Recognizing these patterns is the first step toward managing your emotions effectively.

Visualization Techniques

Spend a few minutes visualizing how you would like to react to a challenging trading situation. Imagine staying calm, following your plan, and making objective decisions. Rehearsing these scenarios mentally prepares you for real-life trading challenges.

Resilience in Action

Losses can be emotional, but they don't have to define you. Develop a ritual to bounce back. After a losing trade, step away from your screen, take deep breaths, and review the trade objectively. Acknowledge what you did well and where you can improve.

Staying Consistent

Consistency is the backbone of resilience. Resilience is not built in one day; it's the cumulative effect of small, consistent actions. Stick to your trading plan, review your progress regularly, and trust the process. When emotions feel overwhelming, remind yourself of your progress and the larger goals you're working toward.

Building resilience takes effort, but the rewards extend beyond trading. It equips you with the mental strength to navigate challenges in any area of life. With practice and intention, resilience becomes your greatest asset, helping you thrive in the unpredictable world of trading.

Avoiding Overtrading & Burnout

Overtrading sneaks in when emotions take the wheel. You feel the rush of a good trade, and suddenly, you're ready for another. Then another. Each trade feeds a growing urge to keep going. But the truth is, this mindset pushes you toward burnout. Emotional triggers are at the root of this behavior—the thrill of winning, fear of missing out, or the desire to recover losses. Recognizing these triggers is your first step toward breaking the cycle.

Emotional Triggers Behind "Just One More Trade"

Every trader has felt the pull of "just one more trade." It often starts with a win. The satisfaction fuels your confidence, and you're sure the next trade will be another victory. Or maybe it's the opposite—a loss makes you desperate to recover what's gone. In either case, emotions cloud your judgment. Overtrading becomes a loop, where reason fades, and impulse takes over. This type of trading is like gambling: you're relying on nothing more than the roll of the dice and luck, throwing the rules out the window. Acknowledging the emotional drive behind this is crucial. Step back and ask yourself, "Am I trading to win or chasing a feeling?"

Setting Daily Trade Caps

A daily trade cap is a simple but effective safeguard. It forces discipline. You decide beforehand how many trades you'll take, and stick to that limit no matter what. This rule protects you from emotional decision-making during the trading session.

Let's say you set a limit of three trades per day. Whether they win or lose, you stop at three. This approach shifts your focus from quantity to quality, helping you evaluate each opportunity with care rather than rushing in.

Planned Breaks to Reset

Breaks are essential. Trading without pauses drains your energy and sharpens emotional responses. Build breaks into your trading routine. After a trade, step away from the screen for a few minutes. Use this time to breathe, stretch, or clear your mind. Longer breaks are just as valuable. Schedule time during the day to rest or review your performance. When you return to the market, your perspective feels refreshed, and you're better prepared to make objective decisions.

Accountability Check-Ins

Accountability keeps you honest. Whether through a mentor, trading group, or even a journal, external feedback helps you stay aligned with your goals. Share your daily limits with someone who understands trading's challenges. A quick check-in after your session—even a text or a brief call—can reinforce your discipline. Alternatively, document your trades and emotions in a journal. Writing down why you traded creates awareness. Reviewing this log regularly reveals patterns and helps you correct them.

CHAPTER 7

CREATING YOUR PERSONAL TRADING PLAN

———— ◆ ————

A trading plan shapes every decision you make in the markets. You might wonder about the point of writing everything down when you could keep it all in your head. The reality hits when emotions run high during market volatility - your clear thinking turns cloudy, and those mental rules fade away. Ask any successful trader about their early days, and they'll tell you about the costly lessons learned before establishing a concrete plan.

Take Alicia, a tech-savvy investor who started trading cryptocurrency in 2021. She relied on YouTube videos and social media tips, jumping into trades whenever she felt excited about a particular coin. Her account grew during the bull market, reinforcing her belief that she could succeed through instinct alone. The crypto winter of 2022 changed everything. Without clear entry and exit rules, she held onto losing positions way too long, hoping they would recover. Her account dropped 70% before she stepped back to reassess.

Why You Need a Plan

Your mind plays tricks when real money sits on the line. The market swings up, and greed whispers to add more to your position. It drops sharply, and fear screams at you to sell everything. There will come a point when you stop trusting everything you've been doing.

A written plan acts as your anchor during these emotional storms. It spells out exactly what you'll do in each situation, removing the burden of making decisions under pressure.

The plan tells you which markets to trade, how much capital to risk per trade, and specific conditions that must align before entering a position. It includes your profit targets and stop-loss levels. Most importantly, it outlines how you'll manage your positions when things go wrong - because they will go wrong sometimes. The market guarantees that fact.

Consider your trading plan as a business document. Professional traders approach the markets as a business, measuring their performance and adjusting their strategies based on solid data. The plan helps you track what works and what falls short. You'll spot patterns in your trading behavior and identify areas for improvement through regular review of your results against your written guidelines.

Your plan evolves as you gain experience. Markets change, and successful traders adapt their approaches while maintaining their core risk management principles. The key lies in making these adjustments thoughtfully, based on careful analysis rather than emotional reactions to recent trades. Write down your reasons for any changes - this creates accountability and prevents impulsive modifications after a losing streak.

The psychological benefits of a trading plan extend beyond decision-making. It builds confidence through consistency. When you follow your rules and see positive results over time, you develop trust in your system. This trust helps you stay patient during drawdowns and avoid the common trap of switching strategies too frequently. The plan becomes your blueprint for long-term success.

Many traders resist creating a detailed plan because it feels restrictive.

Yet structure and discipline create freedom. When you know your parameters for trading, you spend less mental energy second-guessing decisions. The clarity allows you to focus on executing your strategy well rather than constantly questioning your choices. This mental bandwidth matters - trading requires sharp focus and emotional stability.

Alicia's story continued after her harsh lesson. She spent two months developing a comprehensive trading plan with clear rules for position sizing and risk management. She identified specific technical patterns that matched her trading style and documented exact conditions for entries and exits. Her new approach included a maximum loss limit per day and week. Though her returns decreased initially, her account stability improved dramatically. She regained confidence knowing every trade aligned with her predetermined strategy.

Creating your trading plan requires honesty about your goals, capabilities, and limitations. The plan must match your personality and risk tolerance. An aggressive strategy that works for someone else might cause you endless stress. Your available time for market analysis and trading also shapes your approach. The best plan accounts for these personal factors while incorporating sound trading principles.

Your journey toward trading success depends on this foundation. A solid plan transforms abstract ideas about trading into concrete actions. It provides structure during market chaos and helps you maintain perspective when emotions run high. The time invested in developing your plan pays dividends through improved decision-making and reduced stress. Your future trading self will thank you for this preparation.

Steps to Develop Your Trading Plan

A well-structured **trading plan** keeps you steady when markets test your emotions. Creating your plan involves several key elements, each building upon the previous one to form a complete strategy. Many traders skip this crucial step, eager to jump into action - yet those who take time to plan often find greater success in their trading journey.

Define Your Goals

Your **trading goals** shape every aspect of your strategy. Make your goals measurable. Write down specific numbers you aim to achieve each month and year. Maybe you want to grow your account by 2% monthly, or generate $500 in weekly income. These concrete targets help measure your progress and allow you to adjust your approach when needed. Include both financial and personal development objectives - perhaps mastering a particular trading setup or maintaining emotional balance during volatile market periods.

Outline Your Strategy

The strategy section forms the core of your plan. Detail which markets you'll trade and why they match your personality and schedule. Some traders thrive in the fast-paced forex market, while others prefer the slower movements of blue-chip stocks. Specify exact entry conditions - perhaps you enter trades only when price breaks above a 20-day moving average with increased volume. List precise exit rules for both winning and losing trades.

Your **timeframes** matter too. Day trading requires constant market attention, while swing trading allows more flexibility. Choose periods that align with your lifestyle and temperament. Write down position sizing rules - how much capital you'll risk on each trade. Many successful traders limit risk to 1-2% per position, protecting their account from inevitable losing streaks.

Include Psychological Insights

Trading psychology makes or breaks your success. **Document situations** that trigger impulsive decisions. Maybe you overtrade after a loss, trying to recover quickly. Or perhaps you hesitate to take valid setups after several losing trades. Understanding these patterns helps you spot them in real-time and maintain better control.

Keep a trading journal to track both numbers and emotions. Record how you feel before, during, and after trades. Note market conditions and your mental state when you make your best decisions. This data reveals patterns in your behavior and helps refine your approach. Many traders discover their biggest profits come when they feel calm and focused, while losses often follow periods of stress or distraction.

Set a Trading Schedule

Random market participation leads to random results. **Establish specific hours** for analysis, trading, and review. Morning people might scan for setups at 7 AM and trade until noon. Others prefer afternoon sessions when European and US markets overlap. Whatever schedule you choose, stick to it consistently.

Your schedule should include time blocks for different activities. Dedicate 30 minutes to pre-market analysis, identifying potential setups that match your criteria. Set aside time to review your trades weekly, noting what worked and areas for improvement. Include breaks to maintain mental sharpness - even professional traders step away from screens regularly.

Building **discipline** through a structured schedule prevents emotional trading decisions. When you know your dedicated trading hours, you avoid the temptation to chase random market moves at odd times. This structure also helps separate trading time from other life activities, maintaining a healthy work-life balance.

The most effective trading plans evolve through experience. **Track everything** - your successes, failures, emotions, and market observations. Review this data monthly to spot patterns and refine your approach. Consider reviewing your plan quarterly, updating rules based on market changes and your growing expertise. Keep earlier versions to track your progress and remind yourself of lessons learned.

Professional traders treat their activity as a business, and your plan becomes your business blueprint. Include sections on risk management, capital allocation, and performance metrics. Consider adding a checklist for trade validation - specific criteria each trade must meet before you commit capital. This systematic approach removes much of the guesswork from trading decisions.

Weaving Psychology into the Plan

Trading success hinges on your psychological preparation as much as market analysis. A robust trading plan incorporates specific psychological elements to manage emotions and maintain consistency. Your trading psychology framework serves as a personal guidebook, helping you stay grounded during market volatility. By establishing clear psychological guidelines, you create a structure that protects your mental well-being and trading capital.

Emotional management forms the cornerstone of successful trading. When market conditions trigger strong reactions, having predetermined responses prevents impulsive decisions. Your trading plan should specify exact actions for common emotional states. During moments of panic, stepping away from screens for five minutes allows your nervous system to reset. This brief pause creates space for rational thinking to resume, enabling better decision-making when you return to your trading station.

Emotional Trigger

Market movements can spark intense emotional responses, making a detailed trigger management system essential. Your plan should outline specific emotional states and corresponding actions. When experiencing anxiety about a position, taking three deep breaths and reviewing your original trade thesis helps maintain perspective. For moments of overconfidence, checking your position sizing rules prevents overleveraging. These predefined responses transform abstract emotions into concrete, manageable actions.

Trading triggers vary among individuals, so personalizing your response system maximizes effectiveness. Some traders respond strongly to consecutive losses, while others struggle with managing winning streaks. By documenting your unique emotional patterns, you develop targeted coping strategies. Your trigger section might specify: "During winning streaks, I review position sizes twice before increasing exposure" or "After two losses, I reduce position size by 50% for the next three trades."

Pre/Post-Trade Rituals

Structured rituals anchor your trading psychology in consistent behaviors.

Pre-trade rituals prepare your mind for focused decision-making. A five-minute mindfulness practice before market open calibrates your attention. Reviewing your trading rules and stating your intentions aloud reinforces commitment to your strategy. These routines establish a professional mindset and signal to your brain that trading time requires peak mental performance.

Post-trade rituals help process outcomes and maintain emotional equilibrium. Quick journaling after closing positions captures valuable insights about your decision-making process. Recording your emotional state, trade rationale, and execution quality builds self-awareness. This practice highlights patterns in your trading behavior and identifies areas for improvement. Effective post-trade routines might include updating your trade log, reviewing adherence to your plan, and setting intentions for upcoming trades.

Your psychological framework requires regular assessment and refinement. Market conditions change, and your emotional responses evolve with experience. Schedule weekly reviews of your psychological strategies to evaluate their effectiveness. Track which techniques work best for different market scenarios and adjust accordingly. This ongoing optimization process strengthens your psychological resilience and trading performance over time.

Consistency in applying psychological tools makes them second nature. Building these practices into your daily trading routine transforms them from conscious efforts into automatic responses. Your mind learns to recognize emotional triggers and initiate predetermined actions without hesitation. This psychological automation frees mental energy for market analysis and trade execution, improving overall trading effectiveness.

Adaptation & Continual Improvement

Your trading plan must evolve alongside market conditions and your growing expertise. Monthly reviews reveal essential adjustments needed for optimal performance. The markets shift constantly - technology advances, regulations change, and new trading instruments emerge. Through systematic evaluation, you identify which strategies remain effective and which require modification. Tracking these changes helps you stay ahead of market developments while maintaining your competitive edge.

Trading journals provide concrete data for plan improvements. By documenting specific trades, emotional responses, and market observations, you build a personal database of valuable insights. Each journal entry should capture precise details: entry and exit points, position sizing decisions, and the reasoning behind your actions. This detailed record exposes patterns in your trading behavior and highlights areas where your plan needs strengthening.

Review Monthly

Market analysis requires regular assessment of your trading approach. Dedicate time each month to examine your trading results against your documented strategies. Compare your actual trades with your planned executions - did you follow your rules consistently? Which market conditions caused deviations from your plan? This systematic review process exposes gaps between your intended actions and real trading behavior.

Technical developments and shifting market dynamics demand continuous strategic adjustments. Your monthly review should examine emerging trends, new trading tools, and changes in market structure. Pay attention to variations in volatility, volume patterns, and correlation relationships between different assets. These observations guide necessary updates to your trading parameters, position sizing rules, and risk management tactics.

Journal Thoroughly

Detailed journaling creates a feedback loop for strategic refinement.

- Record your thoughts before entering trades, noting specific triggers and expectations.

- Document your emotional state during position management and after exit.

This comprehensive approach reveals psychological patterns affecting your trading decisions. Through consistent journaling, you develop deeper awareness of your trading psychology and decision-making process.

Trading journals should track both quantitative and qualitative factors. Beyond basic trade data, include notes about market conditions, your energy levels, and external factors impacting your performance. This holistic documentation helps identify environmental influences on your trading success. Understanding these connections enables you to optimize your trading schedule and workspace setup for peak performance.

Action Items

Schedule dedicated time blocks for trading plan maintenance.

- Set specific days each week to review your trades and update your strategies.

- Create a structured template for documenting market observations and psychological insights.

- Establish clear metrics for evaluating your plan's effectiveness, such as risk-adjusted returns and consistency in execution.

Your trading success depends on disciplined implementation of these improvements.

- Block time in your calendar for daily journaling and weekly reviews.

- Set up automated reminders for monthly strategy assessments. Develop a systematic approach to incorporating new insights into your trading plan.

This structured routine ensures steady progress in refining your trading approach and psychological preparation.

CHAPTER 8

MOVING FORWARD: BECOMING A MASTER TRADER

———◆———

Long-Term Strategies for a Strong Mindset

If you've made it this far, you already understand how much trading relies on mental discipline. But knowing isn't enough. The real challenge is maintaining that mindset over time. How do you stay sharp when markets shift, your emotions get tested, and the same patterns that once worked start to lose effectiveness?

The answer is constant refinement. You either keep improving, or you start slipping. There's no standing still in trading. If you're not actively strengthening your mindset, your old habits will creep back in, and you'll find yourself making the same mistakes you thought you had outgrown.

I see this happen all the time. A trader builds discipline, follows their plan, sees good results, and then—slowly, almost without noticing—they stop doing the things that made them successful. They stop reviewing trades as carefully. They start skipping their pre-market routine. Their mindset isn't as sharp, and suddenly, they're caught in a cycle of frustration.

So, how do you prevent that? How do you make sure your trading psychology is always improving instead of deteriorating?

Keep Your Mind Sharp by Studying Outside the Charts

There's an easy way to tell which traders will last long-term. They're the ones who are constantly learning, not just about the markets but about themselves. It's easy to get stuck in the habit of only looking at price action, trade setups, and indicators. But the traders who keep growing are the ones who study psychology, decision-making, and high-performance habits just as much as they study technicals.

I had a trader in one of my groups—Noelle—who stood out for this exact reason. She was already profitable, but she wasn't satisfied with just maintaining her results. She made it a point to read at least one book every month, alternating between trading psychology, decision-making, and performance science. She wasn't just reading for entertainment. She was always looking for ideas she could apply directly to her trading.

Some months, she focused on books about cognitive biases—how our brains trick us into making irrational choices. Other months, she studied performance psychology used by top athletes. Over time, I noticed something: while other traders would hit slumps and struggle to recover, she always seemed to stay steady. If she had a bad week, she would reference something she had recently learned and adjust quickly.

That's the difference between someone who trades well for a year and someone who builds a career in this. They don't just wait for experience to teach them lessons. They actively seek out new ways to improve, whether that's through books, courses, or working with mentors.

When was the last time you studied something outside of price action?

The Markets Will Change. Will You?

You might feel like you have a good system now, but how confident are you that it will work five years from today?

Markets evolve. What worked in the past won't always work in the future. The best traders aren't attached to a single method. They adapt. And that adaptability isn't just about strategy—it's about mental flexibility.

I've seen traders who were profitable for years suddenly lose their edge. Not because they became bad traders overnight, but because they refused to adjust when the market changed. They kept forcing the same setups, expecting them to work like they used to. When they started losing, their frustration got the best of them. Instead of reassessing their approach, they kept trading with even more emotion, hoping to make back what they lost.

They weren't mentally prepared for the fact that stability doesn't exist in trading.

How do you avoid falling into that trap?

You train yourself to be flexible before the market forces you to be. You stay curious. You keep testing, questioning, and refining your approach. You remind yourself that no strategy is permanent and that the only real edge you have is your ability to stay mentally sharp.

Ask yourself:

- When was the last time you adjusted your trading strategy based on current market conditions?

- Are you reviewing your performance and making small improvements, or are you assuming that what worked last month will work forever?

Routine is Your Best Defense Against Burnout

One of the biggest threats to a strong mindset isn't just losing trades—it's burnout.

You might not notice it happening at first. Maybe you start feeling a little more frustrated than usual. Maybe you feel exhausted before the market even opens. Maybe you start questioning whether you even enjoy trading anymore.

Burnout doesn't hit all at once. It builds up over time, and by the time you fully recognize it, it's already affecting your performance.

The best way to keep your mind strong for the long haul is to build habits that protect your energy and focus.

A simple routine can make a massive difference. Not just a trading routine, but a routine that supports your overall mental clarity. That means:

- A structured pre-market prep session—so you're not just reacting to the market but going in with a clear plan.

- A review process at the end of each trading session—so you're learning from mistakes instead of repeating them.

- Time away from the screens—so you're not draining yourself mentally with nonstop market exposure.

Some traders act like they need to grind 24/7 to be successful. They think the more time they spend staring at charts, the better they'll perform. But the truth is, some of the worst trading decisions happen when you're exhausted and overexposed.

What are you doing to make sure you're staying mentally fresh?

Emotional Awareness Will Save You Thousands

Emotional intelligence, or EI, is more than just a buzzword that's discussed in psychology classes. It's a honed mental function: the ability to perceive, identify, and manage emotions as they are occurring. Emotional intelligence facilitates clear thinking.

Emotions guide our perceptions, and at the same time, our perceptions or world view can influence our emotional responses and our ability to make quality decisions, often profoundly. It's the voice that tells you to pause; to think before acting; to act rather than react.

Emotional understanding and analysis involve interpreting the causes of emotions. This means not just feeling anger, fear, or frustration but understanding why you're feeling that. "I'm fearful." After that, you should be asking, "What prompted this fear I'm feeling right now?" What perception stuck in your subconscious and predicted, however wrongly, what might come next?

If you've been trading long enough, you already know that your emotions don't just disappear because you've read about trading psychology. You don't wake up one day suddenly immune to fear, greed, frustration, or hesitation.

Those emotions will always be there. The difference between a successful trader and a struggling one isn't the absence of emotions—it's awareness and control.

Ask yourself:

- Can you recognize when you're making a decision out of frustration or desperation?

- Are you aware of when you're trading just to chase the feeling of being right?

- Do you have a process in place to pause before emotional decisions get the best of you?

The stronger your emotional awareness, the better you'll trade. And this isn't something you master once and forget about. It's something you actively check in on every day.

That's why traders who journal consistently improve faster than those who don't. Writing down your thoughts forces you to slow down and see patterns in your own behavior. If you're not tracking how emotions are affecting your trades, how will you ever improve?

Stay Curious, Stay Sharp

The traders who last in this business are the ones who never assume they have it all figured out.

They study not just the market, but themselves. They question their decisions. They look for ways to improve, even when they're winning. They stay open to new ideas but disciplined enough to filter out the noise.

So, where do you go from here?

You can take what you've learned so far and start applying it now, or you can push it to the back of your mind and keep trading the way you always have.

Which choice will make you better six months from now?

Which choice will still have you trading successfully ten years from now?

That's up to you.

Building a Growth Mindset

What do you do when you hit a wall in trading?

Do you step back, analyze, and adjust? Or do you get frustrated, question whether you're cut out for this, and let doubt take over?

The way you respond to setbacks is what separates traders who improve from those who stay stuck. The difference isn't talent, intelligence, or luck—it's mindset.

A growth mindset means believing that skills are developed through effort, practice, and persistence. You aren't limited by what you know today. You can improve if you're willing to put in the work.

Not everyone thinks this way. Some traders assume they have a "knack" for the markets. They know all there is to know. When things go badly, they blame any number of external factors, but never their own unwillingness to learn, adjust, and grow.

Others believe they don't have that gift. When things go wrong, they see it as confirmation that they're just not good enough. They label themselves as bad traders, assume they'll never figure it out, and either quit or continue trading with hesitation and fear.

Then there are those who see setbacks as information. They don't take losses personally. They don't see mistakes as proof of failure. They see them as opportunities to get better. And they don't blame others.

Which mindset do you think will help you succeed long-term?

Your Mindset Controls Everything

Your results don't just come from your strategy. They come from the way you think.

A trader with the best technical system in the world will still fail if they don't have the mental discipline to follow it. On the other hand, a trader with an average system but a strong mindset will continue to refine, adjust, and improve until they succeed.

Think about how this plays out in real-time:

- You take a trade, and it starts going against you. Do you panic and close early, or do you stick to your plan?

- You hit a losing streak. Do you start revenge trading to make the money back, or do you analyze what's happening and adjust?

- You've been trading for months, but your results aren't improving. Do you blame the market and feel stuck, or do you take a hard look at what needs to change?

Your ability to stay disciplined, control emotions, and adapt is what determines whether you grow or stay where you are.

You Are Not Stuck Where You Are

One of the biggest traps in trading is thinking that where you are now is where you'll always be.

Have you ever told yourself:

- •I'll never be able to hold my trades long enough."

- "I always cut my winners too early."

- "I'm just not patient enough."

- "I don't have the discipline to follow my plan."

If you've said anything like this, you're treating your abilities as fixed. You're assuming that how you trade now is how you'll always trade.

But nothing about trading, like life, is fixed. The market evolves, and so can you.

- If you struggle with patience, you can train yourself to be more patient.

- If you have trouble cutting losses, you can develop the discipline to do it.

- If you get emotional after losing trades, you can build mental habits that keep you calm.

None of these skills are locked in. They are developed. There will always be those who are born with certain talents, but that's never the whole story.

How many times have you improved at something in life just because you kept doing it? How often have you struggled with something at first, only to get better over time?

So why would trading be any different?

The Power of Small Improvements

Too many traders think they need one big breakthrough to start seeing success. They assume that if they just fix one major issue, everything will fall into place.

That's not how growth works. Improvement comes from small, consistent changes over time.

If you make tiny adjustments to your trading every day—fixing one mistake, refining one habit, learning one lesson—where do you think you'll be six months from now? A year from now?

It's not about overhauling your entire approach overnight. It's about making small improvements until those improvements compound into something bigger.

What's one thing you can refine in your trading today?

Failure is Not the Opposite of Success

One of the biggest mindset shifts you need to make is how you define failure.

Most traders see failure as proof that they're doing something wrong. They take losses personally. They feel embarrassed when they make mistakes. They think that successful traders don't experience failure.

But failure is not the opposite of success. It's part of it.

If you aren't failing, you aren't pushing yourself enough. You're staying in your comfort zone, avoiding mistakes instead of learning from them.

Think about any skill you've developed in life. Did you get it right the first time? Or did you make mistakes, adjust, and get better?

Trading is no different. Every mistake is feedback. Every loss is data. The only way to fail is to stop learning from them.

What would happen if you started seeing mistakes as stepping stones instead of obstacles?

Rewiring How You Think About Setbacks

If you want to develop a growth mindset, you have to change the way you respond to setbacks.

Instead of saying, "I always do this wrong," shift your thinking to:

- "I can figure this out."

- "I'm improving every day."

- "Every mistake is teaching me something."

- "I get better with every trade."

This might seem small, but the way you talk to yourself matters. If you constantly tell yourself that you aren't good enough, you'll start believing it. But if you remind yourself that improvement is possible, you'll start taking the steps to make it happen.

Try this:

Write down one mistake you've made recently. Instead of beating yourself up over it, ask:

- What did I learn from this?

- What can I do differently next time?

- How can I turn this into an advantage?

This is how you train your brain to see setbacks as opportunities instead of failures.

Commit to Long-Term Growth

Most traders underestimate how long it takes to become truly skilled at this. They expect results fast. When they don't see immediate progress, they assume they aren't good enough.

But trading is a skill. And like any skill, it takes time to perfect.

- How many hours have you actually spent refining your strategy?

- How often do you review your trades with full honesty?

- How much effort do you put into improving your discipline and emotional control?

If you only focus on short-term results, you'll never build the long-term skills that make a great trader. But if you commit to improving just a little bit each day, you'll be ahead of 90% of traders who give up before they ever reach their potential.

This is the mindset that separates long-term success from short-term frustration.

What kind of trader do you want to be?

Growth Mindset in Action

If you want to start applying this now, here's something simple but powerful:

Start using daily affirmations. Make them specific, not generic.

Generic: "I am successful" or "I am a great trader."

Specific affirmations that reinforce growth:

- "I improve with every trade."

- "I am successful because I stick to my strategy and continue to improve my understanding of my craft."

- "Every setback teaches me something valuable."

- "I am developing the skills to become a disciplined trader."

- "I am in control of my emotions and my decisions because I understand where they're coming from."

Say them out loud. Write them down. Repeat them daily.

You might not believe them at first, but over time, they start shaping how you think.

What you tell yourself matters. What you focus on and put ever-increasing amounts of energy into grows.

Are you going to keep repeating the same negative beliefs that hold you back? Or are you going to start training yourself to think differently?

The choice is yours.

Support Systems & Mentorship

Trading can feel isolating. You sit in front of your screens, make decisions, take risks, and deal with the emotions that come with wins and losses—all on your own. No boss, no co-workers, no one holding you accountable. While that freedom is one of the reasons people get into trading, it also becomes one of the biggest challenges.

Without a strong support system, it's easy to fall into bad habits, spiral after losses, or feel stuck when progress slows down. You might have days where you second-guess everything or weeks where you wonder if you're even improving. That's why having the right people around you is one of the most valuable things you can do for your trading.

- How often do you get real feedback on your trading?

- Do you have anyone you can talk to when you hit a rough patch?

- Are you surrounding yourself with traders who challenge you to get better?

If the answer to any of those is no, you're making this harder than it needs to be.

Trading Alone vs. Trading With Support

I've seen so many traders try to do everything alone. They study on their own, trade on their own, review their mistakes on their own. And while self-reliance is important, there's a limit to how much you can improve in isolation.

Dante was one of those traders. When he started, he spent months grinding by himself. He read books, watched videos, tracked his trades, but his results were inconsistent. He would have great weeks, then terrible ones. He would go on winning streaks, then give everything back. He knew something was missing but wasn't sure what.

Then he joined an online mastermind group. At first, he was hesitant. He thought he had to figure everything out on his own. But within a few weeks, things started to shift.

- He had people who held him accountable when he broke his rules.

- He got real-time feedback on his trades.

- He saw how more experienced traders handled losses, which helped him stop overreacting to setbacks.

- He learned new strategies that fit his style, instead of trying to force methods that didn't work for him.

A few months later, his trading had completely transformed. Not because he magically became smarter, but because he had a system of support that showed him where he was making mistakes and helped him grow faster than he ever could have alone.

That's the power of having a community.

Do you have traders you can talk to who will challenge your thinking and push you to improve?

Why a Support System Changes Everything

It's easy to think that trading is purely technical. You learn a strategy, apply it, and that's all there is to it. But most of your growth doesn't come from learning new indicators or tweaking entries. It comes from the mental side—how you handle emotions, decision-making, and discipline.

When you're alone, your weaknesses stay hidden. You might not realize how much fear affects your trading. You might not notice that you're hesitating on good setups or closing trades too early. But when you have people reviewing your trades, spotting patterns, and giving feedback, your blind spots become clear.

A good support system:

- Holds you accountable when you break your own rules.

- Helps you detach from trades emotionally by giving you an outside perspective.

- Keeps you motivated and disciplined when you start feeling burnt out.

- Helps you improve faster by exposing you to different ways of thinking.

Think about any high-level profession—athletes, musicians, executives. None of them operate in isolation. They have coaches, peers, and mentors who push them to improve. Why should trading be any different?

Who do you have in your corner that challenges you to be better?

Finding the Right Mentors & Peers

Not all trading communities or mentors are helpful. Some are just noise. Others might not align with your trading style or personality. The key is finding the right people—those who actually help you improve, not just tell you what you want to hear.

What should you look for in a mentor or trading group?

- **They align with your style.** If you trade price action, a mentor who relies on indicators might not be the best fit.

- **They provide real feedback.** A good mentor won't just say "good trade" or "bad trade." They'll ask questions, break down your thought process, and challenge your assumptions.

- **They have experience.** A mentor doesn't have to be a millionaire trader, but they should have more knowledge than you and be able to explain why they do what they do.

- **They focus on mindset,** not just strategy. The best mentors help you build the habits, discipline, and emotional control needed for long-term success.

Dante didn't just join any trading group. He found a community where traders were focused on real improvement. They weren't just looking for trade signals or quick wins. They were working on discipline, psychology, and consistency. That's what made the difference.

Are you surrounding yourself with traders who push you to be better, or are you stuck in a cycle of trying to figure everything out alone?

How to Build a Strong Support System

If you don't have a support system yet, where do you start?

- **Find a trading group.** This could be a mastermind, a community of traders who share reviews, or even just a few traders you connect with.

- **Get a mentor.** Someone who has experience and can provide real feedback on your trading. This doesn't mean blindly following someone's trades—it means learning from their insights.

- **Engage in discussions.** Don't just sit in a group and watch. Ask questions, share your trades, and be open to feedback.

- **Review with others.** One of the best ways to grow is to review trades with someone else. They'll see things you miss and help you refine your decision-making.

You don't need a huge network. Even one or two solid traders who help you stay accountable can make a massive difference.

What steps are you taking to build a strong support system around your trading?

Take Action: Who's Keeping You Accountable?

You can keep trading on your own, dealing with the same frustrations, making the same mistakes, and trying to figure everything out yourself. Or you can start building a system that helps you grow.

Which choice will help you improve faster?

Are you willing to do what it takes to find the right people who will push you forward?

This is one of those things you don't realize you need until you have it. But once you do, your trading will never be the same.

Habit of Self-Reflection

Most traders track their P&L but never take the time to evaluate the decisions behind their results. And that's where they go wrong.

If you don't stop to reflect, you repeat the same mistakes.

You might convince yourself that a bad trade was just "bad luck" instead of recognizing that you hesitated on execution or ignored a clear exit signal. You keep making emotional decisions, blaming external factors instead of addressing the real issue—your own habits.

If your decision led to a successful result and you don't reflect on how you got there, you won't know how to repeat that success.

Self-reflection isn't just about looking back. It's about using the past to improve the future. Every mistake carries a lesson. Every hesitation, every overtraded session, every time you broke your rules—there's something valuable in it.

But are you actually paying attention?

The Trader Who Grows and the One Who Stays Stuck

I've worked with traders who stay in the same place for years. They trade the same way, make the same mistakes, and wonder why nothing changes.

Then I've seen traders who improve rapidly. They start at the same level, but in a few months, their results are noticeably different. Their execution is sharper. Their losses are controlled. They aren't perfect, but they're consistently getting better.

The difference? Self-reflection.

The traders who grow are the ones who take the time to evaluate their performance, not just in terms of profits, but in terms of decision-making. They:

- Review their trades with full honesty, not making excuses.

- Look for patterns in their behavior, not just in the charts.

- Identify small adjustments they can make instead of waiting for a huge breakthrough.

The traders who stay stuck? They do none of that. They just move on to the next trade without thinking about what went wrong or what they could have done better.

Which category do you fall into?

How to Build the Habit of Self-Reflection

If you're serious about improving, self-reflection needs to be a structured part of your process. That means setting aside time to review—not just when things go wrong, but on a regular basis.

Start simple:

- **Weekly reviews.** Every weekend, go through your trades from the past five days. Ask yourself: Did I follow my plan? Where did emotions interfere? What mistakes did I repeat?

- **Monthly reflections.** Take a bigger picture look at your progress.

Are you seeing improvement? Are the same problems showing up? What adjustments do you need to make?

Self-reflection isn't just about looking at what's wrong—it's also about recognizing what you're doing well. Too many traders focus only on their mistakes and never acknowledge when they've improved. If you held a trade longer than usual, followed your stop-loss without hesitation, or executed a setup exactly as planned, that's progress. And progress needs to be reinforced.

The more you analyze your own behavior, the more control you gain over your decisions.

Turning Mistakes into Improvements

One bad trade doesn't ruin your trading career. But ignoring the reason behind it can.

A single mistake, if analyzed properly, can lead to some of the biggest improvements you'll ever make.

Think about the last time you made a major error. Did you just move on, or did you break it down? Did you ask yourself:

- Why did I make this decision?

- What was I feeling at the time?

- Have I made this mistake before? If so, why does it keep happening?

- What can I do differently to prevent this next time?

If you aren't asking these kinds of questions, you're missing out on the real lessons in your trading. The market doesn't just teach through wins—it teaches through mistakes. But only if you're paying attention.

Are you willing to turn your setbacks into growth, or are you just trying to forget them and move on?

Holding Yourself Accountable

Nobody is going to make you reflect on your trading. There's no manager checking your performance or boss making sure you stick to your plan.

That's what makes trading so challenging—you are the only one responsible for your improvement.

You can either hold yourself accountable, reviewing your decisions with full honesty, or you can avoid it and keep repeating the same mistakes.

A trader who holds themselves accountable will:

- Track not just their P&L, but their execution and mindset.

- Call themselves out when they break their own rules, without making excuses.

- Stay honest about what's working and what isn't, instead of blaming external factors.

A trader who avoids accountability? They just keep trading, hoping things improve without making any real changes.

Which type of trader are you?

Where Do You Go From Here?

If you're not actively reflecting on your performance, you're leaving massive opportunities for growth on the table.

- Are you willing to commit to weekly and monthly reviews?

- Are you ready to analyze your mistakes instead of avoiding them?

- Are you going to track your execution and mindset, not just your profits?

The traders who improve are the ones who take this seriously. The ones who don't? They stay in the same place, wondering why they aren't seeing results.

Which path are you going to take?

Let's now move into something even deeper—neuroplasticity, cognitive biases, and advanced decision-making science—the next level of trading psychology.

CHAPTER 9
ADVANCED TRADING PSYCHOLOGY CONCEPTS

———— ◆ ————

Neuroplasticity in Depth

Have you ever caught yourself making the same trading mistake over and over again? Maybe you hesitate to enter a trade, even when the setup is perfect. Maybe you move your stop-loss, hoping the trade will turn around. Maybe you cut winners too early because you're afraid of losing profits.

You know these habits hurt your performance, yet you keep doing them. It feels automatic—like you have no control in the moment. But here's the truth: these behaviors are not permanent. They are patterns wired into your brain, and they can be rewired.

That's where neuroplasticity comes in.

Neuroplasticity is your brain's ability to physically change; to reorganize or create new connections in response to learning something new. The more you repeat a behavior, the stronger the neural connections for that behavior become. If you constantly exit trades too early, your brain reinforces that reaction. If you always widen your stop-loss, your brain turns that into a habit. Over time, these actions become instinctive—your default response under stress.

The good news? Just as negative habits can be reinforced, they can also be replaced.

How Your Brain Builds Trading Habits

Every action you take in trading strengthens a neural pathway in your brain. The more you repeat a behavior, the easier and more automatic it becomes. This is why bad habits are so hard to break—your brain has built a strong connection to that behavior.

Think about how this applies to trading:

- If you've trained yourself to exit a trade early every time you see a small profit, your brain will fire that signal automatically.

- If you've trained yourself to overtrade when you're frustrated, your brain will keep repeating that cycle.

- If you've trained yourself to hesitate before taking a valid setup, hesitation will become your default response.

The key to changing these behaviors is intentionally rewiring your brain with new habits. It won't happen overnight, but with repetition, the old patterns will weaken, and the new ones will take over.

How many of your trading habits are helping you, and how many are holding you back?

Rewiring a Negative Trading Habit

Pick one trading habit that you know is hurting you. Don't try to fix everything at once—focus on one specific behavior that you need to change.

Maybe it's:

- Moving your stop-loss because you don't want to take a loss.

- Hesitating to enter a trade even when your setup is valid.

- Closing trades too early out of fear.

- Taking impulsive trades after a loss.

Once you've identified the habit, commit to replacing it with a new behavior. For at least 21 days, you need to train your brain to respond differently in that situation.

Let's say your bad habit is moving your stop-loss. Your new rule might be:

- "Once my stop-loss is set, I will not adjust it unless my strategy specifically allows it."

Every time you feel the urge to move it, stop and recognize what's happening. Your brain is firing an old signal—one that you've strengthened through repetition. But this time, instead of acting on it, pause and reinforce the new rule.

The first few times will feel uncomfortable. Your brain will resist the change because it's used to the old habit. But if you stay disciplined, the new habit will start to take hold. And eventually, it will become your default reaction.

You can also practice this through visualization. See yourself making the change and it will be easier for you to do it in real time.

What's one habit you can start rewiring right now?

The Science of Changing a Trading Habit

There's a reason why breaking old habits and forming new ones takes time. Your brain is physically rewiring itself—creating new neural connections and weakening old ones.

This process follows a clear pattern:

1. Awareness – Recognizing the bad habit as it happens.

2. Interruption – Stopping yourself from acting on the automatic response.

3. Replacement – Implementing the new behavior.

4. Repetition – Reinforcing the new habit through consistent practice.

Most traders fail at step three. They recognize their bad habits, but they don't replace them with a structured plan. Without a new behavior to reinforce, the old habit stays strong.

Let's say you always hesitate before taking a trade. Your new rule might be: "I will execute any valid setup without hesitation, following my predefined entry criteria."

At first, hesitation will still creep in. But if you stick to the rule and force yourself to execute, your brain will start rewiring itself. Over time, hesitation will fade, and confidence will replace it.

How many times have you tried to fix a trading habit but given up too soon?

The Power of Tracking Your Progress

One of the most effective ways to speed up the rewiring process is to track your progress. If you don't measure your behavior, it's easy to fall back into old patterns.

At the end of each trading day, ask yourself:

- Did I follow my new rule today?

- If not, what triggered me to revert to my old habit?

- What can I do differently tomorrow?

If you start tracking your habits, you'll see patterns you didn't even realize were there. Maybe you break your rules when you're trading too large. Maybe hesitation kicks in after a losing streak. Maybe overtrading happens when you skip your morning routine.

The more you analyze your own behavior, the easier it becomes to fix. By seeing your patterns in writing, you can use affirmations to create new thoughts and rewire your brain to substitute that thought for the old behavior that does not serve you. Remember, when creating a new habit:

- See it (write it down).

- Say it (out loud).

- Hear it (by saying it).

- Repeat it (all day throughout the day). Make it the last thing you do after you turn out the lights for bed, and the first thing you do when you open your eyes in the morning.

Are you willing to track your progress and hold yourself accountable?

Commit to the Change

Rewiring your brain isn't complicated, but it does take effort. The hardest part is sticking with the new habit long enough for it to replace the old one.

If you're serious about making a change:

- Pick one habit to work on.

- Define a new behavior to replace it.

- Follow that rule every trading day for at least 21 days.

- Track your progress and adjust as needed.

This is how real improvement happens—not by reading more books or watching more videos, but by rewiring the way you think and act in real-time.

What's the first habit you're going to change?

Let's now move into cognitive biases and advanced decision-making science—the next level of trading psychology.

Cognitive Biases & Their Impact

Have you ever been so confident in a trade that you ignored all signs it was going against you? Or maybe you found yourself only looking for information that supported your position while dismissing everything else. If you've ever caught yourself doing this, you've experienced cognitive biases in action.

Cognitive biases are mental shortcuts your brain takes to process information quickly. They help in daily life, but in trading, they can lead to irrational decisions and costly mistakes. No trader is immune to them, but those who recognize and control them gain an edge over those who don't.

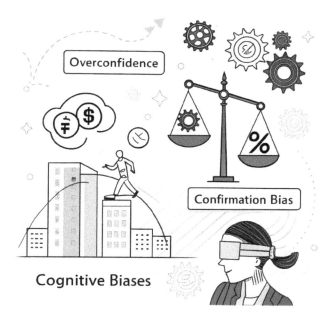

Think about your last few trades. Were you making decisions based on clear, objective analysis, or were your biases creeping in without you realizing it?

The Most Common Cognitive Biases in Trading

If you've been trading long enough, you've likely fallen victim to at least one of these biases. Understanding them is the first step in reducing their impact.

- **Overconfidence Bias** – You believe you're right, even when the market is proving otherwise. You increase your position size because of a few recent wins, assuming you can't be wrong.

- **Confirmation Bias** – You seek out information that supports your trade while ignoring anything that contradicts it. You find a news article that aligns with your thesis and completely dismiss another one that challenges it.

- **Anchoring Bias** – You fixate on a specific price level, such as an entry price, and refuse to adjust your thinking. Even when new information suggests your trade is invalid, you hold on, anchored to that original number.

- **Loss Aversion** – You fear losses more than you value potential gains. Instead of accepting a small loss, you let it grow, hoping it will turn around. When you finally close it, the loss is much worse than it had to be.

Do any of these sound familiar?

Case Study

I once worked with a trader named Ivan who had a strong bias toward buying stocks. No matter what the market conditions were, he looked for reasons to go long.

One day, he spotted a stock that had been trending up for weeks. He was convinced it would keep running. But as soon as he entered, the price started to stall. Then, a few red candles appeared. There were clear signs that momentum was shifting.

Instead of cutting the trade or reconsidering his position, he doubled down. He scrolled through news sources, only reading articles that confirmed his bullish bias. He ignored the technical indicators that showed weakness. He dismissed the high volume on the sell-side, telling himself it was just a temporary dip.

The stock continued to fall, but Ivan refused to accept it. By the time he finally exited, he had taken a massive loss.

What went wrong? His confirmation bias blinded him. Instead of evaluating all the available information, he only focused on what supported his initial belief. If he had been more objective, he could have cut his losses early or even switched his bias to shorting the stock.

How many times have you ignored evidence that contradicted your trade?

How Biases Impact Your Trading Decisions

Biases don't just affect individual trades—they shape the way you approach the market every day.

If you're overconfident after a winning streak, you might take bigger risks without realizing it. If you have confirmation bias, you might dismiss key signals that could save you from a bad trade. If you suffer from loss aversion, you might hold onto losing positions far too long, hoping for a reversal that never comes.

These biases create hidden weaknesses in your decision-making. The only way to control them is to actively check yourself before each trade.

The Cognitive Bias Checklist

If you want to minimize the effect of biases, you need a system in place to question your own thinking. Before entering a trade, run through this checklist to make sure your decisions are based on logic, not emotion:

- Am I considering both bullish and bearish signals objectively?

- Is there any evidence I am ignoring because it contradicts my trade idea?

- Am I anchoring to a specific price level instead of adapting to new information?

- Am I taking on too much risk because I feel confident after a few wins?

- Am I hesitating to take a small loss because I don't want to be wrong?

If you find yourself answering "yes" to any of these questions, pause before entering the trade. Take a step back, reassess the situation, and make sure you're acting on facts, not emotions.

When was the last time you checked your own biases before placing a trade?

Training Your Mind to Be More Objective

You can't eliminate cognitive biases completely, but you can train yourself to recognize them and make better decisions.

- Keep a bias journal. After each trading session, write down whether any biases affected your decisions. Over time, you'll see patterns in your thinking that you weren't aware of before.

- Get an outside perspective. Reviewing your trades with someone else can expose biases you don't notice on your own.

- Set rules for objectivity. If you catch yourself falling into confirmation bias, force yourself to list three reasons why the opposite trade might work. If you're overconfident, scale down your position size until you regain discipline.

The traders who succeed long-term aren't the ones who eliminate emotions entirely. They're the ones who learn how to control them.

Are you willing to question your own thinking to become a better trader?

Let's now move into advanced decision-making science and how to strengthen your ability to make clear, rational choices under pressure.

The Science of Decision-Making Under Pressure

Have you ever noticed how your thinking changes when you're under stress? One moment, you're following your plan with precision, and the next, you're making impulsive decisions that you regret as soon as the trade is over. It's not just a lack of discipline—it's your brain reacting to pressure.

When stress kicks in, your logical thinking takes a backseat. Your body shifts into survival mode, prioritizing quick reactions over rational analysis. In trading, this can lead to all kinds of bad decisions—chasing price, doubling down on losing trades, hesitating when you should act. The worst part? It often happens before you even realize what's going on.

If you've ever looked back at a trade and thought, "Why did I do that?" chances are, stress was influencing your decision-making.

So how do you keep a clear head when the market is moving fast, and emotions are running high?

What Happens to Your Brain Under Stress?

Your brain is wired to protect you from threats. In high-pressure situations, your body releases cortisol, a stress hormone designed to help you respond quickly. In survival situations, this is useful—it sharpens your reflexes and helps you act fast. But in trading, it works against you.

When cortisol floods your system:

- Logical thinking slows down. Instead of processing all available information, your brain locks onto a single detail.

- Emotional reactions take over. Fear of missing out, panic, and frustration become stronger than rational decision-making.

- Risk perception changes. A minor loss might feel unbearable, leading to impulsive trades or revenge trading.

This is why traders who seem disciplined outside of the market suddenly struggle once real money is on the line. The problem isn't knowledge—it's how stress impacts their ability to apply that knowledge in the moment.

Have you ever noticed how differently you think when you're calm compared to when you're in a live trade?

How to Recognize When Stress is Taking Over

Stress doesn't always feel like panic. Sometimes it's subtle—tension in your shoulders, shallow breathing, a feeling of urgency to make a decision. Recognizing these early signs is key to stopping stress from hijacking your trading.

Here are a few indicators that your stress levels are rising:

- You feel your heart rate increasing before or during a trade.

- You feel an urge to act immediately, even when your setup isn't fully confirmed.

- You start second-guessing your plan, looking for reasons to enter or exit impulsively.

- You feel emotionally attached to the outcome of a single trade.

When these signs appear, your brain is shifting into a reactive state. At that moment, you have two choices—let stress control your decisions or take steps to regain control.

Techniques to Stay Clear-Headed Under Pressure

The best traders aren't immune to stress, but they know how to manage it. They have techniques in place to keep their minds clear even when the market is moving fast.

As mentioned earlier, one of the simplest but most effective techniques is **box breathing**—a breathing method used by Navy SEALs and high-performance athletes to stay focused under extreme pressure.

Here's how it works:

1. Inhale deeply through your nose for four seconds.

2. Hold your breath for four seconds.

3. Exhale slowly through your mouth for four seconds.

4. Hold again for four seconds, then repeat.

This technique helps regulate your nervous system, lowering cortisol levels and restoring logical thinking. Just a few cycles of box breathing before or during trading can make a noticeable difference in how you handle high-stress moments.

Another powerful technique is **mindful pauses**. If you feel stress rising, step away from your screen for 30 to 60 seconds. This prevents you from making impulsive decisions and gives your brain a moment to reset.

Some traders also use **heart-rate monitoring** apps to track their stress levels in real time. If they see their heart rate spiking, they pause before making any decisions.

Have you ever considered using physical techniques to manage your trading mindset?

Training Yourself to Handle Pressure Better

Handling pressure isn't just about knowing what to do—it's about training your mind and body to respond differently when stress appears. The more you practice managing your stress, the stronger your decision-making under pressure becomes.

- Start every trading session with a pre-market routine that includes breathing exercises or mindfulness techniques.

- During high-volatility moments, take slow, deliberate breaths instead of reacting immediately.

- If you catch yourself feeling emotional about a trade, step away and reset before making your next move.

The goal isn't to eliminate stress—it's to learn how to control your responses so stress doesn't control your decisions.

Are you willing to build habits that strengthen your ability to stay calm under pressure?

Let's now move into real-time emotional regulation strategies that help you stay in control even in the most unpredictable market conditions.

Real-Time Emotional Regulation

How many times have you acted on emotion in the middle of a trade and immediately regretted it? Maybe you saw a position moving against you and closed it too early, only to watch it reverse in your favor. Or maybe you hesitated on an entry because fear kicked in, and then you sat there frustrated as the trade took off without you.

In those moments, logic takes a backseat. Your emotions take over, pushing you to act impulsively. And by the time you realize what happened, it's too late.

You already know that emotions affect trading. But what are you doing to control them in the moment?

It's one thing to reflect on mistakes after the fact, but if you don't have strategies to regulate emotions in real time, you'll keep making the same costly errors.

The 90-Second Cool-Down

Sasha, a trader I worked with, used to struggle with emotional reactivity. When trades went against her, she would panic and close them prematurely. When she had a winning trade, she would get overly excited and start increasing her risk on the next setup.

One technique completely changed her ability to stay in control: the 90-second cool-down.

Here's what she did:

Whenever she felt an emotional surge—whether it was frustration, excitement, or fear—she forced herself to pause for 90 seconds before taking any action.

No clicking buttons. No adjusting stops. No entering or exiting a trade. Just a deliberate pause.

During those 90 seconds, she would:

- Take slow, deep breaths.

- Step away from her screen (if possible).

- Remind herself that emotions are temporary and will pass.

And they always did.

What she learned is that emotional reactions peak quickly and fade just as fast if you don't feed them. The urge to act impulsively—whether it's closing a trade too early or jumping into something without confirmation—feels overwhelming in the moment. But if you step back and let that peak moment pass, your brain returns to a logical state, allowing you to make a calm, objective decision.

Have you ever noticed how much clearer your thinking becomes after just a short break?

Reframing the Situation

Another trader I know used to struggle with hesitation. Every time a valid trade setup appeared, he would freeze, fearing the potential loss. Even though his strategy had a proven edge, his fear of losing money would overpower his ability to execute.

What finally helped him was a simple mental shift: visualizing both the best-case and worst-case outcomes before entering a trade.

Before clicking the buy or sell button, he would ask himself:

- What's the best thing that could happen? Could this be a great trade that plays out exactly as expected?

- What's the worst thing that could happen? If it fails, what's my actual risk? Would it really be as bad as my emotions are making it seem?

This forced his brain to look at both possibilities instead of only focusing on fear. And once he put things into perspective, the hesitation faded.

A losing trade wasn't catastrophic—it was just part of the process. A winning trade wasn't an excuse to feel invincible—it was simply following the plan.

Do you tend to exaggerate the risk in your mind before entering a trade? Or do you only focus on the reward, ignoring the possibility of loss?

Reframing the situation before emotions take over can help you stay balanced in the moment.

Recognizing Emotional Triggers Before They Control You

Emotional trading isn't random. There are patterns. Specific situations trigger reactions, and if you don't recognize them, they'll keep controlling your decisions.

Take a moment and ask yourself:

- When do you feel the strongest emotional urges in trading?

- Is it after a big win, when overconfidence kicks in?

- Is it after a loss, when frustration tempts you to take revenge trades?

- Is it when you see a trade moving in your favor, but you fear losing profits?

Once you identify your personal triggers, you can start preparing for them before they happen.

For example, if you know you tend to revenge trade after a loss, set a rule: After a losing trade, I will take a mandatory 3-minute pause before even considering another entry.

If you recognize that excitement makes you overtrade, build a habit of lowering your position size after a winning streak to keep your emotions in check.

When was the last time you actively prepared for the emotions you knew were coming?

Building Emotional Resilience Over Time

Emotional regulation isn't something you master overnight. It's a skill—one that you develop with repetition, just like any other aspect of trading.

Every time you successfully resist an emotional impulse, your ability to stay disciplined gets stronger. Every time you pause before acting on fear or greed, you reinforce the habit of making logical decisions under pressure.

Are you willing to do the work to build real emotional control?

No trader can sustain these changes alone. Here's how to build a solid support system to reinforce your growth.

CHAPTER 10

BUILDING A SUPPORT SYSTEM FOR TRADERS

---◆---

Importance of Community & Mentorship

Trading can be one of the most isolating pursuits. You sit in front of your screens, make decisions in real-time, and take full responsibility for every gain and loss. There's no boss overseeing your work, no team to collaborate with, and no one checking to see if you're staying disciplined. While the independence is appealing, it can also be a trap.

Without a community or mentorship, you risk falling into the same mistakes over and over again. You might not even realize what's holding you back because there's no one to point it out. You could be spinning your wheels, making small adjustments to your strategy, thinking that's the problem—when in reality, it's your mindset, discipline, or emotional control that needs work.

How Elena Found Her Breakthrough

Elena had been trading for two years before she saw real progress. She wasn't failing, but she wasn't improving either. Her results were inconsistent—some months were great, others were frustrating. She would win for a while, then give everything back in a short period. She studied charts relentlessly, tested different strategies, and read every book she could find. But nothing changed.

Then she did something different.

She joined a small trading forum and started sharing her trade journal. At first, she hesitated. She wasn't sure if she wanted other traders picking apart her decisions. What if they criticized her? What if she exposed weaknesses she wasn't ready to face?

But once she started posting, something clicked.

Other traders in the forum began pointing out things she hadn't noticed. They asked her questions that forced her to think deeper about her process. They showed her small adjustments that made a huge difference in her execution. She wasn't just trading inside her own head anymore—she had a group of traders holding her accountable, challenging her, and helping her see where she was going wrong.

Within six months, Elena's trading improved more than it had in the previous two years. Not because she found a new strategy, but because she finally had a support system that pushed her forward.

How much faster could you improve if you had people giving you direct, honest feedback?

Why Trading Alone Can Hold You Back

Most traders start out alone, and many stay that way for too long. The problem isn't just the lack of support—it's the lack of perspective.

When you trade in isolation, you:

- Get stuck in repetitive mistakes because no one is there to challenge you.

- Become emotionally attached to your trades without an objective outside view.

- Struggle to stay disciplined because there's no external accountability.

- Miss out on learning from others who have already overcome the challenges you're facing.

A community won't take trades for you, and a mentor won't magically fix your mindset, but having the right people around you accelerates your learning in ways that self-study alone never can.

How much easier would it be to stay accountable if you had a group of traders who expected you to review your trades with full honesty?

The Right Mentor Can Save You Years of Frustration

Not all mentors are equal. Some just throw out generic advice, while others try to push a one-size-fits-all approach that doesn't suit your style. A real mentor doesn't just tell you what to do—they help you think differently, challenge your biases, and guide you toward building your own process.

Finding the right mentor means looking for someone who:

- Trades in a way that aligns with your personality and risk tolerance.

- Can explain concepts in a way that makes sense to you.

- Provides real feedback instead of just vague encouragement.

- Helps you develop both technical and psychological skills.

If you don't have a mentor yet, ask yourself—where could you find one? Could you join a trading group where experienced traders are active? Could you reach out to someone whose approach you respect? The best traders aren't always the loudest ones online, but they're the ones who are consistent and disciplined in their process.

Are you willing to invest time in learning from those who are already where you want to be?

How to Build a Strong Trading Network

If you don't have a community yet, it's time to start building one.

- Join a trading forum or mastermind group where traders actively discuss ideas and review trades.

- Connect with traders who share a similar mindset—those who focus on long-term consistency over quick wins.

- Be open to feedback. The fastest way to improve is to let others challenge your assumptions.

- Contribute. The more you engage, the more you'll gain from the process.

Trading doesn't have to be a solo effort. The more you surround yourself with the right people, the more opportunities you create to sharpen your skills, hold yourself accountable, and push through plateaus.

Who is in your trading network right now? Are they helping you improve, or are you still trying to figure everything out on your own?

No trader succeeds in isolation. Let's now move into creating an accountability network that keeps you focused and disciplined even when motivation fades.

Finding the Right Mentor

How much time have you spent trying to figure things out on your own? How many hours have you put into testing strategies, reading books, watching videos, and still feeling like something is missing?

Every trader reaches a point where they realize they can't do everything alone. Growth comes faster when you learn from someone who has already been through the struggles you're facing now. The right mentor won't just teach you technical strategies—they'll challenge your thinking, point out your blind spots, and keep you accountable in ways you can't do for yourself.

But finding the right mentor isn't as simple as following the most popular trader online. Many self-proclaimed "gurus" flash big profits, but they don't have a structured, repeatable process. Others can trade well but have no idea how to teach.

Some will overwhelm you with information without ever addressing the real issues holding you back.

So how do you find someone who can actually help you level up?

What Makes a Great Trading Mentor?

Not every trader who is successful can be a good mentor. You need someone who fits your style, communicates effectively, and focuses on the things that matter.

When looking for a mentor, ask yourself:

- Do they trade the same markets and timeframes as you? A mentor who trades long-term investments won't be much help if you're a day trader.

- Do they have a track record of consistency? Focus on longevity, not just flashy profits. Have they been profitable across different market conditions?

- Can they clearly explain their process? Someone who truly understands trading should be able to break it down in a way that makes sense to you.

- Do they focus on mindset and discipline, not just strategy?

A great mentor teaches you how to think, not just what to trade.

Many traders waste time chasing signals from people who don't teach them anything about the why behind the trades. A real mentor doesn't just hand you answers—they help you build the skills to find the answers yourself.

Are you looking for someone to do the work for you, or are you looking for someone to push you to become a better trader? How to Approach a **Potential Mentor the Right Way**

If you've identified someone who could be a good mentor, how do you reach out without coming off as just another trader looking for handouts?

First, understand that successful traders value their time. They aren't obligated to mentor anyone, and they definitely won't waste time with someone who isn't serious. If you message someone asking, "Can you mentor me?" without showing effort on your part, don't be surprised if they ignore you.

Instead, show that you're already putting in the work. When reaching out, be specific:

- Mention something they've taught that resonated with you.

- Show that you've applied their concepts in your own trading.

- Ask a well-thought-out question that proves you're serious about improvement.

- Above all, let them know you understand their time is valuable and thank them for any help they can offer.

For example, instead of saying, "How do you trade?" you could say, "I noticed in one of your posts that you focus on waiting for liquidity sweeps before entering. I've been testing this, and I'm struggling with execution timing. Do you have any advice on refining entries for this setup?"

This shows that you've done your research and that you respect their time.

Another smart approach is joining a trading community where they are active. Many great mentors share insights in private groups, webinars, or mastermind programs. If they see you engaging, applying feedback, and improving over time, they're much more likely to take an interest in helping you.

How are you positioning yourself to attract the right mentor? Are you showing that you're committed to growth, or are you expecting someone to hand you all the answers?

The Best Mentorship is Earned, Not Given

The traders who get the most out of mentorship are the ones who bring value back. If you're learning from someone, find ways to contribute—whether that's sharing your own insights, helping other traders in the group, or simply showing gratitude for the lessons you receive.

A mentor-student relationship is a two-way street. The more effort you put in, the more likely a mentor is to invest in your growth.

Are you ready to take mentorship seriously, or are you still searching for shortcuts?

Let's now move into creating an accountability network that reinforces your discipline and keeps you on track even when motivation fades.

Creating an Accountability Network

How many times have you broken your own trading rules, told yourself you'll be more disciplined next time, only to repeat the same mistakes again? Maybe you've overtraded after a loss, moved a stop-loss out of fear, or hesitated on a great setup because doubt crept in.

The truth is, trading alone makes discipline harder. When there's no one checking in on your progress, it's easy to justify bad habits. You tell yourself you'll be more patient, but when no one's holding you accountable, there's no real pressure to change.

This is why some of the most successful traders don't work in isolation—they build accountability networks. A solid group of traders can do what you can't always do for yourself:

- Call out your bad habits before they turn into patterns.

- Provide objective feedback when emotions cloud your judgment.

- Keep you focused on your trading plan, even when motivation dips.

Have you ever considered how much faster you could improve if you had a team of traders keeping you accountable?

Henry's Accountability Group

Henry had been trading for years, but his risk management was inconsistent. Some weeks he stuck to his plan perfectly; other weeks, he let emotions take over. The problem wasn't that he didn't know how to manage risk—it was that he wasn't consistently enforcing his own rules.

Then he made one change that completely shifted his trading: he started a small accountability group.

Every Saturday, he and three other traders met for a one-hour Zoom call. Each person shared their trades for the week—both wins and losses—while explaining their thought process. No one sugarcoated their mistakes. If someone broke their rules, the group called it out. If someone had an emotional reaction to the market, they had to acknowledge it.

At first, Henry felt uncomfortable exposing his weaknesses. But after a few weeks, something happened. He started thinking about how he would explain his trades to the group before placing them. He didn't want to show up on Saturday and admit he had taken reckless trades.

That extra layer of accountability forced him to be more disciplined, even when no one was watching.

Within months, his risk management improved dramatically—not because he found a new strategy, but because he had people holding him accountable to the strategy he already knew worked.

What would change in your trading if you knew you had to explain every decision to a group of traders who expected you to stay disciplined?

How to Build Your Own Accountability Network

You don't need a huge group—just a handful of serious traders who are committed to improvement.

Start by looking for traders who share the same values: discipline, honesty, and long-term success over short-term gains. You want people who will challenge you, not just agree with everything you say.

Once you've found a few traders, create a structure for accountability:

- Set up weekly or bi-weekly calls where everyone reviews their trades.

- Have clear expectations—each person should come prepared with their biggest wins, mistakes, and lessons learned.

- Be honest with each other. If someone is making emotional decisions, call it out. If you're slipping into bad habits, let the group hold you to a higher standard.

The more open and structured your accountability group is, the faster you'll see improvement.

Are you willing to let other traders challenge your thinking, or are you still trying to fix everything on your own?

No trader thrives in isolation. Now, let's move into leveraging online and offline resources to expand your knowledge and stay ahead in the markets.

Leveraging Online & Offline Resources

How much time do you spend consuming trading content? If you're like most traders, you've probably read dozens of books, watched hours of YouTube videos, and scrolled through countless posts in trading forums. But has all that information actually improved your results?

The problem isn't a lack of resources—it's knowing how to filter out the noise. Too many traders get stuck in a cycle of overconsumption, always searching for the next strategy, the next indicator, or the next secret to success. They jump from one idea to the next, never applying anything long enough to see real progress.

If you want to use resources effectively, you have to be intentional. It's not about how much you learn—it's about what you apply.

Quality Over Quantity

Not all trading communities and educational platforms are created equal. Some are filled with valuable insights, while others are just distractions. If you're spending time in forums where traders argue about predictions instead of discussing process and execution, you're in the wrong place.

Ask yourself:

- Is this resource helping me refine my edge, or is it just adding noise?

- Are the traders in this community focused on process and discipline, or are they obsessed with chasing the next big move?

- Am I actively applying what I learn, or am I just collecting more information?

When you focus on high-quality resources, you get better results with less effort.

Are you being intentional about where you spend your time, or are you just absorbing random information without direction?

Using Webinars & Trading Meetups to Expand Your Knowledge

Online resources are great, but there's something powerful about learning from real conversations. Webinars, live Q&A sessions, and local trading meetups allow you to engage with experienced traders in a way that pre-recorded content never can.

Some of the best lessons come from discussing real trades with others. A trader explaining their thought process in real time will give you insights that no book or video ever could.

Have you ever attended a trading meetup, joined a live session, or engaged in a meaningful discussion about the market with other serious traders? If not, you're missing out on an opportunity to accelerate your growth.

Building a Learning Routine That Works for You

It's easy to consume content all day and feel productive without actually making progress. The key is balancing learning and execution.

- Dedicate a specific time each week for studying—whether that's reviewing books, attending webinars, or analyzing past trades.

- Apply one new concept at a time. Don't overwhelm yourself with five different strategies—master one, then move on.

- Spend more time reviewing your own trades than consuming outside information. Your past trades are your best teachers.

The traders who improve the fastest aren't the ones who consume the most—they're the ones who apply what they learn with consistency.

Are you using resources to improve your execution, or are you just collecting more knowledge without applying it?

Finally, remember that a sharp mind requires a healthy body. Let's explore how physical well-being bolsters trading psychology.

CHAPTER 11

THE INTERSECTION OF PHYSICAL HEALTH AND TRADING PSYCHOLOGY

---◆---

Impact of Physical Health on Cognitive Function

Think about the last time you had a bad trading day. Were you tired? Were you stressed? Did you skip meals or drink too much caffeine? Did you party the night before and get little sleep? Small factors like these add up, affecting the way you process information, handle stress, and stick to your trading plan.

Leila's Struggle with Sleep Deprivation

Leila was a trader who prided herself on her work ethic. She would stay up late studying the markets, back-testing strategies, and preparing for the next trading session. Some nights, she only got four or five hours of sleep, thinking she was gaining an edge by putting in extra screen time.

At first, she didn't notice any major problems. But after a few weeks, her trading started to change. She found herself making impulsive trades, second-guessing her decisions, and reacting emotionally to small price movements. Trades she would normally pass on suddenly felt like opportunities she couldn't afford to miss.

One day, after a particularly rough session, she reviewed her trades and saw a clear pattern—her worst trading days were the ones where she had the least sleep. She wasn't losing because her strategy stopped working. She was losing because her brain wasn't functioning properly.

When she made sleep a priority, everything changed. She started thinking more clearly, following her rules with more discipline, and avoiding the emotional trades that had been draining her account.

How many of your trading mistakes could be traced back to exhaustion, stress, or poor focus?

The Science Behind Physical Health and Trading Performance

Research shows that when your body is out of balance, your decision-making ability suffers.

- Sleep deprivation leads to slower reaction times, increased emotional reactivity, and reduced ability to assess risk.

- Poor nutrition causes blood sugar swings, which can make you feel anxious or foggy-headed.

- Lack of exercise reduces circulation to the brain, making it harder to focus.

If you're constantly feeling drained, distracted, or overly emotional while trading, ask yourself: Is my body affecting my trading more than I realize?

There's a reason top-level athletes, CEOs, and high-performance professionals take their health seriously. They know that mental sharpness starts with physical well-being. Trading is no different.

Optimizing Your Body for Better Trading Decisions

You don't need to overhaul your entire lifestyle overnight. But small, consistent changes in how you take care of yourself can dramatically improve your trading performance.

- **Sleep:** Aim for 7-8 hours of quality sleep. Avoid staring at charts or screens late at night. Turning off all electronics one hour before bedtime allows your brain to prepare for sleep. A well-rested brain processes information faster and makes better decisions.

- **Nutrition:** Avoid heavy, processed foods before trading. Stable blood sugar levels help maintain focus and prevent emotional spikes. Don't rely on caffeine for energy. Only real nutrition can supply your body and brain with the fuel it needs to function properly.

- **Exercise:** Even a short walk or light workout before trading can help clear your mind and reduce stress. Physical activity improves cognitive function and decision-making. Take short breaks to regroup when you're feeling frustrated.

Have you ever considered how much sharper you could be if you treated trading like a high-performance skill that requires a strong body and mind?

Most traders look for an edge in the markets, but the real edge often starts with how well you take care of yourself.

Let's now move into specific strategies for managing stress and preventing burnout so you can sustain long-term success.

Exercise & Nutrition for Peak Mental Performance

You already know that trading requires focus, patience, and emotional control. What you might not realize is how much your physical state influences all of these things. Poor nutrition, lack of movement, and excessive caffeine don't just affect your body—they impact your ability to think clearly, manage stress, and stay disciplined.

If you've ever had a trading session where you felt sluggish, impatient, or emotionally reactive, there's a good chance your physical state played a bigger role than you think.

Why Your Body Affects Your Trading More Than You Realize

Your brain is like a high-performance machine, and what you put into your body determines how well it runs. Poor food choices, dehydration, and lack of movement lead to brain fog, slower decision-making, and emotional volatility—all things that make trading harder than it needs to be.

Think about your most disciplined trading days. Were you feeling energized, well-rested, and mentally clear? Now think about the times you made impulsive mistakes. Were you running on caffeine and little sleep? Were you feeling sluggish or mentally drained?

There's a reason professional athletes follow strict routines when it comes to nutrition and exercise. Their performance depends on it. Trading may not be a physical sport, but it demands just as much mental endurance.

Fueling Your Brain for Better Decision-Making

The goal isn't to follow a strict diet but to eliminate the things that interfere with mental clarity. The biggest culprits? Excess sugar, too much caffeine, and processed foods that are loaded with non-nutritive chemicals.

- **Reduce sugar spikes:** High-sugar foods lead to crashes in energy and focus. Instead of reaching for sweets or energy drinks, stick to balanced meals with lean proteins, healthy fats, and slow-digesting carbs to maintain stable blood sugar levels.

- **<u>Watch caffeine intake:</u>** A small amount of caffeine can sharpen focus, but too much can increase anxiety and emotional reactivity. If you rely on multiple cups of coffee to stay alert, consider cutting back and drinking more water instead.

- **<u>Stay hydrated:</u>** Even mild dehydration affects cognitive function. Keep a water bottle next to your trading setup and drink consistently throughout the day.

These small adjustments can make a noticeable difference in how alert and focused you feel while trading.

The Role of Movement in Mental Performance

Trading requires long hours in front of screens, but your brain needs movement to function at its best. Sitting for extended periods leads to mental fatigue, reduced circulation, and increased stress levels—all things that affect your ability to stay disciplined.

Have you ever noticed how much clearer your mind feels after a short walk? That's because exercise increases blood flow to the brain, reducing stress and improving cognitive function.

If you want to sharpen your focus and decision-making:

- Take short breaks, stand up and stretch between trades, shake out your arms and legs, rotate your shoulders and neck, and jump up and down a little to get circulation going.

- Get outside for a quick walk before the market opens to clear your mind. Fresh air does wonders to clear the head. Even if it's raining, negative ions act to recenter the cells energy. If your office has a fountain, go stand by it and absorb the negative ions supplied by moving water.

- Incorporate regular workouts, whether it's weight training, cardio, or even just bodyweight exercises. Dance, play with your kids, or get involved with friends in sports. You'll be amazed how focusing on something other than the market can energize your mind.

You don't need to spend hours in the gym, but moving your body daily will improve how you think and feel during trading sessions.

Your Health Checklist for Optimal Trading Performance

To make this actionable, create a simple checklist to track the key factors that influence your mental and physical state.

- **Sleep:** Did you get at least 7-8 hours of rest?

- **Hydration:** Have you been drinking enough water throughout the day?

- **Meal Quality:** Are you eating balanced meals with real, whole foods?

- **Caffeine Control:** Are you using caffeine strategically instead of relying on it to function?

- **Movement:** Have you taken breaks to stretch or walk during the trading session?

If you're struggling with focus, emotional control, or energy levels, start tracking these factors. You might be surprised at how much of an impact they have on your trading.

Are you willing to make small changes in your health to gain a real edge in your trading performance?

Let's now move into stress management techniques to prevent burnout and keep your mind sharp for the long term.

Stress Management & Burnout Prevention

Most traders don't realize how much stress they carry until it starts affecting their performance. The constant pressure to make the right decisions, recover losses, and stay disciplined can build up in the background. If you don't have a system to manage that stress, it starts to control you.

Burnout doesn't happen overnight. It creeps in slowly. One day, you start feeling frustrated more easily. Your patience wears thin. You force trades that aren't there. Your confidence takes a hit, and suddenly, the strategy that worked before doesn't seem to work anymore—not because the market changed, but because your mindset did.

How much of your trading stress comes from the market, and how much comes from not giving yourself the space to reset?

Chronic Stress Creates Tunnel Vision

When stress builds up, it narrows your thinking. You stop seeing the bigger picture and start reacting to every small market move. You hesitate when you should act and act when you should wait. You get stuck in a loop where every trade feels like it matters too much.

That's when the emotional swings start. You take a loss and feel the need to get it back immediately. You win a trade and suddenly feel invincible, leading to reckless decisions. Instead of sticking to your plan, you let stress dictate your actions.

Have you ever noticed that your worst trading sessions happen when you're mentally exhausted?

This is why managing stress isn't optional. If you don't handle it, it will handle you

.

Scheduled Time Off: The Key to Long-Term Consistency

The best traders don't grind 24/7. They know that trading well requires balance. Taking structured breaks isn't a weakness—it's a strategy.

If you've ever found yourself staring at charts for hours, waiting for the perfect setup, ask yourself: When was the last time I gave my brain a real break?

Small resets throughout the day can make a big difference:

- Step away from the screen between trades, even for a few minutes to regroup and take your brain away from your narrow focus.

- Schedule at least one trading-free day per week where you don't think about the markets. That means don't read books about trading, don't listen to podcasts, and don't talk to other traders about strategy.

- Plan off-screen hobbies that challenge your mind in a different way—exercise, reading, music, anything that isn't trading-related.

- Try learning something completely new. This builds synapses for better cognition. If you like to cook, it doesn't mean learning a new recipe. Learn to cook in a new language, French food for example.

A trader who is mentally refreshed makes better decisions. A trader who never steps away eventually burns out.

Recognizing the Signs of Burnout Before It's Too Late

Burnout doesn't just mean exhaustion—it affects your entire trading process.

- Do you feel irritated or frustrated by small losses that wouldn't have bothered you before?

- Do you have trouble focusing, even when a valid setup appears?

- Do you feel mentally drained before the market even opens?

- Are you losing your temper or experience mood swings even when you're not trading?

If you're feeling any of these, your brain is sending you a warning. Ignoring it won't make it go away. The best thing you can do is build systems now that prevent burnout before it forces you to stop trading altogether.

How much better would your trading be if you worked with your mind instead of against it?

Now, let's move into how to structure work-life balance to maintain peak trading performance while still enjoying life outside the charts.

Work-Life Balance

How much of your life revolves around trading? Do you feel like you're always thinking about the markets, even when you're away from the screens? Do you ever step back and give yourself real space to recharge?

Too many traders believe that working harder means better results. They spend all day staring at charts, constantly checking their positions, and analyzing trades late into the night. But overloading yourself with market exposure doesn't improve performance—it drains you. When there's no balance, trading starts to feel like an obsession instead of a skill.

If you don't create boundaries, trading will consume every part of your life. And when that happens, frustration builds, mistakes increase, and burnout follows.

Sharon's Decision to Set Boundaries

Sharon was an experienced trader, but she was constantly stressed. She would wake up thinking about the market, trade throughout the day, and then spend her evenings analyzing charts and overthinking missed opportunities. Even when she wasn't trading, her mind was stuck in the market.

She started noticing a pattern. The days she spent too much time on trading were the days she performed the worst. She became reactive, overtraded, and made emotional decisions. On the rare occasions when she gave herself space, she traded better—she was more patient, more focused, and less attached to the outcome of each trade.

That's when she made a rule: No trading after 4 p.m. Once she closed her screen, she was done for the day. She spent time with her family, exercised, and did things that had nothing to do with trading. At first, it felt uncomfortable—she worried she might miss something. But after a few weeks, she realized something important:

- She was more relaxed going into the next trading session.

- Her decision-making improved because her mind wasn't constantly overloaded.

- She actually enjoyed trading again instead of feeling trapped by it.

That one simple rule changed everything for her.

What would change for you if you set clear boundaries with your trading?

Creating Balance Without Sacrificing Performance

Taking time away from trading doesn't mean you're less committed. It means you understand that a well-rested mind makes better decisions.

If you're constantly thinking about the markets, here's what you can do:

- Set a daily cut-off time when you're done looking at charts.

- Take at least one full day off per week with zero trading-related activities.

- Prioritize non-trading activities that challenge your mind in different ways— hobbies, exercise, time with friends and family.

The goal is simple: Be fully present when trading, and be fully present when you're not. If you can do that, your performance will improve, your stress levels will drop, and trading will feel like a skill you've mastered instead of something that controls you.

We've come full circle—mindset, strategy, emotional control, physical health, and support systems. Let's wrap up with final thoughts on integrating these lessons into a complete trading framework.

CHAPTER 12

MARKET VOLATILITY AND UNCERTAINITY

---◆---

The Nature of Market Volatility

Volatility is one of the most challenging aspects of trading. It can wipe out accounts in minutes or create massive opportunities—depending on how well you understand it. If you don't know why the market swings the way it does, you'll always feel like you're reacting instead of being in control.

So, what drives these sudden price movements?

Why Markets Move the Way They Do

At its core, the market moves because of buying and selling pressure. But what causes that pressure to shift so aggressively?

- **External Events:** Earnings reports, economic data, central bank decisions, geopolitical tensions—these events change expectations in an instant.

- **Liquidity Gaps:** When there aren't enough buyers or sellers at a certain price level, even a small order can create a sharp move. This is why thinly traded assets tend to be more volatile.

- **Herd Psychology:** When traders panic, they all rush to exit at once. When they get excited, they all chase price higher. Markets aren't just moved by logic—they're driven by emotion and crowd behavior.

Have you ever entered a trade, seen the market move against you in a way that seemed irrational, and then watched price return to where it started? That's volatility shaking out weak hands before the real move happens.

How to Handle Market Volatility Without Letting It Control You

If volatility catches you off guard, it will force you into bad decisions—closing positions too early, widening stops, or chasing entries. But if you learn how volatility cycles work, you can use it to your advantage instead of fearing it.

- Recognize when volatility is expected—around news releases, market open, or key technical levels.

- Reduce position sizes in high-volatility conditions to manage risk.

- Use wider stop-losses strategically instead of getting stopped out by normal market fluctuations.

Volatility isn't good or bad—it's just part of the market. The key is understanding when it's likely to increase and preparing for it.

Are you adjusting your trading approach based on market conditions, or are you treating every environment the same?

Once you accept that volatility is a normal and necessary part of trading, you stop fearing it—and start learning how to work with it. Now, let's move into how to stay mentally flexible and adapt when markets behave unpredictably.

Emotional Regulation During Rapid Market Shifts

How do you react when the market suddenly moves against you? Do you stay calm and reassess, or do you feel an immediate rush of panic, scrambling to make a decision?

Rapid price movements can trigger an emotional response before you even realize what's happening. Your heart rate speeds up, your mind starts racing, and suddenly, you're not following your plan—you're reacting. Whether it's fear causing you to exit too soon or excitement tempting you to chase, emotions can take over in a split second.

If you don't have a system to regulate your emotions during volatile moves, you risk making impulsive decisions that can wreck your account. The market doesn't punish bad strategy as much as it punishes emotional trading.

So, how do you keep control when everything is moving fast?

Recognizing the Physical Signs of Emotional Overload

Before you can regulate emotions, you need to recognize when they're taking over. Stress doesn't just exist in your mind—it shows up in your body first.

- Do you feel your heart pounding when a trade starts moving quickly?

- Are your hands shaking slightly as you go to adjust your position?

- Do you find yourself clicking buttons too quickly, barely thinking through the decision?

These are all signs that your fight-or-flight response is activating. Your brain perceives the market shift as a threat, and it's pushing you to act immediately. But most of the time, acting impulsively is exactly the wrong move.

The traders who stay calm under pressure aren't naturally unemotional—they've just trained themselves to recognize when emotions are creeping in and use strategies to stay in control.

The 30-Second Cool-Down

One of the most powerful tools you can use in a fast-moving market is the 30-second cool-down. When the market suddenly spikes or drops, your instinct might be to react immediately. Instead, train yourself to pause before making any decisions.

During those 30 seconds:

- Take a slow, deep breath—inhale for four seconds, hold for four, exhale for four.

- Look at the chart objectively—is this move part of a larger pattern, or is it just noise?

- Ask yourself: Am I making this decision based on my strategy, or am I reacting to fear or excitement?

By forcing yourself to pause, you give your prefrontal cortex (the rational part of your brain) time to catch up before your emotions make the decision for you.

Have you ever exited a trade in panic, only to watch price reverse in your favor moments later? That's exactly what this method helps prevent.

Building Long-Term Emotional Stability in Fast Markets

The goal isn't to eliminate emotions—you can't. The goal is to develop habits that allow you to process emotions without acting on them impulsively.

- If volatility makes you anxious, reduce your position size so the dollar amount at risk doesn't trigger panic.

- If you tend to overtrade when the market moves fast, set a rule to limit how often you can enter after a major price swing.

- If you feel frustration taking over, step away from the screen for a few minutes. Let the emotion pass before you make another trade.

The traders who thrive in volatile markets aren't the ones who predict every move correctly—they're the ones who keep their emotions under control while everyone else panics.

Look around at those who are panicking. Keep that picture in your mind.

Are you letting emotions dictate your trades, or are you building the discipline to pause, assess, and make rational decisions—even in the fastest markets?

Now, let's move into how to adjust your trading approach in high-volatility conditions so you can capitalize on market swings instead of getting caught in them.

Tactical Adjustments to Your Trading Plan

A static trading plan might work in ideal conditions, but markets are constantly shifting. Volatility expands and contracts, liquidity changes, and price action becomes more unpredictable. If you don't adjust, you'll find yourself getting stopped out too often, entering positions that are too large, or reacting emotionally to price swings.

Your strategy isn't failing—you're just not adapting to what the market is giving you.

Why You Need a More Flexible Approach

Most traders assume that a stop-loss or position size should always stay the same. But different market conditions require different risk management techniques. A tight stop might work well when price action is slow and controlled, but during volatile periods, it will get hit before the real move even starts.

Have you ever entered a trade, only to get stopped out seconds before price moves in your favor? That's a sign that your stop-loss is too tight for current market conditions.

The same applies to position sizing. If you trade the same size in a fast-moving market as you do in a slow one, your risk exposure increases dramatically. What felt like a manageable loss in a calm market can quickly turn into something much larger when volatility spikes.

Are you adjusting your approach, or are you using the same risk settings no matter how the market is behaving?

How to Adjust Your Trading Plan for Volatility

If you're trading in high-volatility conditions, you need to modify your risk parameters to prevent unnecessary losses and give your trades enough room to breathe.

- **<u>Widen Your Stop-Loss Slightly:</u>** If the market is making bigger swings, a wider stop prevents you from getting shaken out before the trade has a chance to work. But don't just widen stops without adjusting risk—balance it by lowering position size.

- **<u>Reduce Your Position Size:</u>** If price movements are twice as large as usual, your risk per trade is automatically higher. Trading smaller keeps your risk the same while allowing you to stay in the game longer.

- **<u>Be More Selective With Entries:</u>** In volatile conditions, waiting for confirmation becomes even more important. Entering too early can lead to unnecessary drawdowns, making it harder to stick to your plan.

By making these tactical adjustments, you reduce unnecessary losses and improve your ability to stay in profitable trades longer.

Are you willing to adapt, or are you letting rigid rules hold you back from improving your results?

Trading successfully isn't about forcing the market to fit your plan—you can't. It's about adjusting your plan to fit the market. Now, let's move into how to set realistic expectations for trading in high-volatility environments so you stay confident and disciplined.

Setting Realistic Expectations for High-Volatility Environments

How do you approach trading when the market starts moving fast? Do you see the potential for bigger profits, or do you focus on the increased risk?

High-volatility environments create some of the best opportunities, but they also expose traders to more emotional swings, faster price movements, and larger-than-expected losses. If you enter these conditions expecting the same level of predictability as a low-volatility market, you'll end up frustrated, overreacting to price action, and making impulsive decisions.

The key is adjusting your expectations. Instead of seeing volatility as something to fear or chase, you need to understand how to balance risk and reward without getting caught in emotional extremes.

Why Volatility Changes the Game

When the market is moving fast, everything is amplified. Small miscalculations become big mistakes. Minor hesitations turn into missed opportunities. A trade that might normally take hours to develop now plays out in minutes.

If you're not mentally prepared for these shifts, you'll either:

- Get shaken out too early, thinking every pullback is a reversal.

- Overstay your welcome, expecting a move to go further than it realistically can.

- Overleverage yourself, thinking the increased movement means "easy money."

Have you ever entered a trade in a volatile market, taken a small profit, and then watched it move five times further than you expected? Or held on too long, only to see it reverse and wipe out your gains?

This happens when you fail to adjust your expectations for how price behaves in different conditions.

Balancing Risk and Reward in Volatile Markets

Instead of assuming that every big move will continue indefinitely, you need to accept that price swings will be larger and adjust accordingly.

- **Set wider targets and stops** – When volatility increases, a normal move might be two or three times larger than usual. If you use the same small stop-loss and take-profit levels, you'll either get stopped out too early or exit a winning trade before it has a chance to run.

- **Don't chase every breakout** – High volatility can create false moves before the real trend emerges. If you enter too aggressively, you might find yourself on the wrong side of a sudden reversal.

- **Expect rapid shifts in momentum** – Just because the market is moving quickly in one direction doesn't mean it will last. Be ready for sharp pullbacks and don't let greed or fear dictate your next move.

The best traders anticipate volatility rather than react to it. They don't get attached to a single outcome—they stay flexible and adapt as the market evolves.

Are you treating high-volatility environments as opportunities to be managed, or are you letting them pull you into emotional decisions?

The key to succeeding in fast-moving markets isn't just technical skill—it's having the right mindset and expectations. Now, let's move into how to balance risk and opportunity when volatility spikes so you can trade with confidence instead of fear.

Balancing Risk and Opportunity

How do you feel when the market starts moving fast? Do you see it as a chance to capitalize on big swings, or does it trigger hesitation and second-guessing?

Volatility gets a bad reputation because it brings uncertainty, but the reality is that without volatility, there's no opportunity. Every major trend, breakout, and profitable setup happens because price moves. The key isn't avoiding volatility—it's learning how to manage it so that it works in your favor rather than against you.

If you only see risk when markets are volatile, you'll constantly be on edge, reacting emotionally to every price movement. But if you understand how to control risk while staying open to opportunity, you'll be able to trade with confidence instead of fear.

Why Volatility Creates Both Risk and Reward

A market that barely moves doesn't offer much potential. But when price starts accelerating, traders get emotional—some panic, some chase, and some freeze up completely.

Volatility exposes weaknesses in traders who haven't developed emotional control. Have you ever:

- Exited a trade too early because a sudden spike made you uncomfortable?

- Hesitated to enter because price was moving too fast, only to watch it take off without you?

- Rushed into a trade out of excitement, without fully confirming your setup?

All of these reactions come from the same issue—not balancing risk and opportunity. When you focus too much on one, you either play too safe and miss out or take on too much risk and get burned.

So how do you find the middle ground?

How to Stay in Control When Markets Move Fast

Managing risk doesn't mean avoiding volatility—it means being strategic about when and how you engage with it.

- **Define your risk before entering:** Instead of adjusting stops on the fly or making decisions based on emotions, set clear risk parameters for every trade. If a market is moving faster than usual, reduce position size so the dollar amount at risk stays manageable.

- **Be patient with entries:** The biggest mistakes happen when traders feel like they have to act immediately. If you see a strong move, let price settle before jumping in—many times, the best entries come after the initial volatility spike.

- **Trust your plan:** When emotions rise, uncertainty creeps in. If you've already tested your strategy in different market conditions, stick to it. Your job isn't to predict every move—it's to execute with discipline.

The best traders don't avoid volatility, and they don't chase it blindly either. They recognize that risk and opportunity exist together—and the only way to profit consistently is by staying balanced between the two.

Are you letting volatility dictate your decisions, or are you learning how to control risk while staying open to potential gains?

Now, let's move into how to cultivate mental flexibility so you can quickly adapt when the market behaves unpredictably.

Cultivating Mental Flexibility

How do you react when the market doesn't do what you expect? Do you freeze, hoping it turns back in your favor? Do you scramble to adjust your trade on impulse? Or do you recognize the shift, accept the new conditions, and pivot accordingly?

Trading is not about predicting the market—it's about reacting effectively to uncertainty. No matter how much experience you have, there will always be times when price moves in ways you didn't anticipate. If you can't adapt, you'll find yourself stuck, watching profits disappear or taking unnecessary losses simply because you couldn't accept that your original plan wasn't working.

The best traders aren't the ones who are right the most—they're the ones who adjust the fastest when they're wrong.

Why Mental Flexibility is Non-Negotiable

Markets change. What worked yesterday might not work today. A setup that looked perfect can fail without warning. If you treat your analysis as absolute truth instead of a framework that needs adjustment, you'll always be behind.

Think about the last time you hesitated to cut a loss because you were convinced price would come back. Or the time you ignored a new trend because it didn't fit your original bias. These situations don't just cost money—they create frustration, emotional exhaustion, and self-doubt.

Have you ever caught yourself saying, "This trade should have worked"? That thought alone shows resistance to change. The market doesn't care about "should." It only cares about what is actually happening.

So, how do you train yourself to pivot instead of freeze?

How to Develop a More Flexible Trading Mindset

The goal isn't to abandon your strategy every time things get uncertain—it's to recognize when conditions have changed and adjust before it's too late.

- **<u>Detach from your initial bias:</u>** Once a trade is placed, it doesn't matter if your original idea was good. All that matters is how price is behaving right now.

- **<u>Have an exit plan for being wrong:</u>** If the market invalidates your setup, don't hold onto hope. Cut the loss and wait for a better opportunity.

- **Use real-time feedback:** Instead of reacting emotionally, step back and ask, "What is the market telling me?" If price is acting differently than expected, take that as information—not a personal attack on your analysis.

Mental flexibility isn't about second-guessing yourself—it's about making objective adjustments while staying emotionally neutral. Think about this as though you are the mentor to someone else. What would you tell them about what you've observed in their behavior?

Are you resisting change, or are you learning to flow with the market's movement?

With volatility managed, let's move on to building your own structured trading plan so you can execute with confidence in any market condition.

CHAPTER 13

SUSTAINING LONG-TERM PERFORMANCE AND LIFELONG LEARNING

———— ◆ ————

Revisiting Your Trading Progress: A Yearly Audit

Many traders get caught up in short-term results, evaluating their skills based on immediate outcomes rather than long-term progress.

The problem is, a few good or bad trades don't define your ability. If you only judge yourself in the moment, you'll either become overconfident too quickly or discouraged too easily.

The real picture of your trading success is revealed over months and years, not just days or weeks. If you don't take time to analyze your progress properly, you'll keep repeating mistakes without realizing how far you've actually come—or where you need to improve.

Are you tracking the right things, or are you letting short-term results dictate your confidence?

Why Long-Term Reviews Matter More Than Daily Wins and Losses

If you look at any single day or week in your trading, it might not tell you much. Even profitable traders have losing streaks, and even bad traders can have lucky wins. But when you zoom out and analyze your performance over six months to a year, patterns start to emerge.

- Are you consistently profitable over time, or do you have occasional big wins that hide poor risk management?   Are you improving in key areas like discipline, execution, and emotional control?

- Are your best trades coming from planned setups, or are you making more from impulsive decisions?

By reviewing longer-term trends in your trading, you stop obsessing over every individual trade and start focusing on sustainable improvement.

How to Conduct an Effective Yearly Trading Audit

A yearly review isn't just about looking at your profits and losses—it's about identifying the strengths and weaknesses that actually affect your long-term growth.

- **Review your trade journal:** Are you following your plan consistently, or do you see repeated mistakes?

- **Analyze your biggest wins and losses:** What patterns emerge? Are your losses coming from the same types of errors?

- **Assess your mindset throughout the year:** Did emotions interfere with your trading decisions? Have you developed better discipline over time?

Instead of focusing on whether you "had a good year," focus on whether you became a better trader.

Are you just hoping you improve, or are you actively measuring your growth?

Building on What You Learn From Your Audit

Once you see where you're improving—and where you're struggling—you can adjust your strategy, refine your habits, and focus on real progress.

If your results are improving, keep reinforcing what's working. If you're seeing negative trends, correct them before they compound.

A trader who reviews their progress regularly is always evolving. One who avoids self-assessment is doomed to repeat the same mistakes.

Are you taking your development seriously, or are you just hoping things will eventually click?

Now, let's move on to how to transition from part-time to full-time trading by making strategic adjustments to your mindset and risk management.

Scaling Up: Transitioning from Part-Time to Full-Time Trading

Have you ever thought about what it would take to go full-time as a trader? Not just the idea of quitting your job and trading every day, but the actual process of shifting from part-time trading to making it your primary source of income?

Many traders dream of the freedom that comes with full-time trading, but few consider the psychological, financial, and lifestyle adjustments required to make it work. Trading full-time is not just about placing more trades—it's about managing your mental state, structuring your day, and ensuring financial stability even when the markets aren't favorable.

The difference between those who succeed and those who struggle isn't just skill—it's preparation. Are you truly ready to trade full-time, or are you assuming more time in the market will automatically lead to more success?

The Psychological Shift

When you trade part-time, you have a safety net. You may have another source of income covering your expenses, which means your trading decisions aren't based on immediate financial pressure. But when you go full-time, every loss, every bad week, and every slow market condition has real consequences.

This shift requires a completely different mindset. Instead of viewing each trade as a way to grow your account, you must start seeing your trading as a business.

- Do you have a structured routine, or are you trading randomly throughout the day?

- Are you tracking expenses, performance metrics, and risk exposure like a professional?

- Can you remain disciplined even when you're not making money for weeks at a time?

If you haven't mastered emotional control as a part-time trader, those weaknesses will only get worse when trading is your sole source of income.

Risk Management Adjustments for Full-Time Trading

One of the biggest mistakes traders make when transitioning to full-time is assuming they can just trade more often to make up for bad days. This mindset leads to overtrading, revenge trading, and taking setups that wouldn't normally fit your criteria.

The truth is, trading full-time means you need even stricter risk management because your capital is not just for growth—it's for survival.

- **<u>Maintain a financial buffer:</u>** Do you have at least 6-12 months of living expenses saved in case of a drawdown period?

- **<u>Lower risk per trade:</u>** You don't need to swing for huge wins every time. Keeping risk small allows you to trade sustainably.

- **<u>Be okay with sitting out:</u>** If market conditions aren't ideal, can you resist the urge to force trades just because it's "your job" now?

Full-time trading isn't about trading more—it's about trading smarter and knowing when to step back.

Lifestyle Considerations

Trading full-time isn't just about replacing a paycheck. It's about building a sustainable routine that prevents burnout, emotional fatigue, and decision fatigue.

- Do you have a daily schedule that keeps you focused and disciplined?

- Are you balancing screen time with mental recovery? Sitting in front of charts all day can drain you.

- How will you handle the isolation of trading alone? Many traders struggle without co-workers or external structure.

Your entire life structure changes when you trade full-time. The better you prepare for that shift, the smoother the transition will be.

Are you treating your trading like a professional career, or are you still approaching it with the mindset of a hobby?

Going full-time is not about trading more—it's about trading with more precision, more discipline, and more control over your risk. Now, let's move into how to stay ahead in a constantly evolving market so you remain profitable long-term.

Staying Ahead: Adapting to Technological and Market Changes

The financial world never stands still. Market conditions shift, algorithms evolve, and new technologies emerge that can either give you an edge or leave you behind. If you refuse to adapt, your strategy that worked last year might become completely ineffective tomorrow. The best traders don't just react to change—they anticipate it and adjust before it becomes a problem.

Are you staying ahead of market developments, or are you slowly falling behind without realizing it?

Why Market Adaptability Matters

Traders who struggle over time usually aren't bad at trading—they're just too attached to a single way of doing things. They resist updating their strategies, dismiss new tools, and assume that what worked before should always work. But markets are constantly evolving, and the traders who succeed long-term are the ones who stay flexible.

Have you noticed that certain setups don't work as well as they used to? That price action behaves differently than it did a year ago? These aren't random occurrences. They are signs that liquidity, market structure, and trader behavior have shifted.

If you aren't paying attention to these changes, you'll keep making the same mistakes, wondering why things "feel different" without realizing the market has already adapted—you just haven't. How to Stay Flexible Without Chasing Every New Trend

Keeping up with market and technological shifts doesn't mean jumping on every new tool or strategy that comes out. It means being aware of changes, testing them objectively, and making informed decisions about whether they can enhance your trading.

- **Regularly review your trading performance** – Are you still getting the same results, or are you seeing signs that your strategy needs refining?

- **Stay informed on technological advancements** – Are there new tools that improve execution speed, market analysis, or risk management?

- **Learn from other traders** – You don't need to reinvent the wheel. Observing what experienced traders are adjusting in their strategies can provide valuable insights.

Adapting doesn't mean abandoning what works—it means refining it, improving it, and staying sharp before the market forces you to change.

Are you actively evolving with the markets, or are you waiting until your strategy stops working before realizing you need to adjust?

The traders who thrive long-term aren't the ones who stick to the past—they are the ones who embrace continuous learning and refinement. Now, let's move into how to commit to lifelong learning so you keep sharpening your edge year after year.

Lifelong Learning: The Ongoing Quest for Mastery

The best traders never stop learning. They know that mastery isn't a destination—it's a process. No matter how skilled you become, there will always be new insights to gain, new strategies to test, and new ways to refine your approach. The moment you think you've figured everything out is the moment you start falling behind.

Are you treating trading like a fixed skill, or are you developing a mindset that keeps you sharp, adaptable, and always improving?

Why Mastery is an Ongoing Process

Many traders plateau because they stop learning after reaching a certain level of competence. They find a method that works, gain some consistency, and then assume they don't need to study anymore. But the market is always evolving, and traders who stop growing eventually get left behind.

Think about the last time you learned something that completely changed how you trade. What if you had never come across that piece of information? How much longer would it have taken for you to make that breakthrough?

Mastery doesn't come from repeating the same things over and over—it comes from continuously refining, questioning, and pushing yourself beyond your current level.

Building a Habit of Continuous Learning

If you want to stay at the top of your game, learning needs to become a structured part of your routine—not something you only do when things aren't going well.

- **<u>Read widely:</u>** Study market history, trading psychology, and technical advancements. The more perspectives you expose yourself to, the more complete your understanding becomes.

- **<u>Analyze your past trades:</u>** Regular reviews allow you to see patterns in your mistakes and successes, making each trade an opportunity to improve.

- **<u>Engage with other traders:</u>** Discussing ideas, comparing strategies, and challenging your assumptions keeps you from becoming too rigid in your thinking.

Lifelong learning isn't just about gaining new knowledge—it's about staying curious, questioning your methods, and constantly refining how you approach the markets.

Are you actively investing in your own growth, or are you assuming that what you know today will always be enough?

The best traders don't wait for setbacks to force them into learning. They make continuous improvement a priority. Now, let's move into how to apply everything you've learned to create a trading mindset that stays strong, adaptable, and consistently profitable.

Final Words of Wisdom: Embracing Uncertainty with Confidence

How comfortable are you with not knowing what will happen next? Can you place a trade, manage your risk, and accept the outcome—without letting emotions take over?

Uncertainty is the one thing that never changes in trading. No matter how much experience you gain, how many strategies you master, or how much data you analyze, there will always be unknowns. The market doesn't owe you a clean pattern, a predictable reaction, or a guaranteed outcome.

Many traders struggle because they seek control where none exists. They want to eliminate uncertainty rather than learning how to operate within it. But the truth is, your edge doesn't come from knowing the future—it comes from how you respond to what unfolds in real time.

Are you trying to fight uncertainty, or are you learning how to move forward despite it?

Confidence Comes From Preparation, Not Prediction

Traders often think confidence means being certain about a trade, but real confidence is knowing that even when uncertainty is present, you are prepared.

- You have a risk management plan in place, so no single trade can hurt you.

- You have a process for reviewing and improving, so every trade—win or lose— teaches you something.

- You have the emotional discipline to stay in control, even when the market is unpredictable.

When you trust your ability to adapt, you don't need certainty. You don't need the perfect setup or the perfect market conditions. You just need to follow your plan and let the probabilities play out over time.

Are you focusing on controlling your execution, or are you wasting energy trying to control the market?

Moving Forward With Clarity and Purpose

The traders who last in this business are not the ones who always win. They are the ones who accept uncertainty, manage risk, and refine their skills without hesitation.

If you've put in the work to understand the market, build strong habits, and develop the right mindset, you already have what you need. The question is: Are you willing to trust yourself and take action?

Uncertainty is part of the game, but it doesn't have to shake your confidence. You can trade calmly, decisively, and with clarity—no matter what the market throws at you.

With the core framework in place, let's conclude by reiterating key takeaways and looking at future directions for your growth as a trader.

CHAPTER 14

THE POWER OF TRADING AS A CAREER

———◆———

Trading Treats Everyone Equally

The market doesn't care about your education, your job history, or who you know. It doesn't care if you're a former CEO or if you've never worked in an office before. It doesn't reward people based on status, and it doesn't hold back opportunities from those willing to put in the work. The only thing that matters is how well you manage risk, control your emotions, and execute your strategy.

Are you telling yourself that something outside of you is holding you back, or are you recognizing that trading success is completely in your hands?

Skill and Discipline Are the Only Equalizers

Think about two traders: one spent years running a business and has a degree in economics, while the other worked as a janitor with no formal financial education. They both open a trading account with the same amount of capital and start placing trades.

Who has the advantage?

Not the person with the fancy resume. The only trader who succeeds is the one who learns to:

- Follow a plan without letting emotions interfere.

- Respect risk instead of chasing quick wins.

- Adapt to changing market conditions without hesitation.

There are no shortcuts, no special privileges, and no guarantees. The same market that rewards disciplined traders will crush those who trade based on ego, impulse, or lack of preparation—regardless of their background.

So, if trading is one of the few fields where past experience doesn't define your success, why would you let self-doubt stop you?

Anyone Can Succeed—If They Commit to Mastering Their Mindset

The only thing separating successful traders from struggling ones is commitment to the process.

- Are you actively learning, testing, and refining your strategy?

- Are you developing the mental strength to handle wins and losses the same way?

- Are you focusing on long-term consistency rather than short-term results?

- Your past doesn't dictate your future in trading—your habits, discipline, and mindset do.

Are you ready to stop focusing on what you lack and start building the skills that actually matter?

The Freedom & Rewards of a Trading Career

What would your life look like if you didn't have to answer to a boss, follow a set schedule, or commute to an office every day? What if your income wasn't limited by a salary, and your time was truly your own?

Trading offers something most careers can't—complete freedom over how, when, and where you work. It's one of the few professions where success isn't determined by connections, seniority, or company politics. Your growth depends entirely on your skills, discipline, and mindset.

Are you trading just to make money, or are you working toward a lifestyle where you control your time, your location, and your financial potential?

Time Freedom

Most people spend their lives working set hours, answering to managers, and structuring their days around someone else's demands. They live and die by the clock and someone else's schedule. But as a trader, you set your own schedule.

Your workday doesn't need to be eight hours long. If you trade efficiently, you can spend just a few focused hours in the market and have the rest of the day to live on your terms.

- Want to work mornings and have the afternoons free? You can.

- Prefer to trade at night and enjoy your days? That's an option too.

- Need a break? The market will be there when you return—there's no boss asking for permission.

Time is your most valuable asset. Are you using trading as a tool to buy back your time, or are you still thinking like someone stuck in a traditional work structure?

Location Independence

If you have a laptop and an internet connection, you have everything you need to trade. You're not tied to an office or a specific location.

Want to trade from a quiet home office? A beachfront café? A different country every few months? It's all possible.

Most careers require you to be in a specific place at a specific time. Trading removes that limitation. Your work follows you wherever you go, allowing you to design a life that fits you, rather than fitting your life around work.

Have you considered how powerful it is to have a skill that allows you to make money from anywhere in the world?

Financial Upside: No Salary Cap, Only Growth Potential

Traditional jobs limit how much you can earn. You work a set number of hours, and you get paid a fixed amount—no matter how much value you create. In trading, your income potential is directly tied to your skill level.

There's no salary cap. No annual review to determine if you get a raise. The better you become, the more opportunities you create for yourself.

That's not to say trading is easy. The market doesn't hand out money just because you want it. But if you're willing to put in the work, refine your strategy, and master your mindset, your earning potential is completely in your control.

Are you treating trading like a true profession, where growth leads to higher rewards, or are you stuck thinking like an employee who waits for a paycheck?

Freedom Requires Discipline

Yes, trading offers freedom. But that freedom comes with responsibility. No one will hold you accountable except yourself. You have to manage your time, stay consistent, and control your risk.

If you can develop the right habits, the rewards go far beyond money. You gain control over your time, location, and income in a way that most people never will.

Are you committed to building the skills and discipline required to fully take advantage of everything trading can offer you?

My Personal Story

Have you ever felt like you weren't meant to succeed? Like no matter how hard you tried, you weren't the person who had the natural talent or intelligence to make it? That was me.

If you had met me in high school, you wouldn't have seen someone who was destined for success. I wasn't the smartest kid in the class, and I definitely wasn't the one teachers expected to go far. I was average at best, and to be honest, I didn't even have the confidence to think otherwise.

Math? I struggled with it. When people talked about finance or numbers, I tuned out because I didn't believe I could ever understand it.

After college, I faced reality head-on—and it wasn't pretty. I applied for jobs, hoping to land something stable, but nothing worked out. The rejection emails kept piling up, and I started questioning my future. What was I going to do with my life?

I had no clear path. No backup plan. No confidence in myself.

Discovering Trading

I didn't wake up one day and decide, "I'm going to be a trader." I didn't have a mentor guiding me. I fell into it almost by accident—and at first, I was terrible.

The market chewed me up and spit me out. I lost money, doubted myself, and questioned whether I was even capable of succeeding in something that felt so unpredictable.

I tried strategy after strategy, thinking I just needed to find the "perfect method." I bought courses, followed other traders, and mimicked what they were doing. But no matter what I tried, my results didn't improve.

It wasn't until I started focusing on the mental side of trading that everything changed.

I realized that success had nothing to do with the perfect entry or indicator—it had everything to do with controlling my emotions, sticking to a plan, and removing ego from my decisions.

The moment I shifted my focus to mastering my psychology instead of just chasing trades, I saw my performance improve dramatically.

Where I Am Today

Looking back, I sometimes can't believe where trading has taken me.

- I now coach hedge fund managers—people who pay over $50,000 just for a consultation.

- I've built a global community of traders who are committed to mastering both strategy and mindset.

- I wake up every day knowing that I have full control over my time, income, and freedom.

And to think—I almost quit when things got tough.

So if you ever feel like you're not smart enough, not skilled enough, or not "built" for trading, ask yourself this: What if I'm wrong?

Because if I—a kid who struggled with math and couldn't get a job—can succeed in trading, why not you?

You just have to be willing to put in the work, train your mind, and stay in the game long enough to see the results.

The Final Lesson: Psychology + Strategy = Success

How many times have you heard traders say, "Trading is all about psychology," or, "Mindset is everything"? While there's truth in that, let's be real—psychology alone won't make you a successful trader.

You can have the strongest mindset in the world, but if you don't have a strategy that actually works, no amount of discipline will turn a losing method into a winning one. At the same time, even the best trading strategy won't make you profitable if you lack the mental control to execute it properly.

Success comes from combining both—a proven strategy and a mindset that allows you to execute with discipline, patience, and confidence.

Are you putting equal effort into both, or are you leaning too heavily on one while neglecting the other?

The Balance Between Psychology and Strategy

If mindset alone created great traders, every self-help book reader would be a millionaire. But trading requires something deeper—a structured system that gives you a statistical edge.

- You need a strategy that works in today's market. If your system is outdated, no amount of mindset training will make it profitable.

- You need to follow that strategy with discipline. A perfect plan is useless if you let emotions push you into impulsive trades.

- You need to constantly refine both. The market evolves, and so must your approach. If you're not improving, you're falling behind.

This book has provided you with a framework—the tools to build both your psychology and strategy. Now, the real question is: Are you going to apply it?

Your Next Steps

Understanding this material isn't enough. You have to apply it, test it, and refine it over time.

- Are you tracking your trades, not just by results but by execution and mindset?

- Are you holding yourself accountable to follow your system, even on difficult days?

- Are you continuously learning, adapting, and improving both your strategy and your mental approach?

No book, mentor, or course can trade for you. This is now in your hands.

So ask yourself: Are you ready to commit to mastering both psychology and strategy, or will you stay stuck in the cycle of inconsistency?

Success is possible—but only if you take what you've learned and do the work.

The Best Way to Learn: Mentorship & Community

Have you ever felt like you're trading in isolation, trying to figure everything out on your own? You spend hours studying charts, testing strategies, and watching market movements—yet when things go wrong, you have no one to turn to for guidance.

The truth is, trading doesn't have to be a lonely pursuit. In fact, the fastest way to accelerate your growth is by learning from those who have already mastered the game.

Think about it—if you wanted to become an elite athlete, would you train alone without a coach? If you wanted to master a skill, would you ignore those who had already done it successfully?

So why would trading be any different?

Why Community and Mentorship Matter

No matter how much knowledge you gain from books, courses, or back-testing, nothing replaces real-world experience. The best way to develop the skills and mindset of a professional trader is by observing one in action.

- Watching how a professional executes trades in real time teaches you more than studying charts alone.

- Seeing how an experienced trader manages risk, controls emotions, and makes adjustments gives you a level of insight that no textbook can provide.

- Being part of a community of traders keeps you motivated, accountable, and constantly learning.

When you surround yourself with people who are committed to growth, you absorb their mindset, discipline, and approach to the markets.

Are you trying to reinvent the wheel alone, or are you putting yourself in an environment where success is the standard?

Evolve Mastermind: Learn, Grow, and Trade with Professionals. This is exactly why I created Evolve Mastermind—a community where serious traders come together to learn, develop, and refine their skills.

Inside, you get:

- Access to real-time trades—see exactly how professional traders execute entries, manage risk, and handle uncertainty.

- Live coaching sessions—where we break down market conditions, trading psychology, and strategy refinements.

- Emotional management insights—because mastering psychology is just as important as perfecting execution.

With today's technology, you no longer need to sit in a physical office to learn from top traders. You can be anywhere in the world and still get direct access to mentorship, trade breakdowns, and a network of like-minded traders who push you to get better every day.

Are you serious about mastering trading, or are you just hoping to figure it all out on your own?

If you're ready to take your learning beyond books and charts, the best thing you can do is put yourself in the right environment—where success isn't just talked about, but actively demonstrated.

CHAPTER 15

BUILDING SUCCESSFUL TRADING HABITS

———◆———

Mark, a former corporate executive who decided to try his hand at trading. Like many beginners, he jumped in with dreams of quick riches, watching YouTube videos about traders making millions overnight. He opened his trading account with $50,000 and lost $20,000 in his first month trying to chase "hot stocks" and following social media tips.

This story is all too common, but it doesn't have to be your story. The truth about trading success isn't about finding that one perfect trade or having a "natural talent" for the markets. It's about something far more fundamental: your daily habits.

The 1% Edge: Your Path to Trading Mastery

Think about the most successful hedge fund managers and day traders you know. Do you think they became successful overnight? Consider Renaissance Technologies, one of the most successful hedge funds in history. They didn't achieve their remarkable returns through a single brilliant trade or a magic formula. Their success came from consistently applying robust processes, day after day, year after year.

The secret? Improving just 1% each day. Here's what that looks like in trading:

- Day 1: Learning to read one new chart pattern

- Day 2: Understanding one new technical indicator

- Day 3: Improving your position sizing by a small margin

- Day 4: Refining your entry criteria slightly

- Day 5: Enhancing your exit strategy

While each improvement seems minor, the compound effect is powerful. After one year, you're not just 365% better—due to compounding, you're multiple times better than when you started.

Identity Transformation: The Core of Trading Success

The Identity Shift

Stop thinking "I want to learn trading" and start thinking "I am a trader." This isn't just positive thinking—it's about fundamentally changing who you are. Let me share a story about Sarah, one of my mentees:

Sarah struggled with consistency until she made this identity shift. She stopped saying "I'm trying to trade" and started saying "I am a trader." This simple change led to profound behavioral shifts:

- She started waking up at 6 AM to prepare for the market open, not because she had to, but because "that's what traders do"

- She began keeping a detailed trading journal, not because someone told her to, but because "that's what traders do"

- She started reviewing her trades every weekend, not as a chore, but because "that's what traders do"

Professional vs. Amateur Mindset

Consider these contrasts:

Amateur Trader:

- Trades based on emotions

- Chases hot tips and trends

- Inconsistent with analysis

- Focuses on profits only

- Trades without a plan Professional Trader:

- Trades based on their system

- Follows their own analysis

- Consistent daily routine

- Focuses on process

- Always follows their plan

Building Your Trading System

The Three Pillars: Goals, Systems, and Tools

1. Goals:

- Example: "Generate consistent 1% monthly returns with maximum 0.5% risk per trade"   NOT: "Make a million dollars trading"

2. Systems:

- Pre-market routine

- Trading plan execution

- Post-market analysis

- Risk management protocol

- Journal keeping process

3. Tools:

- Trading platform

- Analysis software

- Journal template

- Risk calculator

- Market scanners

Real-World Example: Let me tell you about Tom, a successful day trader I know. His morning system looks like this:

- 6:00 AM: Market overview

- 6:30 AM: News analysis

- 7:00 AM: Watchlist creation

- 7:30 AM: Strategy refinement

- 8:00 AM: Final preparations

The Four Laws of Trading Habit Formation
1. Make It Obvious

Creating Your Trading Environment (TE)

Your trading environment is crucial. Here's how John, a profitable swing trader, sets up his TE:

- Physical Setup:

- Dedicated trading desk

- Dual monitors

- Proper lighting

- Ergonomic chair

- Trading journal within reach Digital Setup:

- Clean desktop

- Organized bookmark bar

- Preset chart layouts

- Saved scanner settings

- Ready-to-go journal templates

Implementation Strategy:

Morning Routine Stack:

1. Wake up

2. Exercise

3. Shower

4. Trading desk setup

5. Market analysis

2. Make It Attractive

The Dopamine-Driven Trader

Understanding the role of dopamine in trading is crucial. Many traders get addicted to the "rush" of trading—that's dopamine working against you. Instead, learn to channel it properly:

Wrong Way:

- Getting excited about potential profits

- Feeling the rush of a big position

- Celebrating winning trades Right Way:

- Feeling satisfied about following your plan

- Getting excited about good analysis

- Celebrating consistent execution

Reward System Examples:

1. Process-Based Rewards:

*   Perfect execution = favorite coffee

*   Week of journal keeping = movie night   Month of plan adherence = new trading book

1. Learning Rewards:

*   Completing analysis = special breakfast

*   Reading trading book = social activity

*   Reviewing trades = favorite snack

3. Make It Easy

The 2-Minute Trading Start

Begin with simple, 2-minute tasks:

*   Day 1: Open your trading platform

*   Day 2: Look at one chart

*   Day 3: Analyze one indicator

*   Day 4: Paper trade one position

*   Day 5: Journal one trade

Maria, a new trader, started with just reading one candlestick pattern daily. Within three months, she could analyze entire charts in minutes. Why? Because she made it easy to start and built up gradually.

Environment Design

- Friction Removal:

- Create chart templates

- Save scanner settings

- Prepare watchlist criteria

- Automate journal entries

- Set up price alerts

4. Make It Satisfying

Immediate Reward System

Trade Analysis Protocol:

1. Complete trade: Immediate journal entry

2. Follow plan: Check mark in tracker

3. Weekly review: Progress chart update

4. Monthly assessment: Skill rating update

Success Story:

David, a forex trader, created a "trading score card" where he got points for:

- Following his plan: 5 points

- Proper position sizing: 3 points

- Complete trade journal: 2 points

- Weekly review: 10 points

He made it into a game, and his consistency improved dramatically.

Advanced Habit Strategies

Dealing with Boredom: The Professional's Edge

Story Time: Meet Lisa, a consistently profitable trader for over a decade. Her secret? She embraced boredom. While others chase excitement, she:

- Trades the same setup daily

- Uses the same position sizing

- Follows the same routine

- Never deviates from her plan

"Trading should be boring," she says. "If you're excited, you're probably doing something wrong."

Creating Your Trading Tribe

Community Building Strategy:

1. Join online trading communities

2. Find an accountability partner

3. Participate in trading webinars

4. Share your journal with peers

5. Create a mastermind group Example Structure:

- Daily check-ins with trading partner

- Weekly group reviews

    - Monthly performance sharing

    - Quarterly goal setting sessions

Progress Tracking System

The Complete Trading Journal

Daily Entries:

1. Market Analysis

- Overall market condition

- Sector analysis

- Key levels identified

1. Trade Details

- Entry/exit points

- Position sizing

- Risk parameters

- Setup quality rating

1. Emotional State

- Pre-trade mindset

- During trade emotions

- Post-trade reflection

1. Plan Adherence

- Rules followed/broken

- Process rating   Areas for improvement

Monthly Review Template

1. Performance Metrics

- Win rate

- Risk/reward ratio

- Profit factor

- Maximum drawdown

2. Behavioral Analysis

- Emotional control rating

- Plan adherence percentage

- System execution score

- Areas for improvement

3.   Skill Development

- New patterns learned

- Strategies refined

- Knowledge gained

- Next month's focus

CONCLUSION

---◆◆---

You've made it this far. You've absorbed the lessons, the strategies, and the mindset shifts that separate successful traders from those who struggle. But now comes the real question: What are you going to do with it?

Information alone doesn't create success—action does. If you don't apply what you've learned, nothing will change. You'll keep making the same mistakes, battling the same emotions, and wondering why your results aren't improving.

The difference between traders who stay stuck and those who break through isn't intelligence, luck, or background. It's the willingness to execute, refine, and stay consistent.

Are you going to be one of the traders who takes this knowledge and uses it, or will this just be another book you read without action?

Take Your Trading to the Next Level

If you're serious about mastering trading—not just understanding it but actually becoming consistent, confident, and profitable—then you need more than just knowledge.

You need:

- Ongoing mentorship to refine your execution and eliminate blind spots.

- Real-time insights so you can see professional traders manage risk and make decisions under pressure.

- A network of committed traders who hold you accountable and push you to improve.

That's exactly what the **Evolve Mastermind** is designed for.

It's not a course. It's not just theory. It's a community of traders who are actively improving, sharing real trades, and applying proven strategies in today's market.

If you're ready to stop guessing and start growing, you can learn more about joining the Evolve Mastermind here: [https://go.anmol.net/evolve-mastermind-apply]

Your next steps are simple: Commit. Take action. Execute.

Will you do what most traders won't—put in the work and take control of your success? The decision is yours.

Where do you go from here? You've gained insights into trading psychology, strategy, discipline, and risk management. You've seen how mindset and execution work together to create success. But knowledge alone isn't enough—what matters is what you do next.

Trading is not about reaching a finish line. It's a constant process of learning, refining, and adapting. The market is always changing, and so must you. Some days will test your patience, some weeks will challenge your discipline, and some months will make you question everything. That's part of the process. The traders who succeed are the ones who commit to progress, not perfection.

Are you willing to keep pushing forward, even when things don't go as planned?

Keep Learning, Keep Refining

No trader has it all figured out. Even the most experienced professionals continue to study, test, and adjust.

- Every loss is data. Instead of dwelling on mistakes, analyze them and improve.

- Every win is a test of discipline. Success isn't about making one great trade—it's about repeating good decisions over time.

- Every moment in the market is an opportunity to refine your edge. The more you learn, the stronger your confidence and execution become.

You don't need to be perfect to be successful. You just need to stay committed to growth, show up every day, and execute with discipline.

So ask yourself: Are you ready to keep evolving, or are you going to let hesitation hold you back?

Your success in trading—and in life—comes down to your ability to keep moving forward, no matter what.

How often do you acknowledge your progress? Do you celebrate the small wins, or are you always chasing the next big moment?

Trading isn't just about making money—it's about becoming the kind of person who can handle uncertainty, manage risk, and stay disciplined under pressure. Every trade, whether a win or a loss, is part of your growth. The traders who last in this game are the ones who learn to see setbacks as stepping stones and small victories as proof that they're on the right track.

If you've made it this far, you already have what it takes. You're committed. You're willing to learn. You're showing up when many others quit. That alone puts you ahead of most.

Every Loss is Data. Every Win is Fuel. Keep Going.

The market will test you. There will be times when you feel like you're making no progress, times when you want to give up, and times when self-doubt creeps in. That's when you have to remind yourself why you started.

- Every loss teaches you something. If you're paying attention, you're always improving.

- Every win proves that your work is paying off. Even small successes add up over time.

- Every day you stay committed, you separate yourself from those who give up too soon.

You don't need to be perfect. You don't need to have it all figured out. You just need to keep showing up, keep refining, and keep believing in yourself.

Are you willing to push through the tough moments, knowing that each step forward is bringing you closer to success?

This is your path. Own it. Keep going.

ABOUT THE AUTHOR

———◆———

Who would have thought that someone who struggled with math and couldn't land a job after college would go on to coach hedge fund managers and help thousands of traders worldwide?

If you had told me years ago that trading would become my passion, my career, and my platform to impact others, I wouldn't have believed you. But the truth is, trading changed my life, and now my mission is to help others develop the skills and mindset to take control of their own success.

I didn't come from a background in finance. I didn't have connections on Wall Street. I wasn't someone who was "born" for this. I built myself into a trader. And if I can do it, so can you.

My Trading Background & Coaching Experience

After years of struggling to find direction, I stumbled into trading. At first, I was like most new traders—chasing strategies, making emotional decisions, and learning the hard way. I took losses that felt devastating at the time, but they taught me the lessons I needed to move forward.

Once I understood that psychology was the missing link to consistency, everything changed. Mastering my emotions, refining my process, and developing discipline turned my results around.

- I went from feeling lost to trading full-time with confidence.

- I built a coaching program that now helps traders at all levels develop their edge.

- I work with hedge fund managers who pay over $50,000 for private consultations, proving that no matter how advanced you are, mindset is everything.

But my real passion isn't just trading—it's helping others break through the barriers that hold them back.

How You Can Learn More & Work With Me

If you've made it this far, you're serious about taking your trading to the next level. And I want to help you go beyond just reading about success—I want to help you experience it.

- Join the **Evolve Mastermind**—A private community where traders learn directly from me, access real-time market insights, and build the habits needed for long-term success.

- Explore my coaching programs—If you need personalized mentorship, I offer structured guidance to help traders at every stage refine their approach.

- Check out additional resources—I share insights, lessons, and strategies through my website and online content. https://go.anmol.net/evolve-mastermind-apply

The market doesn't care about where you started. It only cares about how well you execute. If you're ready to commit to your growth, I'm here to help you make it happen.

Let's get to work.

PRACTICAL EXERCISES & ACTION ITEMS

———•———

Emotional Log: Track Your Emotional State & Trading Triggers

Purpose:

This log will help you become more aware of the emotions influencing your trading decisions. By tracking your state before, during, and after trades, you'll identify patterns in how emotions impact your execution, risk management, and overall performance.

Trade Entry: Pre-Trade State

Date & Time:

Trade Setup: (Breakout, pullback, trend continuation, etc.)

Market Conditions: (Volatile, ranging, strong trend, news event) Emotional State Before Entering:

- Calm & Focused

- Anxious & Hesitant

- Overconfident

- Fearful (Avoiding risk)

- Revenge Trading (Trying to recover losses)

- Impulsive (Rushing to enter)

- Neutral

Trigger for Entry: (What made you take the trade?)

- Followed my strategy exactly

- Entered late due to hesitation

- FOMO—Didn't want to miss out

- Entered because of recent losses/wins

- External influence (news, chatrooms, social media)

During the Trade: Emotional Fluctuations How did you feel as price moved?

- Confident and patient

- Nervous and doubting my entry

- Wanted to exit too early

- Regretted taking the trade

- Overexcited about potential profits

Did you adjust your plan mid-trade?

- Yes, I stuck to my original stop-loss/take-profit

- No, I moved my stop-loss to avoid a loss

- No, I closed too early due to fear

- No, I let a winning trade turn into a loss

Trade Exit: Post-Trade Reflection Outcome:

- Win

- Loss

- Break-even

Did you follow your plan?

- Yes, executed exactly as intended

- No, exited early due to emotions No, held too long trying to make more

Emotional State After Exit:

- Satisfied & Disciplined

- Frustrated & Regretful

- Overconfident (Tempted to overtrade)

- Fearful of taking the next trade

- Biggest Takeaway from This Trade:

(Write a short reflection on what you learned and how you'll adjust next time.)

Weekly Emotional Review:

- Most common emotional trigger?

- How often did emotions interfere with my execution?

- What changes can I make to improve my discipline next week?

Mindfulness Drills: Pre-Trading Breathing & Meditation Exercises

Purpose:

Trading requires mental clarity, emotional control, and focus. If you enter the market feeling anxious, distracted, or overly eager, your decision-making will suffer. These 5-minute mindfulness drills will help you reset, reduce stress, and sharpen your focus before placing any trades.

1. 5-Minute Breathing Exercise (Box Breathing Method)

Why it works:

Box breathing is used by athletes, military personnel, and high-performance professionals to calm the nervous system, lower stress, and increase focus.

How to do it:

1. Find a quiet place and sit comfortably.

2. Close your eyes or lower your gaze.

3. Inhale through your nose for 4 seconds.

4. Hold your breath for 4 seconds.

5. Exhale slowly through your mouth for 4 seconds.

6. Hold your breath for 4 seconds before repeating.

7. Repeat this cycle for 5 minutes, keeping your breaths smooth and controlled.

Focus on:

- The sensation of air entering and leaving your body.

- Letting go of any tension or racing thoughts.

- Feeling centered and present in the moment.

2. Pre-Trading Grounding Meditation (Body Scan Technique)

Why it works:

A body scan helps bring awareness to physical tension and emotions that might impact your trading. If you feel tension in your chest, shoulders, or hands, it could be a sign of stress, fear, or over-excitement.

How to do it:

1. Sit or stand comfortably, keeping your spine straight.

2. Close your eyes and take a deep breath in through your nose, then exhale slowly.

3. Shift your attention to your head—relax your forehead, jaw, and neck.

4. Move to your shoulders—let them drop and release tension.

5. Continue down to your chest and stomach—breathe deeply and soften any tightness.

6. Scan your arms, hands, legs, and feet—relax each area before moving on.

7. Finish by taking three deep breaths and setting a calm, focused intention for your trading session.

3. Visualization Drill: Mental Rehearsal for Execution Discipline

Why it works:

Visualization trains your brain to stay disciplined under market pressure. By mentally rehearsing your trade execution before the session starts, you strengthen the neural pathways that support confident decision-making.

How to do it:

1. Close your eyes and imagine yourself sitting at your desk, ready to trade.

2. Picture the market opening and price moving on your screen.

3. See yourself analyzing setups calmly, executing trades with confidence, and following your plan.

4. Imagine a moment of market volatility—you stay composed, stick to your risk management, and make decisions based on logic, not emotion.

5. Visualize ending your session feeling disciplined and in control, regardless of your P&L.

Mindfulness isn't about eliminating emotions—it's about recognizing them and staying in control. Taking just 5 minutes before trading to breathe, center yourself, and mentally prepare can mean the difference between acting impulsively and executing with precision.

Commit to making mindfulness part of your pre-trading routine and watch how it transforms your focus, patience, and consistency.

Cognitive Reframing: Transform Negative Thoughts into Constructive Alternatives

Purpose:

Your mindset determines your execution. If you let self-doubt, fear, or frustration dictate your decisions, you'll struggle to stay consistent. Cognitive reframing helps you shift negative thoughts into constructive perspectives, allowing you to trade with clarity and confidence.

How Cognitive Reframing Works:

When you experience a negative thought related to trading, pause and challenge it. Ask yourself:

- Is this thought based on facts or emotions?

- Would I say this to another trader in my position?

- What is a more balanced, constructive way to think about this?

By shifting your mindset, you replace self-sabotage with logical, disciplined thinking.

Common Negative Thoughts & How to Reframe Them

Negative Thought: "I always lose. I'm just bad at trading."

Reframed Thought: "Losing trades are part of the process. If I follow my edge consistently, my results will improve over time."

Negative Thought: "I should have made more money on that trade. I exited too early!"

Reframed Thought: "I followed my plan and locked in profits. There will always be more opportunities, and I'm here for the long game."

Negative Thought: "I can't believe I lost money today. I need to make it back."

Reframed Thought: "Losses happen. My job is to manage risk, learn from mistakes, and stay disciplined for the next trade."

Negative Thought: "This setup looks perfect, I'll risk more than usual."

Reframed Thought: "No setup is guaranteed. I will follow my risk management rules no matter how confident I feel."

Negative Thought: "I missed a great trade. I feel like I'm falling behind."

Reframed Thought: "Opportunities come every day. My goal is to trade well, not catch every single move."

How to Make This a Habit

Write down any negative thoughts that come up during trading.

- Challenge those thoughts using the three questions above.

- Reframe them into a constructive, logical alternative.

- Review your reframes before your next session to reinforce the habit.

Your thoughts shape your actions. If you train yourself to think like a disciplined, successful trader, you will start executing like one.

Visualization Routines: Mentally Rehearse Disciplined Trade Execution

Purpose:

Your mind doesn't differentiate between real and vividly imagined experiences. By visualizing your ideal trading behavior, you train your brain to execute with confidence, discipline, and emotional control. Given enough details, your mind will believe this is a real experience. Professional athletes, elite performers, and top traders use visualization to reduce hesitation, strengthen decision-making, and improve consistency.

How to Use Visualization for Trading Success

Step 1: Set the Scene (2 Minutes)

1. Sit in a quiet place, close your eyes, and take a few deep breaths.

2. Imagine yourself sitting at your trading station, focused and prepared.

3. Feel the calmness in your body as you step into the role of a disciplined trader.

Step 2: Mentally Rehearse a Flawless Trading Session (3 Minutes)

1. See yourself scanning the market with clarity and patience. You are not rushing—you're waiting for high-probability setups.

2. Visualize identifying a setup that meets your criteria. You don't hesitate. You execute confidently because you trust your edge.

3. Picture managing the trade with discipline. You are not reacting emotionally. You let the trade play out according to your plan.

4. If the trade moves against you, visualize handling it calmly. You respect your stop-loss, accept the outcome, and move on without frustration.

5. If the trade is a winner, see yourself locking in profits responsibly. You follow your exit strategy instead of getting greedy or fearful.

Step 3: Reinforce the Mindset of a Consistent Trader

1. Remind yourself: "I trade with confidence. I follow my plan. I execute without hesitation."

2. Feel the emotions of a disciplined, patient, and focused trader—not someone chasing or reacting impulsively.

3. Open your eyes and carry this mindset into your live trading session.

Making This a Daily Habit

- Practice before every trading session to reinforce discipline and mental clarity.

- Use it after a tough trading day to reset and refocus for the next session.

- Review your visualization notes if emotions start affecting your execution.

Your trading results will always reflect your mindset. The more you train your brain to act with discipline, the more automatic it becomes in live markets.

Loss Recovery Plan: Structured Reflection After Drawdowns

Purpose:

Experiencing a drawdown is inevitable, but how you respond determines whether you recover efficiently or spiral into emotional decision-making. This Loss Recovery

Plan will guide you through structured journaling and reflection so that you can regain confidence, refine your strategy, and prevent repeated mistakes.

Step 1: Immediate Emotional Reset (Before Analyzing Your Trades) Take a break. Step away from your screen for at least 15-30 minutes.

- Regulate your emotions. Use breathing exercises or mindfulness drills to reduce frustration and avoid revenge trading.

- Accept the losses. Remind yourself that trading is about probabilities, and losses are a normal part of the process.

Step 2: Review the Drawdown Objectively

What is the total percentage loss over this drawdown? (Keep perspective—small drawdowns are part of the game.)

How many trades contributed to this drawdown?

- Were the losses due to poor execution or normal variance?

- Followed my plan, but the market didn't cooperate (Normal variance).

- Deviated from my plan (Emotional trading or undisciplined mistakes).

Step 3: Identify the Root Causes

Go through each trade in your journal and ask:

- Did I enter for the right reasons?

- Was I too aggressive with risk?

- Did I hesitate, exit early, or let emotions interfere?

- Did I take setups outside my strategy?

- Did I revenge trade after a loss?

Pattern Recognition:

Are there any repeated mistakes?

- Was I trading under stress, fatigue, or emotional pressure?

- Was my market read off, or was I forcing trades?

Step 4: Define Corrective Actions

Once you've identified what went wrong, establish a clear action plan:

- **If risk management was poor:** Reduce position sizes and reinforce strict stop-loss adherence.

- **If emotions interfered:** Implement mindfulness drills before every session.

- **If overtrading was an issue:** Set a max trade limit per session to prevent unnecessary exposure.

- **If discipline broke down:** Commit to reviewing your trading rules before every session.

Step 5: Rebuild Confidence With Simulated & Small-Size Trading If Your Confidence is Shaken:

Trade in simulation or with reduced size until discipline is fully restored.

- Focus on execution over results. Wins and losses don't matter—following your plan does.

- Journal every trade, especially when emotions arise.

Final Thought: Losses Are Lessons

Every drawdown is an opportunity to refine, adjust, and improve. The difference between traders who recover and those who spiral into deeper losses is the ability to step back, review objectively, and take corrective action.

Are you reacting emotionally to losses, or are you using them as stepping stones toward a stronger trading approach?

Cognitive Bias Checklist: Pre-Trade Checks for Mental Clarity

Purpose:

Cognitive biases distort objectivity and therefore decision-making, leading to impulsive trades, poor risk management, and missed opportunities. This checklist will help you recognize and correct biases before executing a trade, allowing for more objective and disciplined trading.

Step 1: Pause & Assess Your Mindset Before Placing a Trade

<u>Ask yourself:</u> Am I making this decision based on logic and strategy, or am I falling into a mental bias?

<u>Overconfidence Bias:</u> Am I risking too much because of a recent winning streak?

Solution: Stick to my pre-defined risk rules regardless of recent performance.

<u>Confirmation Bias:</u> Am I ignoring evidence that contradicts my trade idea?

<u>Solution:</u> Actively seek reasons why this trade might fail before entering.

<u>FOMO (Fear of Missing Out):</u> Am I chasing price because I'm afraid of missing a move?

<u>Solution:</u> If the setup is valid, wait for a proper entry. If not, let it go. There will always be another trade.

<u>Recency Bias:</u> Am I assuming this trade will succeed or fail based on my last trade?

<u>Solution:</u> Treat every trade as an independent event with its own probabilities.

<u>Loss Aversion:</u> Am I hesitant to take a valid trade because I just had a losing streak?

<u>Solution:</u> Losses are part of the process—stick to my plan and execute without fear.

<u>Anchoring Bias:</u> Am I fixating on a specific price level because of past data rather than real-time market conditions?

<u>Solution:</u> Focus on the current structure, not outdated expectations.

<u>Revenge Trading Bias:</u> Am I trading emotionally to "make back" my losses?

<u>Solution:</u> Reset, review my strategy, and only take high-quality setups that meet my criteria.

Step 2: Make a Clear Trading Decision

- If I checked any of the biases above, I will pause, reassess, and only take the trade if it aligns with my strategy.

- If the trade meets all my technical, fundamental, and risk management criteria, I will execute with confidence.

- I will accept any outcome without attachment, knowing that probabilities—not emotions—determine my success.

Cognitive biases affect every trader, but self-awareness and discipline separate the professionals from the impulsive.

Are you trading your plan, or are you letting mental biases shape your decisions? This checklist will keep you accountable—use it before every trade.

Physical Health Checklist

Purpose:

Your ability to trade with clarity, discipline, and emotional control is directly impacted by your physical health. Poor sleep, lack of movement, and improper nutrition can lead to mental fatigue, poor decision-making, and increased emotional reactivity. Use this checklist to track and improve the physical factors that influence your trading performance.

Daily Health Checklist

1. <u>Sleep:</u> Did I Get Enough Rest to Trade With a Clear Mind?

- 7-9 hours of quality sleep (not just time in bed, but deep, restorative sleep)

- Avoided screens (phone, laptop) at least 30-60 minutes before bed

- Slept in a cool, dark, and quiet environment Woke up feeling refreshed (not groggy or sluggish)

- If my sleep was poor, I will adjust my bedtime routine and avoid caffeine late in the day.

2. <u>Exercise:</u> Did I Move My Body Today?

- At least 30 minutes of physical activity (walking, gym, yoga, or stretching)

- Took breaks between trading sessions to stand, stretch, or move around

- Maintained good posture while sitting at my desk

- If I was sedentary all day, I will schedule movement breaks and set a reminder to walk or stretch.

3. <u>Nutrition:</u> Am I Eating for Mental Clarity & Energy?

- Had a balanced breakfast before trading (healthy fats, protein, complex carbs)

- Avoided excessive sugar, processed foods, and heavy meals before trading

- Ate whole, nutrient-dense meals to sustain energy throughout the day

- Avoided emotional eating after a bad trade (stress-based snacking or binge eating)

- If I ate poorly, I will prepare healthier meals and snacks for better focus and mood stability.

4. Hydration: Did I Drink Enough Water?

- Drank at least 2-3 liters of water throughout the day

- Avoided excessive caffeine, energy drinks, or alcohol that can cause dehydration

- Kept a water bottle at my desk to sip regularly while trading

- If I didn't hydrate properly, I will prioritize water intake and set reminders to drink more fluids.

End-of-Day Review:

- How did my physical state affect my trading today?

- Did I feel sharp, focused, and disciplined, or sluggish, anxious, and reactive?

- What can I improve tomorrow to optimize my mental and physical performance?

You can have the best trading strategy, but if your body and mind aren't functioning at their best, your execution will suffer. Treat yourself like an elite performer—because trading requires just as much focus and discipline as any high-stakes profession.

Support System & Network: Finding Mentors & Trading Buddies

Purpose:

Trading can feel isolating, but success is rarely achieved alone. A strong support system—whether through mentors, trading buddies, or a trading community—helps keep you accountable, provides new perspectives, and accelerates your growth. This checklist will help you identify, connect with, and build relationships with the right people.

Step 1: Identify What You Need in a Support System

- Ask yourself: What type of support would help me grow as a trader?

- A mentor – Someone more experienced who can guide me, provide insights, and help me refine my approach.

- A trading buddy – A peer at a similar level who can hold me accountable, review trades with me, and share ideas.

- A community – A group of like-minded traders where I can learn, ask questions, and stay motivated.

- Accountability partners – Traders who help me stay disciplined and focused on my goals.

- If I don't have these people in my network yet, I will actively seek them out.

Step 2: Finding Potential Mentors & Trading Buddies Where to Look:

- Online trading communities (Discord groups, Telegram, Twitter trading circles, forums like Elite Trader or Trade2Win)

- Educational platforms (Masterminds, coaching groups, or structured mentorship programs)

- Local trading meetups (Networking events, trading workshops, conferences)

- Social media & YouTube (Following experienced traders who actively teach and engage with their audience)

- I will reach out to at least one potential mentor or trading buddy this week.

Step 3: How to Approach a Mentor or Trading Buddy

- <u>Be specific</u> about what you're looking for. Instead of just saying, "Can you mentor me?" explain what you want to learn and how you've already been working on your trading.

- <u>Offer value where possible.</u> Even if you're seeking guidance, show that you're serious about trading by sharing your progress, insights, or trade reviews.

- <u>Be consistent and engage actively.</u> Whether it's checking in with your trading buddy daily or showing up in a community, consistency strengthens relationships.

- <u>Respect their time.</u> If reaching out to a mentor, come prepared with well-thought-out questions, not just generic ones.

- I will <u>send a message</u> or join a discussion today to start building my network.

Step 4: Maintaining & Strengthening Your Support System

- <u>Review trades together</u> – Set up weekly or monthly calls to discuss setups, execution, and emotional control.

- <u>Hold each other accountable</u> – Set goals and check in on progress regularly.

- <u>Share knowledge</u> – Keep an open dialogue about what's working and what needs improvement.

- <u>Stay professional</u> – Avoid drama, negativity, and emotional venting—focus on growth.

- I will <u>commit to maintaining strong relationships</u> with my trading network and continuously learning from them.

Final Thought:

Surrounding yourself with serious, disciplined traders will push you to level up faster than trading alone. A strong support system helps you stay accountable, focused, and constantly improving.

Trading Plan Creation: A Structured Framework for Consistent Execution

Purpose:

A trading plan acts as your roadmap, keeping you focused, disciplined, and accountable. Without one, trading becomes impulsive and inconsistent. This structured framework will help you define your goals, strategy, risk rules, trading schedule, and emotional management techniques to ensure long-term success.

1. Define Your Trading Goals Financial Goals:

- What is your monthly/quarterly/yearly profit target?

- How much are you willing to risk per trade and per week to achieve this?

Skill Development Goals:

- What specific skills do you want to improve (e.g., risk management, patience, execution discipline)?

- How will you track and measure your improvement?

Process-Oriented Goals:

- How will you ensure consistency in your trading (e.g., following rules, sticking to max trades per day, reviewing performance regularly)?

- If my goals are vague, I will refine them into clear, measurable objectives.

2. Outline Your Trading Strategy

Markets Traded: (Forex, Stocks, Crypto, Options, Futures)

Preferred Timeframes: (Scalping, Day Trading, Swing Trading, Position Trading) Setup Criteria:

- What specific conditions must be met before taking a trade?

- What indicators, price action signals, or confluences confirm your entry?

Entry Rules:

- What signals confirm your trade execution?

- Do you wait for confirmation or enter immediately?

Exit Rules:

- When do you take profits? (Fixed target, trailing stop, partial exits?)

- When do you cut losses? (Fixed stop-loss, time-based exit, invalidation of setup?)

- If my strategy isn't clearly defined, I will refine it and backtest before trading live.

3. Risk Management: Define Your Risk Rules Per Trade Risk:

What percentage of your capital will you risk per trade? (1%, 2%?) What is your maximum dollar loss per trade?

Daily/Weekly Max Loss:

- How many consecutive losses will trigger a break from trading?

- What's the maximum loss you'll accept in a day/week before stepping away?

Position Sizing:

- How do you determine lot size or contract size based on risk percentage?

- Do you adjust size based on volatility?

Trade Review Process:

- How will you track and analyze each trade to improve execution?

- If my risk rules aren't clearly defined, I will immediately create firm boundaries to protect capital.

4. Trading Schedule: Set Consistent Trading Hours. What are your dedicated trading hours?

- Pre-market analysis: ___ AM

- Active trading session: ___ AM - ___ PM

- Post-market review: ___ PM

Which market sessions do you focus on?

- London? New York? Asian?

- Do you avoid low-volume hours?

Breaks & Rest Periods:

- How will you prevent overtrading and burnout?

- When will you take scheduled screen breaks?

- If my schedule is inconsistent, I will commit to a structured routine to maintain discipline.

5. Emotional Management: Preventing Mental Mistakes Pre-Trade Routine:

- Do you practice mindfulness or breathing exercises before trading?

- How do you mentally prepare to trade without distractions?

Emotional Check-In Before Entering Trades:

- Am I feeling rushed, impatient, or stressed?

- Am I chasing a trade out of FOMO?

Handling Losses:

- How do I reset after a losing streak?

- What steps do I take to avoid revenge trading?

Managing Wins:

- Do I adjust risk after a winning streak, or do I stick to my plan?

- How do I avoid overconfidence and impulsive trades?

- If I am not actively managing my emotions, I will implement techniques to build emotional resilience.

Final Step: Commit to Following Your Plan

- Print and review your trading plan before every session.

- Track your trades and journal how well you follow your rules.

- Review and refine your plan monthly based on real results.

A trading plan only works if you follow it. Are you treating your trading like a structured business, or are you still making random decisions?

Take ownership of your process, and success will follow.

APPENDIX I:
LEARNING TO BREATHE

---◆---

For most of us, breathing has become an incomplete, superficial and sometimes hasty procedure. The action of breathing is a powerful driving force in circulation. It moves oxygen deeply through the bloodstream. If you have a sedentary job or lifestyle, you've likely developed congestion in one organ or another. With complete breathing, the bloodstream in organs is prevented from slowing down to the point where it stagnates and degenerates from "stream" to "marsh".

When you breathe in, blood is moved through every tissue in the body. The optimum interchange of gases in the lungs—the absorption of oxygen and the giving off of carbon dioxide—is at its most efficient when breathing is deep, complete and slow. The large vein continuously pouring blood from the liver into the heart is emptied regularly through suction developed by the lungs in breathing. When the venous blood from the liver can't circulate freely, it becomes congested and causes repercussions throughout the body.

It's best to practice breathing lying down.

• • First remove any article of clothing or jewelry that will constrict your neck, chest, lungs, belly, or diaphragm.

- Lie on your back on a firm surface (not your bed).

- Legs should be straight and arms comfortably down along your sides, palms up and elbows gently tucked near the waist.

- Tuck your shoulder blades under to lift your chest a bit and open up your rib cage.

- Do not arch the neck or tuck the head or chin. Your head should be in a natural position with chin pointed toward the opposite wall.

- If necessary, place a low soft pillow under your knees to diminish the lumbar arch.

- Closing your eyes will help you concentrate.

- Relax all the organs and muscles designed to hold things in or hold you up.

1. Exhale first through your nose, pushing out as much air as possible.

- Until a receptacle is empty, it cannot be filled, so in the act of respiration, a slow and complete exhalation is an absolute prerequisite of correct and complete inhalation.

- Slowly and calmly exhale through your nose, forcing all air out of your lungs. The chest is depressed by its own weight, expelling air. This out-breath must be slow. At the end of the expiration, use your abdominal muscles to force remaining air out. To do this, pull your abdominal muscles inward, in a contraction toward your back to expel the last traces of tainted air. Because the spongy nature of the lungs does not allow them to fully empty, they will always retain some impure air. You're attempting to minimize that residue.

2. Breathe in through your nose.

- Fill your lungs with air. Fill the diaphragm first, then the chest. You're not attempting to blow yourself up like a balloon. Breathe easily, slowly and silently. Think about the action of your lungs, rib cage, diaphragm, clavicle, and intestines as they rise and lower. You may need to yawn. This is a good sign, showing that your lungs are relaxed.

3. Hold inspiration (in-breath) for 5-20 seconds.

- When you breathe deeply, the surface of the tiny air sacs (alveoli) in your lungs is increased. All the normally inactive alveoli, unused in everyday breathing, are brought into service. When air remains in contact with lung alveoli, you receive the maximum degree of aeration.

4. Putting it all together.

- Lie on your back, exhale through your nose and then inhale through your nose. Begin breathing slowly and deeply from your diaphragm. When you feel that it's impossible to raise your diaphragm any more, expand your ribs and allow more air to enter your lungs. Once the ribs are fully extended, raise your collar bones so a little more air can enter. Remember, don't try to blow yourself up like a balloon. The whole process should be easy and comfortable.

- Avoid tensing your hands, face and neck.

- For this practice, hold the in-breath for 5-20 seconds and then slowly release air through the nose for a slow count of 5. When you reach 5, force the air from your lungs through the nose using the abdomen to press out any remaining air.

- Allow 2 short ordinary breaths before beginning again. Repeat 3 times.

There's a natural immunity attributed to the ionic balance in the blood that, in great part, depends on breathing. This exercise will teach you to focus on the diaphragm rather than primarily using the chest in shallow breathing, which is the way many people breathe on a daily basis. By learning to breathe properly, you'll learn to relax properly, ultimately leading to less stress and better objectivity during trades.

TIPS FOR
TEACHING
ONLINE

Helping Students Think, Learn, and Grow—

No Matter Where They Are!

ALEX KAJITANI

Solution Tree | Press

a division of

Solution Tree

555 North Morton Street
Bloomington, IN 47404
800.733.6786 (toll free) / 812.336.7700
FAX: 812.336.7790

email: info@SolutionTree.com
SolutionTree.com

Visit **go.SolutionTree.com/technology** to download the free reproducibles in this book.

Printed in the United States of America

Library of Congress Cataloging-in-Publication Data

Names: Kajitani, Alex, author.
Title: 101 tips for teaching online : helping students think, learn, and
    grow-no matter where they are! / Alex Kajitani.
Other titles: One hundred one tips for teaching online
Description: Bloomington, IN : Solution Tree Press, [2022] | Includes
    bibliographical references and index.
Identifiers: LCCN 2022002834 (print) | LCCN 2022002835 (ebook) | ISBN
    9781954631076 (Paperback) | ISBN 9781954631083 (eBook)
Subjects: LCSH: Internet in education. | World Wide Web. |
    Computer-assisted instruction. | Communication in education. |
    Instructional systems--Design. | Blended learning.
Classification: LCC LB1044.87 .J25 2022 (print) | LCC LB1044.87 (ebook) |
    DDC 371.33/44678--dc23/eng/20220215
LC record available at https://lccn.loc.gov/2022002834
LC ebook record available at https://lccn.loc.gov/2022002835

Solution Tree
Jeffrey C. Jones, CEO
Edmund M. Ackerman, President

Solution Tree Press
President and Publisher: Douglas M. Rife
Associate Publisher: Sarah Payne-Mills
Managing Production Editor: Kendra Slayton
Editorial Director: Todd Brakke
Art Director: Rian Anderson
Copy Chief: Jessi Finn
Production Editor: Alissa Voss
Content Development Specialist: Amy Rubenstein
Text and Cover Designer: Laura Cox
Associate Editor and Proofreader: Sarah Ludwig
Editorial Assistants: Charlotte Jones and Elijah Oates

Acknowledgments

I am deeply grateful to the educators, students, and their families who have inspired this book. Thank you for your willingness to share with me what is and is not working with online teaching, and how it could be better. I hope that your thoughts, ideas, and solutions leap off the pages of this book and land with impact.

Huge gratitude to the team at Solution Tree for all of your hard work and diligence in getting this book from "101 Post-it Notes on My Wall" to the beautiful book it is today, especially to Claudia Wheatley, Douglas Rife, and Alissa Voss for your guidance and expertise.

And to my fabulous family—my wife, Megan, who is always willing to look over "just one more draft"; our children, who have encouraged me throughout this process (often giving me their opinions on their own online learning experiences); my mother, Loren, who always asks how things are going; and Karen and David, who got me over the finish line. Thanks to all of you for helping to turn a fun idea into something that makes the world better. What is best in me, I owe to all of you.

Solution Tree Press would like to thank the following reviewers:

Johanna Josaphat
Social Studies Teacher
The Urban Assembly
 Unison School
Brooklyn, New York

Kristina Nichols
Instructional Coach/Reading
 Specialist
Savannah Elementary School
Aubrey, Texas

David Pillar
Assistant Director
Hoosier Hills Career Center
Bloomington, Indiana

Rachel Swearengin
Fifth-Grade Teacher
Manchester Park Elementary School
Olathe, Kansas

Table of Contents

About the Author ix

Introduction 1

    About This Book. 3

    Tip 1: Remember What Teachers Do. 4

1   **Looking Good on Camera** **5**

    Tip 2: Look Directly Into Your Camera 6

    Tip 3: Let the Light Shine on You. 7

    Tip 4: Have Your Laptop Camera at Eye Level. 9

    Tip 5: Sit (at Least) an Arm's Length Away. 10

    Tip 6: Mix Up Your Background. 11

    Tip 7: Use Props. 12

    Tip 8: Consider a Mic and a Good Camera 13

    Tip 9: Be Professional on the Top; Relaxed on the Bottom. 14

    Tip 10: Use a Do Not Disturb Sign 15

    Where to Go From Here 16

2   **Building Relationships With Students** **19**

    Tip 11: Take the Time (Don't Take Shortcuts) 20

    Tip 12: Be Interested, and Be Interesting 21

    Tip 13: Remember the Three Types of Relationships in a Class 22

    Tip 14: Help Students Get to Know Your Stories 23

    Tip 15: Help Students Get to Know Your Surroundings. 24

    Tip 16: Help Students Get to Know Your Stuff 25

    Tip 17: Know Your Students' Interests. 26

    Tip 18: Make a Student Your Cohost. 27

    Tip 19: Show Up. 28

    Where to Go From Here 30

3   **Engaging Students**. **33**

Tip 20: Greet Students "at the Door" 34

Tip 21: Say Students' Names 35

Tip 22: Wave Your Arms 36

Tip 23: Increase Your Enthusiasm by 20 Percent 37

Tip 24: Make Videos Interactive 38

Tip 25: Use Cards and Hand Signals 39

Tip 26: Mix It Up. 40

Tip 27: Keep 'Em Moving 41

Tip 28: Make Phone Calls Home 42

Where to Go From Here 43

4   **Managing Your Classroom**. **47**

Tip 29: Set Your Expectations High 48

Tip 30: Establish Class Procedures. 50

Tip 31: Establish Routines 51

Tip 32: Monitor the Chat 52

Tip 33: Make Sure Your Settings Are Safe 53

Tip 34: Use Multiple Monitors 54

Tip 35: Be Consistent 56

Tip 36: Turn Classroom Jobs Into Online Roles 57

Tip 37: Prerecord a Welcome Message 59

Where to Go From Here 60

5   **Pulling in Parents and Guardians** **63**

Tip 38: Give Parents and Guardians Questions They Can Ask 64

Tip 39: Invite Them to 65

Tip 40: Teach Parents and Guardians Some Simple Teaching Strategies . 66

Tip 41: Check In on Them 68

Tip 42: Create Ways for Parents and Guardians to Help 69

Tip 43: Include Parents and Guardians in Family Projects 70

Tip 44: Promote Curiosity 71

Tip 45: Find Out Their Preferred Method of Contact 72

Tip 46: Use a Translator 73

Where to Go From Here 74

6 **Creating a Community** **77**

Tip 47: Use the Word *Community* 78

Tip 48: Invite Special Guests 79

Tip 49: Get Students (and Yourself) Out Into the Community 80

Tip 50: Acknowledge Which Communities We're Part Of 82

Tip 51: Break the Class Up Into Smaller Teams That Can Work Together . 83

Tip 52: Connect With the Quiet Ones 84

Tip 53: Create Ways to See and Hear Each Other 85

Tip 54: Have Students Check in on Students 86

Tip 55: Plan Virtual Gatherings 87

Where to Go From Here 88

7 **Organizing Your Lessons** **91**

Tip 56: Boil It Down, But Don't Water It Down 92

Tip 57: Chunk It 93

Tip 58: Keep. It. Simple. 94

Tip 59: Separate When You Need to Be There and When You Don't 95

Tip 60: Provide an Agenda 96

Tip 61: Talk Less (and Listen More) 97

Tip 62: Give Think Time 98

Tip 63: Relate Lessons to Their World 99

Tip 64: Show What Different Levels of Success Look Like 100

Where to Go From Here 101

8 **Assessing Students** **105**

Tip 65: Monitor Faces and Body Language 106

Tip 66: Use Hand Gestures, Emojis, and Polls 107

Tip 67: Take a Photo 108

Tip 68: Use (Google) Surveys 109

Tip 69: Assess Via Video 110

Tip 70: When Providing Feedback, Be Specific and Timely 111

Tip 71: Provide Feedback Via Video or Voice Recording 112

Tip 72: Have a Back Channel Where Students Can Ask for Help 113

Tip 73: Rethink What Counts as Cheating 114

Where to Go From Here 115

9 Ensuring Equity 119

Tip 74: Pronounce Students' Names Right (and Learn to Say "Hello!") . 120

Tip 75: Be Conscious About (Camera) Backgrounds 121

Tip 76: Know Your Students' Living Situations 122

Tip 77: Find the Reason Behind the Reason. 123

Tip 78: Embrace Race and Diversity 124

Tip 79: Commit to Culturally Responsive Teaching. 125

Tip 80: Be Diverse in Your Video and Photo Selections 126

Tip 81: Create Teams With Equity in Mind. 127

Tip 82: Ensure Access to the Internet and a Reliable Device. 128

Where to Go From Here 129

10 Differentiating Learning 133

Tip 83: Hold Online Office Hours 134

Tip 84: Make and Take Appointments 135

Tip 85: Send Care Packages 136

Tip 86: Teach Students to Pause and Go Back 137

Tip 87: Understand Depth of Knowledge 138

Tip 88: Ask Three Questions 139

Tip 89: Surround Students With Visuals 140

Tip 90: Add Subtitles to Your Videos. 141

Tip 91: Give Them Tomorrow, Today! 142

Where to Go From Here 143

11 Taking Care of Yourself 147

Tip 92: Stand Up! 148

Tip 93: Lean on Others for Help 149

Tip 94: Set Time Boundaries 150

Tip 95: Picture Your Happy Place (and Put a Frame Around It). 151

Tip 96: Don't Compare Your Insides to Someone Else's Outsides 152

Tip 97: Ditch the Guilt 153

Tip 98: Share the Work 154

Tip 99: Understand What Burnout Is (and Isn't). 155

Tip 100: Surround Yourself With Good People 156

Where to Go From Here 157

Final Thoughts 161

Tip 101: Create the World as It Can Be. 162

References and Resources 163

Index 169

About the Author

 **Alex Kajitani** is the 2009 California Teacher of the Year and a top-four finalist for National Teacher of the Year. He speaks internationally on a variety of education and leadership issues and delivers powerful keynote speeches and workshops to educators and business leaders. Also known as "The Rappin' Mathematician," Alex's songs, videos, and online programs are used around the world to help students succeed.

Alex is the author of *Owning It: Proven Strategies to Ace and Embrace Teaching* and coauthor of *Chicken Soup for the Soul: Inspiration for Teachers*. He also has a popular TEDx Talk and has been featured in many media stories, including the *CBS Evening News*, where Katie Couric declared, "I *love* that guy!"

To learn more about Alex's work, visit www.AlexKajitani.com.

To book Alex Kajitani for professional development, contact Solution Tree at pd@SolutionTree.com.

Introduction

It was my first year of teaching, and I was sinking. I had several degrees and credentials, yet I couldn't seem to get my students to pay attention or remember any of the mathematics I had just taught them. At the same time, I realized that my students could remember every word to every rap song on the radio.

One day, while teaching (or, what I thought was teaching) my class to add and subtract decimals, I decided to create my own rap song, which I named "The Itty-Bitty Dot," after the decimal point. I practiced it all night (I admit, in front of the mirror) and performed it in front of my class the next morning.

It was a complete disaster.

My middle school students laughed hysterically at me. Then they couldn't run out of the room fast enough to tell their other friends about what was sure to be the end of my short-lived teaching career. *Oh, well.*

But then, a funny thing happened as I was walking to the teachers' lounge for lunch. I walked by the students' lunch tables, and they were all singing "The Itty-Bitty Dot." The next day, they entered my room with the same level of excitement usually reserved for when the bell rang to end my class. They were saying things like, "Yesterday was the best day ever in math class. Are you going to rap again?"

As their interest in mathematics seemed to skyrocket (along with their test scores), my students insisted that I start creating rap music videos about the mathematics concepts I was teaching. And with their help, we posted them all over the internet. "The Rappin' Mathematician" was born, and those videos have now been viewed hundreds of thousands of times in homes and classrooms around the world (and eventually featured on the *CBS Evening News*).

I also started getting emails and calls from students in other countries, letting me know how their teachers were using the videos to teach them in class.

That's when my online teaching career began.

Since we filmed that first video, I've been busy recording videos and creating online programs that help students do everything from master their times tables to higher-level algebra concepts. These videos have been incredibly well-received and effective. But I always longed for one more dimension of them—a live component.

When schools across the globe abruptly shut down due to the COVID-19 pandemic, I knew there would be many students who might struggle to stay engaged in mathematics—and many parents who would struggle to help their kids understand the concepts. Wanting desperately to help, I quickly created "Wacky Math Hour," a free, weekly, live Zoom class that anyone could join. Being one of the first teachers to offer something like this, I had the terrifying pleasure of working out some major kinks early on. (Who knew, at the time, that students would figure out how to draw on the teacher's screen?)

Even with the early Zoom mix-ups, thousands of teachers and parents from around the world signed up to join us and enthusiastically asked for more. Each week of those early pandemic months, I—along with a few of my amazing teaching colleagues—delivered engaging, effective mathematics instruction directly into the hearts and minds of students around the world.

And that's when I realized the true power of online teaching.

I've watched my own children take online classes over the years, with mixed results. I've seen them completely engaged and engrossed in their online class, and I've seen them half asleep and utterly disengaged as the teacher struggles to command the online environment.

So, I set out on a journey to learn from amazing teachers who are teaching online. (Yes, I am a trainer of teachers around the United States, and some people like to know that I was California Teacher of the Year and a top-four finalist for National Teacher of the Year. But I still look to learn from other teachers every day.) I sought out highly effective online teachers who are not merely taking the traditional ways of teaching and transporting them into online classrooms but rather building a new reality—taking advantage of the unique qualities of the online environment to engage and educate students in a multitude of ways that work for them creatively and successfully. Now, I've

combined my own experiences with online education with what I've learned from these highly successful online teachers and condensed them into this book for you, the next generation of online educators (no matter where you are in your teaching career!).

About This Book

101 Tips for Teaching Online is an easy book to read. It's filled with practical tips for teachers, from teachers, that you can implement immediately to be highly effective in your online classroom, while still doing the critical work that teachers do. It draws on the wisdom (and specific experiences) of teachers, some of whom have been teaching online for many years and some who've jumped in with fresh ideas in just the past couple of years. And it draws on the commonsense ideas that some of us quickly discovered as we pivoted to online learning at the beginning of the pandemic.

This book is divided into eleven chapters, each containing several tips relating to the following topics.

1. Looking good on camera
2. Building relationships with students
3. Engaging students
4. Managing your classroom
5. Pulling in parents and guardians
6. Creating a community
7. Organizing your lessons
8. Assessing students
9. Ensuring equity
10. Differentiating learning
11. Taking care of yourself

Each tip in this book will help you do what you need to do to explain things to students, engage them in learning, and help them feel safe, loved, and confident as a member of your class.

Throughout the book, you'll find Teacher Feature and Advice From Students feature boxes. The Advice From Students feature boxes have quotes from real students about the different ways they find learning online helpful. In each feature, I've sculpted my conversations with the students down to just one thought, with the hope that it's something that you can implement immediately in your own work—because as teachers, we're masters at adopting and adapting our colleagues' ideas, right?

As you read each chapter, reflect on how you might use the chapter's tips in your own teaching. At the conclusion of each chapter, a Where to Go From Here section provides a quick self-assessment, with space to jot down notes on your reflections. In addition, this section includes suggested resources to consult if you want to dig deeper into the chapter topic.

Before we get to chapter 1 (page 5), let me start us out with the first important tip—a foundation for them all: remember what teachers do.

TIP 1
Remember What Teachers Do

I'll never forget something my first principal, David Geck, said to me during my very first week of teaching. He said:

"A truly great teacher can teach with a plot of sand and a stick."

That was over twenty years ago, and over those years, I've used a lot of tools to teach students. From word walls to hundreds charts, and from cutouts to SMART Boards, I've used 'em all.

And yet, what unlocks the learning isn't the tool—it's our ability, as teachers, to explain things to students.

As teachers, we've been trained to explain. Of course, inextricably linked to that ability is the need to build relationships with students, the need to monitor and assess their learning, the need to . . . well, you know how long this list goes on. But at the core of it all is our ability to explain things.

When schools across the world closed their physical doors due to the pandemic and switched to remote learning, many teachers had to scramble. A move to remote learning meant new online platforms, new apps, new classrooms (like our kitchen tables), and of course, new struggles. But what did we discover at the end of all that? Simply this: all the tools required to deliver online learning are just technologically evolved versions of a plot of sand and a stick.

Our ability to explain things to our students is what sparks in them the true ability to think, learn, and grow.

Let's do this.

Looking Good on Camera

As teachers, we need to look good (McCombs School of Business, 2020). I don't mean this to sound self-centered or egotistical, but it is very important. Why? *Because we're professionals* (Morris, 2020).

As teaching professionals, we don't just have credentials and degrees—we have opportunities, every day, to show students what a professional looks and sounds like. Not just when we're physically standing in front of them, but when we're interacting with them virtually as well. And it's hard to give the impression that you're a professional when you're not looking and sounding your best!

The tips in this chapter will help you look good, sound good, and make a good impression on your students—so you can be a highly effective online teacher. (See page 18 for additional research supporting the following tips on looking good on camera.)

TIP 2
Look Directly Into Your Camera

I know, I know—we're all so stunningly beautiful that it's very hard to resist looking at ourselves while we're teaching online. Making the shift from looking at ourselves to looking directly into our camera might seem a bit awkward at first, but it makes a huge impact on our online presence.

Because here's the thing: when we are busy looking at ourselves, we're not making eye contact with our students (from their perspective, we're looking away from them). And it's really hard for them to learn from someone, stay engaged, and build a relationship with someone who isn't giving them eye contact.

When we look directly into the camera, our students see us looking right at them, and they're much more likely to pay attention, stay engaged, and take class seriously (Walden, 2021).

If this is challenging for you, consider drawing an arrow and writing "Look Here" on a sticky note, and then placing it next to where your camera is with the arrow pointing directly to the camera. Or, in most virtual teaching programs, you can set up your view so you can see everyone in the class except yourself.

Of course, there will be times when you need to look away from your camera, such as when you're reading something that's not on your screen or when you're focused on a slide (of course, you'll want your students looking at that slide as well!), but that will be the exception, not the norm. The following are three times that you should *definitely* be looking directly into your camera.

1. When you call on a student or are speaking with a student directly (more on that in tip 21, page 35)

2. When you're giving directions to the class

3. When you need to address something serious

And don't worry—when class ends, you'll still be stunningly beautiful!

TIP 3
Let the Light Shine on You

Having proper lighting while teaching online doesn't mean you need to have a Hollywood studio setup or any sort of expensive equipment. You can use a few lamps or invest in a cheap ring light—there are lots of different options and sizes! But get the lighting right, and you'll be looking like your favorite actor in the soon-to-be-released sequel of your favorite movie. (Well, maybe not exactly, but your students will be able to see you much better.)

Here are three suggestions to help you look your best (see figure 1.1, page 8).

1. Avoid having a window directly behind you, which can be distracting for the viewer and give you a washed-out look (McCombs School of Business, 2020). Instead, simply rotate yourself and your laptop or computer 180 degrees, so that you are sitting facing the window (Graham, 2020). The natural light will give you and your skin a nice, soft glow and will brighten up what students see behind you. If you just can't avoid sitting with the window at your back, consider covering it with a curtain and using the lights in the room.

2. Use a lamp. While many of us have one big light that shines down on us from the ceiling, placing a lamp that can "spotlight" you directly can help you shine even brighter. Of course, *too* much brightness can be distracting, so a simple trick is to point the lamp at the wall that is in front of you, so that the light bounces off the wall. This trick softens the light (called diffusion) before it hits your face.

3. Use 45-degree angles. When you shine a light directly at your face, it lights your face equally. While this might be nice for makeup tutorials, it's not ideal for teaching. Instead, try shining the light at yourself from a 45-degree angle. This will create some shadows on your face, which will give your overall look some depth. It also helps you avoid having to look directly at a bright light while you're teaching (O'Donnell, 2020).

Shine on!

Figure 1.1: Let the light shine on you.

TIP 4
Have Your Camera at Eye Level

Ever tried to have a conversation with someone standing a few feet above or below you? It might be OK for a little while, but then it gets distracting (especially if you're looking up and into someone else's nose!). When teaching online, be sure to line your camera up at eye level, so that you can look directly into your students' eyes (see figure 1.2). Eye level = right level (McCombs School of Business, 2020; Morris, 2020).

Most laptops have their camera at the top of the screen. So, when your laptop is sitting flat on a desk, your eyes are well above the camera level. This means you need to raise your device up about six inches to be at eye level.

For desktop computers, the camera's location can vary. Using a detached webcam (or even your phone's camera) can help you to position your camera exactly where you need it and give you the flexibility to move it as needed!

You don't need a fancy laptop or computer stand (although they're nice). Just grab a small crate or a handful of books and stack them underneath to raise the laptop up to the necessary height. Of course, be sure to use books that are big and sturdy enough to support the device you're using (Burgess, 2016).

Figure 1.2: Have your camera at eye level.

TIP 5
Sit (at Least) an Arm's Length Away

Generally, sit about an arm's length away from your camera. This will allow you to be close enough for your students to see you clearly while giving the camera enough room to see what's around and behind you, which offers framing and context.

Once you're an arm's length away from your camera, picture a 3 × 3 grid across your screen, and position yourself so that your eyes are at the bottom of the top three squares, while still leaving a bit of space between the top of your head and the top of your screen (see figure 1.3). At the same time, your armpits should be at the very bottom of your screen (Burgess, 2016). Remember: eyes on the top line, pits at the bottom.

Figure 1.3: Sit (at least) an arm's length away.

TIP 6
Mix Up Your Background

In a traditional, in-person classroom, students report to the same classroom day after day. As teachers, we switch up what's on the walls, but students know that they're still in the same physical place.

Teaching online is an opportunity to mix it up and change where you're teaching from.

Teaching about fractions? Consider holding class from your kitchen, where you can pull out different measuring cups, and discuss how to double your favorite cookie or tamale recipe!

Teaching about science? Head out to your backyard or the field near your house (and consider telling the students to head outside for the day's class as well!). Of course, heading outside means you might also be dealing with loud and unplanned noises like wind or the howl of wolves. Putting in some headphones (many have an internal microphone) can help minimize distracting noise. Alternatively, if you teach in a rural area without a reliable internet connection, or an urban area with limited access to natural settings, consider using a virtual background that displays the lesson's theme—your students could find you in the Amazon rain forest on Monday, and at the top of Mount Kilimanjaro on Tuesday!

And maybe one day, try filming from a "mystery location" where you give clues about your location throughout the class and students can try to guess where you are. (This is a great way to keep students engaged.)

Teacher Feature

Throughout her class period, Dorina Sackman-Ebuwa, a middle school literacy teacher, changes what's behind and around her and challenges her students (most of whom are English learners) to identify what's different from when class began.

Some days, she begins with an unlit candle, and by the end of class, it's lit. Other days, while students are working in breakout rooms, she switches out the photos that are behind her on the wall. According to Dorina, "It's a great way to keep kids engaged, keep them alert, and keep them focused on what's happening in front of them!" (D. Sackman-Ebuwa, personal communication, November 19, 2020)

TIP 7
Use Props

As awesome and engaging as you are, having a few props can help you go beyond simply being a talking head throughout your class. They're also extremely helpful when teaching English learners (ELs) and students who struggle with vocabulary (a strategy known as *realia*).

You don't need any fancy props—they can be as simple as the cover of a book that you're quoting, which you can hold up to show students. Teaching about a faraway place? Show students a trinket you bought when you visited there.

Of course, props can include items that you use frequently to teach, such as a whiteboard for demonstrations, flash cards, or even finger puppets or stuffed animals for some occasional comic relief (Teach and GO, n.d.).

You might need to have your whiteboard on a wall that is not directly behind you. Consider getting a simple swivel tray (know commonly as a *lazy Susan*) and put your laptop on top of it. When you need to switch your camera to focus on the whiteboard, simply swivel your laptop toward the whiteboard, and *voilà*—instant camera change (Flynn, 2020).

TIP 8
Consider a Mic and a Good Camera

For the most part, the camera and microphone that come installed inside your computer or laptop will work for teaching online. However, have you ever tried to listen to a podcast that's a bit muffled or watch a video that's a bit grainy? It can be distracting and frustrating.

Investing in a higher-quality video camera and microphone will help you look and sound even better, which will engage your students at a much higher level while increasing the overall production value of your content. Plus, you'll feel really cool with a microphone and camera in front of you. And if you combine this with some of the lighting suggestions in tip 3 (page 7), you'll start each class feeling like you've got your own Hollywood production studio!

TIP 9
Be Professional on the Top;
Relaxed on the Bottom

Let's be honest: one of the greatest joys of online teaching is getting to wear sweatpants, flip-flops, or *whatever you want*—as long as it's not in the camera's sight line. (Though, do choose carefully and be very mindful of what's showing if you need to stand up to grab something or write something on the whiteboard.)

As for what *is* showing on camera, sticking with wearing solid colors and simple prints helps to reduce distractions (Lufkin, 2020; Sprecher, n.d.). However, try to avoid wearing something that is all black or all white, as those can give you a washed-out look. Jewelry that dangles and sparkles can also be distracting. However, if that's part of your style, then wear what you need to wear (V. Brown, personal communication, March 15, 2021).

TIP 10
Use a Do Not Disturb Sign

It's happened to all of us, and we've seen it happen to pretty much everyone. Behind the teacher's shoulder, the door opens, and a family member walks across the room, the kids run in screaming, or the family pet makes a cameo appearance.

Hanging a *Do Not Disturb* sign on the door outside wherever you're teaching can at least give pause to the person who is about to enter. Taking the time to explain to your kids, partner, or others *why* that sign is there, and what is happening in the room, can be a big help toward them taking the sign seriously. Just be sure to remove the sign when it's OK to enter, so nobody gets too used to seeing it.

Of course, there might inevitably be times when a surprise guest appears in your teaching area. When that happens, consider doing any of the following.

1. Ignore it.

2. Mention it, but then keep teaching. (For example, "Please ignore the dog that just ran across the room and keep working on finding that common denominator!")

3. Stop and introduce the person—especially if you can link it to something you're teaching. (For example, "Hey, perfect timing; my wife used to work in politics, so maybe she can help us understand the three branches of government a little better.")

Advice From Students

My teacher asks us to pin her on the video, which makes her video bigger and keeps her on the screen. That helps me stay focused on her, and I pay more attention.

—Cora, Third Grade (personal communication, November 4, 2020)

Where to Go From Here

The best reason to implement this chapter's tips for looking good on camera is simple: you can stop worrying about how you look and start focusing on your teaching!

Using figure 1.4, reflect on the tips in this chapter. To what degree do you currently achieve the goal in each tip? Are there some tips you are interested in using in your classes? How would you implement them? The figure has space for notes on your reflections.

Tips in This Chapter	To What Degree Are You Already Following the Tip?	Your Plans for Implementing the Tip
Look directly into the camera.	☐ Already nailing it! ☐ Following it some but should do more. ☐ Not following it at all but should try. ☐ Not following it at all and not interested.	
Let the light shine on you.	☐ Already nailing it! ☐ Following it some but should do more. ☐ Not following it at all but should try. ☐ Not following it at all and not interested.	
Have your camera at eye level.	☐ Already nailing it! ☐ Following it some but should do more. ☐ Not following it at all but should try. ☐ Not following it at all and not interested.	
Sit (at least) an arm's length away from the camera.	☐ Already nailing it! ☐ Following it some but should do more. ☐ Not following it at all but should try. ☐ Not following it at all and not interested.	

Mix up your background.	☐ Already nailing it! ☐ Following it some but should do more. ☐ Not following it at all but should try. ☐ Not following it at all and not interested.	
Use props.	☐ Already nailing it! ☐ Following it some but should do more. ☐ Not following it at all but should try. ☐ Not following it at all and not interested.	
Consider a mic and a good camera.	☐ Already nailing it! ☐ Following it some but should do more. ☐ Not following it at all but should try. ☐ Not following it at all and not interested.	
Be professional on top, relaxed on the bottom.	☐ Already nailing it! ☐ Following it some but should do more. ☐ Not following it at all but should try. ☐ Not following it at all and not interested.	
Use a "Do Not Disturb" sign.	☐ Already nailing it! ☐ Following it some but should do more. ☐ Not following it at all but should try. ☐ Not following it at all and not interested.	

Figure 1.4: Reflection chart for chapter 1.

*Visit **go.SolutionTree.com/technology** for a free reproducible version of this figure.*

If you want to go beyond the tips in this chapter and dig deeper into looking good on camera, the following are two resources to consider.

1. Zoom has a series of design guides, including a March 2021 "Lighting Concepts" article (available at https://support.zoom.us/hc/en-us/articles /360028862512-Lighting-Concepts). This guide gives tips on how to achieve optimal lighting in your space using a light meter app on your phone to measure the illumination on your face and the wall behind you. This can help you find the right lighting to adjust the illumination to optimal levels.

2. There are a number of detailed advice books for business professionals about creating your best on-camera appearance. These books have lots of tips that can apply to teaching online. For example, Karin M. Reed (2017), a broadcast journalist who now coaches Fortune 500 business executives on how to present on camera, includes an entire chapter on wardrobe and another chapter on makeup in her book *On-Camera Coach: Tools and Techniques for Business Professionals in a Video-Driven World*.

CHAPTER 2

Building Relationships
With Students

Depending on who you ask, there can be a lot of different definitions of *relationship*. My favorite definition is simply, *a connection*.

You can have connections (and, thus, relationships) with people that are strong or weak, growing or falling apart. Every time we connect with our students, we are building the relationship (Smith, Fisher, & Frey, 2019). Every time we fail to connect, the relationship weakens. Fortunately, those connections don't need to be in person (Ditch That Textbook, 2020; Hellerich, 2020; O'Block, 2020). And the tips in this chapter will show you that teaching online is a fabulous opportunity to build relationships with our students—in small and large ways! (See page 32 for additional research supporting the following tips and to go deeper as you build relationships with students online.)

TIP 11
Take the Time (Don't Take Shortcuts)

We live in a time of what futurist Ray Kurzweil calls *accelerating change*, with technological, cultural, social, and environmental change taking place exponentially faster than in any other period in the known history of our planet (Baer, 2015). We are feeling the effects of this firsthand in almost every aspect of our lives. And while technological advances allow us to connect, travel, share, and even produce vaccines at staggering rates, building meaningful, significant relationships with our students takes time. Sometimes, lots of time.

Of course, it doesn't mean we have to devote large chunks of time, all at once, to building these relationships. We can build relationships with students in small, consistent, and meaningful ways. And we don't need to be physically present in the room where it happens.

The remaining tips in this chapter will give you some ideas and strategies to authentically connect with your students so highly effective learning takes place. And the bottom line comes down to three words:

Take. The. Time.

Taking the time doesn't mean taking all, or even a lot of, our time. It can happen in the small things we do, every day. It happens when we:

- Take the time to pronounce a student's name correctly.

- Connect what we're covering in class with our students' interests.

- Tell them a story that they'll remember and relate to.

The remainder of this chapter is dedicated to how you can use these examples, and several others, to build authentic and powerful relationships with students—even if there's a screen between you!

TIP 12
Be Interested, and Be Interesting

In the late 1800s, Jennie Jerome (Winston Churchill's mother) attended a dinner party where she met Benjamin Disraeli and William Gladstone, who were both competing to be prime minister of the United Kingdom. Ms. Jerome spent much of the evening speaking with them both. When a journalist later asked her what her impression of the two men was, she responded: "When I left the dining room after sitting next to Gladstone, I thought he was the cleverest man in England. But when I sat next to Disraeli, I left feeling that I was the cleverest woman" (Mening, 2016).

Building strong relationships with our students works two ways: it means that (1) we need to see them as the fascinating, wonderful people that they are, and (2) we need to build opportunities for them to see us as the fascinating, wonderful people that we are (because we really, really are!). Put another way, it's not very fun to build a relationship with someone we think is boring, and certainly none of us want to *be* the boring person in the relationship.

Building relationships with students while teaching online should never involve a one-way flow of information. Think of the screen between you and your students as a two-way valve: sharing happens both ways. Of course, students might sometimes be too intimidated to share information about themselves, but a few well-placed questions are all you need to get to know your students.

The following are two easy ways to get the ball rolling.

1. Notice something in the frame around or behind the students, and ask them about it. A simple "Hey, tell me about that picture that's on the wall behind you!" can send an immediate message to your students that you're interested in them.

2. Have an object that is meaningful to you nearby, and show it to your students along with telling them how you came to own the object. Then, ask them to go grab something that is meaningful to them. You can even put fun requirements on the object they must gather, such as, "It must be able to fit inside a coffee cup!"

And any time you can bring up something you've learned about your students at a later date shows not only that were you listening, but that you also found what they had to say interesting and relevant.

So, which should you be for your students—Disraeli or Gladstone?

Both.

TIP 13

Remember the Three Types
of Relationships in a Class

At any given moment, there are three types of relationships happening in your online classroom.

1. The relationship between the student and the teacher.

2. The relationship between the student and other students.

3. The relationship between the student and the content. (Believe me, I've been a middle school mathematics teacher for many years and have encountered many students with a less-than-ideal relationship with numbers!)

Understanding these three relationships can help us determine how we structure our online classrooms and content (see chapter 7, "Organizing Your Lessons," on page 91 for more on that). And nurturing all three of these types of relationships helps create a thriving online classroom.

Some examples of what this looks like are as follows.

- Having students post videos of themselves talking about something they're learning about in class (on a program like Flipgrid) is a great way for students to build their relationship with the content. They can also use photo editing programs (such as Canva) to create photos with words overlaid to describe a particular piece of the content being covered.

- When students are then directed to view their classmates' work and provide replies (in either video or written form), we are giving them an opportunity to build their relationships with each other. Taking the time to allow them to chat in smaller groups (such as breakout rooms) also gives them this opportunity.

- And of course, when we comment and provide replies, the student-teacher relationship continues to grow and strengthen. Whenever possible, referencing something a student has said or done in the past and relating it to something that is happening now is a powerful way to show students that we're paying attention to them, and all they bring to our class!

TIP 14
Help Students Get to Know Your Stories

There are few things more memorable than a great story. When we tell stories about our experiences or struggles or the situations we've encountered, we make ourselves much more memorable to our students. And we accelerate their ability to get to know us, thereby strengthening the relationship (Jarzabek, 2020).

Our stories don't need to be stories of epic proportions or heroics—sometimes the best stories are those that are humbling or trivial but honest, authentic, and real. In an online environment, students want to know who that teacher on the other side of the screen is, and every time we tell them a story about ourselves, that person becomes more real and more relatable.

In addition, if you can link a story with the academic content the students are learning, even better. My own children still talk about their online science teacher, who, while teaching about spiders, told them about the time he killed one of the world's deadliest spiders (the Brazilian wandering spider, to be exact). The students joyfully repeat how their teacher doesn't like to kill any animals, but this spider's venom can paralyze a human in five seconds, so he had to smash it!

After you tell a few stories, you can even use an online poll feature (such as the poll feature in Zoom, or Poll Everywhere) to ask students to vote on their "favorite (fill in your name) story from the past month." Not only will this reinforce the stories you've been telling, but it also reinforces the relationship you're building with your students.

And of course, taking the time to hear your students' stories (whether in spoken words or in writing) will help you see your students as the amazing people they are—far more than little boxes onscreen!

TIP 15
Help Students Get to Know Your Surroundings

As mentioned in tip 6 (page 11), it's great to mix up your background and give students an opportunity to see you in different locations. While this can be an effective way to highlight content (fractions with measuring cups in your kitchen or a science lab out on your back patio), it's also a great way to help students get to know *you*.

Where appropriate, let students in on what your surroundings look like. Perhaps every Friday, you read the day's story out in your garden (see figure 2.1), with your cute dog sitting at your feet. If internet access permits, perhaps you can head out to somewhere that you like to go—the local library (during the nonfiction unit), the woods near your house (photosynthesis, anyone?), or maybe just the middle of your living room (let's talk calculating square footage!).

It's also important to remember that you might be teaching students who live far away, or in neighborhoods far different than your own. What a golden opportunity to show our students a different geographical location or neighborhood, and when appropriate, learn a bit about theirs as well. Just be sure to be aware of equity issues before doing this. (Read tip 75, page 121, Be Conscious About [Camera] Backgrounds.)

When teachers and students learn about each other's surroundings, we go far beyond the walls that often confine us in a physical classroom.

Figure 2.1: Help students get to know your surroundings.

TIP 16
Help Students Get to Know Your Stuff

Along with sharing your stories and surroundings, sharing things that are important to you can help build relationships between teachers and students, and between the students' themselves.

If you're a crafter or a maker, you can share things you created. If you're a traveler, you can share things you've bought or found from different places. If you're a collector, share your collections. If you're a book lover or art lover, share your bookshelves or your art pieces.

When we share things that are important to us, we share parts of ourselves that are unique and fun and help set us apart. And when our "stuff" makes regular appearances during our online classes, it helps to build a culture and climate that is positive and memorable!

Teacher Feature

Trevor Todd, a fifth-grade teacher in Wilmington, North Carolina, shares his love for bow ties with his students. Each day he wears a different bow tie (over the years, he's amassed hundreds of them) during his online class, each with its own unique story about how he obtained it (some were made for him, some were sent to him, and others he purchased on his own). At the end of the year, he sends each of his students their own bow tie, and of course, anytime students see a bow tie, they think about Mr. Todd! (T. Todd, personal communication, October 1, 2020)

TIP 17
Know Your Students' Interests

One of the easiest and most effective ways to build relationships with students while teaching online is to find out *their* interests and hobbies. Then, refer to those interests throughout the school year, semester, or class.

Finding out your students' interests is easy. You can ask a simple question and have them type responses into the chat to start class one day, or it can be part of a larger activity.

The real magic happens when you take that information and *use it to build a relationship with the student* (Ditch That Textbook, 2020). You can keep a simple list of your students' names, along with their favorite activity, on a sheet of paper and hang it up behind your computer for easy reference (see figure 2.2).

Take any opportunity (it can be preplanned or spontaneous) that you can link to one or more of your students with something they love to do. Not only does this help make the academic content culturally responsive (see tip 79, page 125, for more on that), your students will be very impressed with your ability to instantly recall something that's very important to them!

Figure 2.2: Know your students' interests.

TIP 18
Make a Student Your Cohost

As teachers, we just can't do everything (although we seem to keep trying, don't we?). With this in mind, let's use online learning as an opportunity to build relationships with students by trusting and empowering them to take a leadership role in our online classrooms.

Depending on the number and age of your students and the structure of your class, you can have a different cohost each day, week, or whatever works for you. Just make sure everyone gets an opportunity.

A few of the duties of the cohost could include:

- Taking over if you happen to lose internet connection for a while

- Starting discussions or giving directions (maybe we'll even help create some future teachers!)

- Starting or ending class in an uplifting way

When we create opportunities for our students to take leadership roles in our online classes, we're sending the strong message that we trust them. When trust is present, we're able to build powerful relationships with students while teaching online.

TIP 19
Show Up

As a student, did you ever experience the thrill of seeing one of your teachers outside of school? Maybe it was in the grocery, and you marveled at how they too bought food! Or maybe their kid also played the same sport as you, and you came to realize that they also spent their Saturday mornings somewhere other than their classroom.

Even with all of today's technology and opportunities to connect online, there might be times when showing up in person helps create opportunities to build powerful relationships with students. Not only does it show students how much you care, but it also allows them to see you as a real person who exists beyond the four corners of their computer screen.

Of course, distance, health or safety, and your own personal preferences for seeing students in person must be taken into consideration, but the following are just a few ways remote teachers have "shown up" for their students outside of their computer screens (Vulpo, 2021).

- Heather Tuttle, a special education teacher in Manhattan Beach, California, wanted to surprise a student on his birthday. After driving up to his house and getting the student's attention, Ms. Tuttle got out of the car dressed up like a unicorn and started dancing to "One More Time" from the movie *Trolls*.

- Linda Wright, a second-grade teacher in Greensboro, North Carolina, puts small flower-shaped signs in the front yards of her students, letting them know how much she values them. One of the students' fathers even posted about it on social media, stating, "My son got an awesome surprise from his teacher this morning. . . . Such a sweet and above and beyond gesture from her!" (Vulpo, 2021).

- Unable to show up in person? Consider mailing a cutout mini teacher version of yourself, which students can place next to their computer during online class time when they're completing work independently (or whenever they need a little more of you in their life).

Advice From Students

I really like feeling like my teachers are my friends; and I like when they get to know us, by talking to us. One of my teachers sends us messages if she can't speak with us directly. She also shares books with me that she knows I might like to read.

—Becca, Eighth Grade (personal communication, February 3, 2021)

Where to Go From Here

Building relationships with students is central to the art of teaching, whether in person or online. As Carl Jung (1981) notes:

> One looks back with appreciation to the brilliant teachers, but with gratitude to those who touched our human feelings. The curriculum is so much necessary raw material, but warmth is the vital element for the growing plant and for the soul of the child. (p. 144)

Or, as comedian Lily Tomlin puts it, "I like a teacher who gives you something to take home to think about besides homework" (Wagner, 1995, p. 32).

Reflect on the tips in this chapter. To what degree do you currently achieve the goal in each tip? Are there some tips you are interested in using in your classes? How would you implement them? Figure 2.3 has space for notes on your reflections.

Tips in This Chapter	To What Degree Are You Already Following the Tip?	Your Plans for Implementing the Tip
Take the time (don't take shortcuts).	☐ Already nailing it! ☐ Following it some but should do more. ☐ Not following it at all but should try. ☐ Not following it at all and not interested.	
Be interested, and be interesting.	☐ Already nailing it! ☐ Following it some but should do more. ☐ Not following it at all but should try. ☐ Not following it at all and not interested.	
Remember the three types of relationships in a class.	☐ Already nailing it! ☐ Following it some but should do more. ☐ Not following it at all but should try. ☐ Not following it at all and not interested.	

Help students get to know your stories.	☐ Already nailing it! ☐ Following it some but should do more. ☐ Not following it at all but should try. ☐ Not following it at all and not interested.	
Help students get to know your surroundings.	☐ Already nailing it! ☐ Following it some but should do more. ☐ Not following it at all but should try. ☐ Not following it at all and not interested.	
Help students get to know your stuff.	☐ Already nailing it! ☐ Following it some but should do more. ☐ Not following it at all but should try. ☐ Not following it at all and not interested.	
Know your students' interests.	☐ Already nailing it! ☐ Following it some but should do more. ☐ Not following it at all but should try. ☐ Not following it at all and not interested.	
Make a student your cohost.	☐ Already nailing it! ☐ Following it some but should do more. ☐ Not following it at all but should try. ☐ Not following it at all and not interested.	

Figure 2.3: Reflection chart for chapter 2.

continued ▶

Tips in This Chapter	To What Degree Are You Already Following the Tip?	Your Plans for Implementing the Tip
Show up.	☐ Already nailing it! ☐ Following it some but should do more. ☐ Not following it at all but should try. ☐ Not following it at all and not interested.	

*Visit **go.SolutionTree.com/technology** for a free reproducible version of this figure.*

If you want to go beyond the tips in this chapter and dig deeper into building student relationships, there are several books that translate academic research on student-teacher relationships into strategies and techniques for classroom use. Three examples to consider are as follows.

1. *The On-Your-Feet Guide to Building Authentic Student-Teacher Relationships* by Dominique Smith, Douglas Fisher, and Nancy Frey (2019) is a six-page loose-leaf guide showing teachers how to implement techniques that research has shown to improve student-teacher relationships. The three authors are from the Educational Leadership program at San Diego State University.

2. In *Building Bridges: Engaging Students at Risk Through the Power of Relationships*, Don Parker (2019), an experienced principal from Illinois, focuses on ways to build relationships with students at risk.

3. *Youth Culture Power: A #HipHopEd Guide to Building Teacher-Student Relationships and Increasing Student Engagement* by Jason Rawls and John Robinson (2019) presents the research and science behind Rawls and Robinson's philosophy of using hip-hop culture as pedagogy. There is an accompanying hip-hop album as well—*Youth Culture Power*. Rawls and Robinson are both educators and entertainers, and together, they form the hip-hop duo Jay ARE.

CHAPTER 3

Engaging Students

You are not engaged until you are emotionally involved (Walden University, n.d.). Think about what it's like to be engaged to a person or engaged in an activity. It requires us, at least on some level, to be emotionally invested in the time we are spending, the person we're spending it with, and the outcome we hope it leads to.

As teachers, we know that the time we spend with students can produce important and memorable experiences that have the potential to transform their lives (and ours!; DeVito, 2016; Kennedy, 2020). While engaging students in an online environment can be challenging, the tips in this chapter will give you some real, easy-to-implement things you can do to get your students engaged, keep them engaged, and maybe even keep them thinking about class long after they've logged off. (See page 45 for additional research supporting the following tips and to go deeper in your practice of student engagement.)

TIP 20
Greet Students "at the Door"

One of the quickest, easiest, and most effective ways to engage students is to greet them immediately upon entering your online classroom. And make sure to greet them by name (more on that in tip 21, page 35).

As students appear in your class, greeting them can be as simple as the following.

- "I see Marisela is joining us—welcome, Marisela!"

- "Looks like Owen is back for another day—so glad you're here, Owen!"

- "Aaaah, back for more learning, I see Tamika is here—I hope you're ready for a great class today!"

Just as we greet students when they enter our physical classrooms, when we greet students (by name) as they enter our virtual classrooms, it immediately engages them. And it sends them the clear message that their teacher sees them, values them, and is ready to roll for another fabulous day of online learning.

TIP 21
Say Students' Names

Nothing gets someone's attention like hearing their own name. When we hear our name, we become immediately engaged in the conversation at hand (O'Block, 2020)—no wonder it's a tactic used by the best salespeople, politicians, and, of course, parents and teachers!

The following are a few tips to naturally incorporate saying students' names into your teaching, to help keep them engaged throughout the entire class.

- Make sure you pronounce their name correctly (more on that in tip 74, page 120).

- After the initial greeting at the beginning of class, try to say every student's name at least once during the class. It helps to keep a simple list of your students' names next to your computer, and just check off each name as you use it.

- Using their names can be as simple as saying, "All good, Devin?" or, "OK, Monica, I think you're going to like this next video . . ." When students hear their name from time to time, they know you're looking out for them and are much more likely to stay engaged.

- Train students to say *each other's* names. When teaching students to respond to each other (see more on classroom procedures in tip 30, page 50), train them to refer to their classmate by name. Teaching them to use statements like, "I agree with what Mikko said because . . ." not only keeps Mikko highly engaged, but also teaches students to listen closely to each other.

TIP 22
Wave Your Arms

While the numbers vary based on which study you consult, most communication experts agree that 70 to 93 percent of all communication is nonverbal (Advaney, 2017). Nonverbal aspects of communication can include your vocal tone, mannerisms, facial expressions, head movements, body posture, and physical distance.

While it's unlikely that you're going to invade someone's personal space while teaching online, issues like body posture, facial expressions, and hand movements are amplified on the screen.

An effective way to avoid *talking head syndrome* while teaching online is to mix up how you're sitting, what you're doing with your arms, and the expressions on your face. You don't need to bust out the latest dance moves (although if you do, your students will probably love it!) or do celebrity impressions. However, mixing in a few of the following will help keep your online teaching style fresh and engaging.

- Answer with your hands. Ask questions where you and the students hold up a certain number of fingers to answer. Or use open fists or closed fists for true-or-false answers. You can also incorporate some hand signals to signify class procedures.

- Describe with your hands. Whenever possible, use hand motions to describe the content you're discussing. Use one finger to draw a circle in the air or use two fingers in a walking motion to describe when someone is walking.

- Emote with your hands. From time to time, it can be fun and effective to lean in very close to your camera and whisper while you motion with your hands like you're telling them a secret. When talking about something that excites you, wave your arms in the air or strike a triumphant pose. And if you can mix in a few hand gestures with some funny facial expressions, engagement will skyrocket (hand motion like a skyrocket!; Smith, 2020).

TIP 23
Increase Your Enthusiasm by 20 Percent*

In an in-person classroom, students can see our body movements as we buzz around the classroom. They're constantly gauging our proximity, mood, and confidence based on our posture, movement, and ability to physically interact with students across the classroom.

With online teaching, all of this is reduced to a face and some shoulders on a small box of a screen. Without all the energy from physical cues, we've got to compensate somehow. One way is by increasing our enthusiasm! We can do this with the tone and volume of our voice, with music, and with creativity and surprise.

It doesn't mean that fireworks always need to be going off in your classroom, or that every lesson plan needs to be an Oscar-worthy performance. However, when we increase our enthusiasm, we simultaneously increase our passion, our energy, and our students' engagement.

*OK, maybe it doesn't need to be exactly 20 percent, but hopefully you get the point I'm making.

TIP 24
Make Videos Interactive

Utilizing videos in engaging, effective ways is a critical component to teaching online. But simply showing videos can result in just entertainment—or students checking out—without any actual learning taking place.

When we transform those videos into interactive ones, research shows that it becomes one of the most effective ways to teach with digital technology (Fisher, Frey, & Hattie, 2020). And good news: making videos interactive doesn't mean you have to create every video yourself.

You can take an existing video and make it interactive in some simple ways.

- Teach students that they can always use the *pause this video and go back* strategy. One of the greatest advantages that teaching online has over in-person teaching is that students no longer need to worry about absorbing everything teachers say the first (and often only) time they teach it.

  In 2020, I watched my own daughter suffer through a few live, online classes with a ukulele teacher, only to finish class feeling lost and unengaged. (And it wasn't cheap, either!) However, when she began watching YouTube video tutorials about playing the ukulele, she began working at her own pace, skipping what she already knew, and repeating what she needed extra help on. Her skills soared! She now plays for us nightly and tells others how easy it is to learn to play.

- When watching a video together, intentionally pausing at certain points to reflect, practice, discuss, or do some writing is another effective way to make videos interactive, while at the same time holding students accountable for the learning.

- There are some fantastic online programs, such as Nearpod, Seesaw, and Pear Deck, that allow you to make interactive videos and make videos interactive.

And here's another advantage to using interactive videos: you only need to create the video once (though you might find ways to improve it), and then you can use it as often as you need!

TIP 25
Use Cards and Hand Signals

Just as teachers can engage students by waving their arms and using well-timed gestures, we can keep students engaged online by giving them simple tasks that keep them moving. These tasks also keep them thinking and learning, all while we are assessing their learning. (See chapter 8, page 105, for more on assessment.)

Throughout class, you can do periodic check-ins, where students display one of three cards on their screen.

- Green ("I'm totally following along right now.")

- Yellow ("Hmmm . . . I'm getting a bit confused.")

- Red ("Eeeek! I need help!")

Based on the cards students are holding up, teachers can stop and address individual students or the class. Giving students an opportunity to continually self-assess keeps them present and engaged. An alternative to color cards could be a 1–10 rating system, where students evaluate their understanding based on numerical criteria.

Another idea is to have a class set of hand signals where students hold up their responses based on your question. Consider going beyond a simple thumbs-up or thumbs-down approach and teach them a bit of sign language. You could teach them American Sign Language (ASL) signs for "I understand" and "I'm confused" (both simple and easy to see on video). You could get creative with younger students by using fun ASL signs for animals—are they feeling like a clever cat (cat sign) or a confused cow (cow sign)? Or, you could try teaching them signs for different emotions and do a periodic check-in on their social and emotional well-being.

Now, what's that hand signal for "engaged?"

TIP 26
Mix It Up

With every buzz, ping, and ring, our attention spans seem to be getting shorter by the . . . uh . . . what were we talking about?

Online teaching requires us to constantly *mix it up* when it comes to what we're putting in front of the students on the screen and what we're asking them to do during class. One way to do this is with the concept of *chunking*. We do this in our everyday lives without even realizing it.

Case in point: did you ever notice how much easier it is to watch two forty-five-minute episodes of your favorite show than to find the time to commit to an entire movie that's going to run an hour and a half? Sure, it's the same amount of time, but it definitely seems easier to watch the two episodes (and then contemplate whether you have enough time for a third!).

So, rather than thinking of your one-hour class as one sixty-minute chunk, design it as six ten-minute chunks that are all related. Of course, you can even break each chunk up into *micro-chunks*.

Here's an example of how a class might mix it up by being broken up (obviously, this is a totally general example; all times are approximate, and you would need to tailor it to you and your students' needs).

- **Minutes zero to ten:** Welcome, class meeting, and review of last class

- **Minutes eleven to twenty:** Four-minute video clip, followed by six minutes in small breakout rooms discussing the clip

- **Minutes twenty-one to thirty:** Eight minutes for whole-class discussion, followed by a two-minute Brain Break activity

- **Minutes thirty-one to forty:** Quick poll to assess student learning so far (two minutes), followed by interactive lecture with note-taking

- **Minutes forty-one to fifty:** A game, activity, or app that reinforces the learning and gives students an opportunity to think more deeply about the learning

- **Minutes fifty-one to sixty:** Wrap-up, review, and exit ticket activity (and maybe a quick preview to get students excited for the next class)

TIP 27
Keep 'Em Moving

Keeping students engaged means keeping them moving. As teacher Dee Kalman said, "If the bum is numb, the mind is dumb!" (Pica, 2015, p. 54). In a traditional, in-person classroom, students can get up and move from class to class or move during recess. When teaching an online class, we have very little control over what students do before and after our class. Students who have spent the hour leading up to our class playing video games are now entering their second hour of stagnation just when our class is beginning!

Utilizing small opportunities to get students moving (regardless of their age) can help keep them engaged and learning. In addition to small things like having them use gestures (tip 25, page 39), we can build in times throughout the class to give them an opportunity to move.

- Have students stand up and go retrieve something from their house ("All right—before we start talking about radius and diameter, everyone stand up and go grab a plate or cup. If you don't have one, just stand up and draw a plate or cup on your paper. You have one minute . . . go!").

- Play a song for thirty seconds. While the music is playing, instruct everyone to stand up, dance, stretch, or move however they want. The only rule is you can't just sit there. You can even instruct students to turn off their cameras if they're self-conscious (but it's on their honor that they must be moving!).

- Play chair yoga. Teach students a few stretches that they can do while sitting in their chair—and encourage them to use these stretches any time they're sitting somewhere for a while. You can even have some fun by giving the stretches funny names, like the "(insert your last name) Shoulder Stretch!" or the "Numb Bum Stand-Up Stretch."

TIP 28
Make Phone Calls Home

While all of chapter 5 (page 63) is devoted to "Pulling in Parents and Guardians," one tool involving parents has great power for engaging students—the all-powerful phone call home.

We all remember the feeling: there's nothing quite like hearing that phone ring and knowing it's your teacher calling. Of course, *why* your teacher is calling might depend on a lot of factors, but either way, when that phone rings, engagement is sky-high!

You don't even need a specific reason as to why you're calling. It might be just to check in with the parents, see how they think things are going with online learning, or let them know that you enjoyed (or didn't enjoy!) something their child did during class.

Regardless, when we call home, there are two immediate results.

1. The students know that you've spoken with their parents, and they are more likely to be and stay engaged throughout class.

2. Word gets around from student to student that you are "the kind of teacher who calls home," which increases the likelihood of everyone's engagement increasing.

Important note: It may seem like some parents are very hard to get a hold of. See tip 45 (page 72) and tip 46 (page 73) for some concrete strategies you can try.

Advice From Students

Have compassion for students who are sitting in front of their computers all day and understand that it's hard to stay focused and engaged—especially if it's our second or third online class of the day. It's really easy to zone out.

—Senna, Ninth Grade (personal communication, January 21, 2021)

Where to Go From Here

As teachers, keeping students (and ourselves!) engaged throughout a live class is critical to helping them stay interested, involved, and learning. When students are connecting to your online class from home, they have many potential distractions, such as TV, games, snacks, and music in addition to the distractions that can happen as part of your class! For some students, it can be easier to hide in an online gallery of students than in a grid of desks in a classroom.

Reflect on the tips in this chapter. To what degree do you currently achieve the goal in each tip? Are there some tips you are interested in using in your classes? How would you implement them? Figure 3.1 has space for notes on your reflections.

Tips in This Chapter	To What Degree Are You Already Following the Tip?	Your Plans for Implementing the Tip
Greet students "at the door."	☐ Already nailing it! ☐ Following it some but should do more. ☐ Not following it at all but should try. ☐ Not following it at all and not interested.	
Say students' names.	☐ Already nailing it! ☐ Following it some but should do more. ☐ Not following it at all but should try. ☐ Not following it at all and not interested.	
Wave your arms.	☐ Already nailing it! ☐ Following it some but should do more. ☐ Not following it at all but should try. ☐ Not following it at all and not interested.	

Figure 3.1: Reflection chart for chapter 3.

continued ▶

Tips In This Chapter	To What Degree Are You Already Following the Tip?	Your Plans for Implementing the Tip
Increase your enthusiasm by 20 percent.	☐ Already nailing it! ☐ Following it some but should do more. ☐ Not following it at all but should try. ☐ Not following it at all and not interested.	
Make videos interactive.	☐ Already nailing it! ☐ Following it some but should do more. ☐ Not following it at all but should try. ☐ Not following it at all and not interested.	
Use cards and hand signals.	☐ Already nailing it! ☐ Following it some but should do more. ☐ Not following it at all but should try. ☐ Not following it at all and not interested.	
Mix it up.	☐ Already nailing it! ☐ Following it some but should do more. ☐ Not following it at all but should try. ☐ Not following it at all and not interested.	
Keep 'em moving.	☐ Already nailing it! ☐ Following it some but should do more. ☐ Not following it at all but should try. ☐ Not following it at all and not interested.	

Make phone calls home.	☐ Already nailing it! ☐ Following it some but should do more. ☐ Not following it at all but should try. ☐ Not following it at all and not interested.	

*Visit **go.SolutionTree.com/technology** for a free reproducible version of this figure.*

If you want to go beyond the tips in this chapter and dig deeper into engaging students in an online classroom, there are books written during the COVID-19 pandemic to help both novice and experienced online teachers. Two examples to consider are as follows.

1. Check out *Connecting With Students Online* by Jennifer Serravallo (2020). Jennifer
   Serravallo is a prolific author of books about teaching reading and writing. She wrote this book during the COVID-19 pandemic shutdown and donates a portion of the proceeds to organizations serving children directly impacted by COVID-19. The book is particularly directed toward new teachers and teachers new to technology.

2. At the opposite end of the spectrum, if you are an experienced online teacher looking to use every bell and whistle in Zoom to engage your students, take a look at *Teaching Effectively With Zoom: A Practical Guide to Engage Your Students and Help Them Learn* by Dan Levy (2020), a senior lecturer in public policy at Harvard University.

CHAPTER 4

Managing Your Classroom

Any teacher who has stood in front of thirty students knows that effective classroom management is the make-it-or-break-it skill that determines whether you're going to have a long year—or a verrrrrrrry long year.

Harry and Rosemary Wong (2018) define classroom management as, "The practices and procedures that a teacher uses to maintain an environment in which instruction and learning can occur" (p. 8), and this applies to the online environment as well. While teaching online might give you the ability to press mute a few times, without solid classroom management skills in place, you could find yourself *wishing* your screen would freeze, just so you can slow things down!

The tips in this chapter will help you run your online classroom efficiently and effectively, so you can stress less and teach more. (See page 62 for additional research supporting the following tips and to go deeper in your implementation of managing your online classroom.)

TIP 29
Set Your Expectations High

In any class, at any level, regardless of the topic or age of students, it is critical that teachers set their expectations high. As Harry and Rosemary Wong (2018) state in *The First Days of School*:

> The expectations you have of your students significantly influence what they are capable of achieving in class and in life. (p. 48)

When creating and communicating your expectations for students in your online classroom, remember that your expectations for students are not just what you want them doing and saying in class, but also characteristics of the kind of people you want them to be. Expectations go far beyond the technology you'll be using and the content the students will be learning. They help students to live in a world where they are safe, confident, and loved.

Only you can determine the expectations that you have for your students, but here are three tips to incorporate them into your practice.

1. Write them in a positive way, letting students know what they should be doing (as opposed to what they should *not* be doing).

    For example, expecting that your students will "Always arrive prepared" communicates a positive expectation, as opposed to communicating that you are expecting forgetfulness when you tell students, "Don't forget to bring everything."

2. In an in-person classroom, many teachers choose to post their expectations in large letters on the wall as a constant, visible reminder for all to see. While this might not work in an online class, here are a few creative ways to make sure your expectations are visible and communicated.

    a. Begin class by reviewing the expectations with your students (how often you review them depends on how often it's needed). Coming up with a brief, call-and-response way to review them can be helpful.

    b. If you have a class website, make sure the expectations are clearly visible on the home page.

    c. Create virtual backgrounds that the students can use, each displaying one of the expectations.

3. Make expectations work both ways. As teachers, we often communicate what we expect of our students. But what can our students expect of us? It may be the same as what you expect of your students, but taking that extra step to let students know that helps to establish a culture of mutual respect and accountability.

TIP 30
Establish Class Procedures

Ever been somewhere and had to wait behind someone who clearly didn't know the procedures? (I travel a lot, and my heart goes out to those people as I walk through the airport TSA checks.) Taking the time to teach, rehearse, and reinforce the following five critical procedures, along with a few questions all students should know how to answer, will make sure that your online class runs smoothly, from sign-on to sign-off.

1. How the class begins.

    a. What materials will I need before I sign in?

    b. What should I do as soon as I enter my online classroom?

2. How to answer a question.

    a. What do I do if the teacher calls on me to answer a question? (Unmute myself and answer aloud? Type my response in the chat box?)

    b. What can I say if I don't know the answer?

3. How to ask for help.

    a. What do I do if I need help or am confused? (Raise my hand on video or push the "hand raised" emoji? Type something into the chat—directly to the teacher or to everyone?)

4. How to work with classmates.

    a. When the teacher puts us into breakout rooms, how should we communicate with each other?

    b. What should I do if I end up in a breakout room by myself?

5. How the class ends.

    a. What will I be expected to do at the end of class?

    b. What should I do after I sign off and class is over?

TIP 31
Establish Routines

What's the difference between a procedure and a routine?

A *procedure* is something that you teach students how to do, such as line up outside your classroom door (during in-person teaching) or type an appropriate response in the chat area (during online teaching), when prompted. A *routine* is when students complete the procedure with regularity (while meeting your high expectations!). For example, knowing how to brush your teeth correctly is a procedure. Brushing your teeth every night before you go to bed is a routine. Routines rock (especially when given a cool name).

Have some fun with your classroom routines by giving them a cool name. For example, a simple procedure I teach my students is how to have their finger hover above the "unmute" button, so that when I call on them to answer a question, they can immediately unmute themselves and begin answering (and avoid the awkward "I think you're still muted, we can't hear you" delays).

As I teach this procedure, I tell students that it's called the *fast fingers* routine, so any time they hear me say, "Fast fingers," they automatically know what to do.

TIP 32
Monitor the Chat

Ever pass a secret note under your table to a friend in class or whisper something to a classmate when the teacher isn't looking? While this might not happen in an online class, the chat area is where all the action is. Just as the teacher in an in-person classroom might move to intercept that note or deter students from whispering, it's important to monitor the chat area as best you can.

From the first moments of meeting a new class, it's critical to proactively take the time to clearly communicate with your students what you intend the chat area to be for. What topics will you allow in the chat? And when are students allowed to use the chat? If students know exactly what you consider appropriate and inappropriate use of the chat room, you will reduce how much you need to monitor.

Figure 4.1 contains a few examples of what is (and isn't!) an appropriate use of the chat feature.

Appropriate Use of the Chat Feature	Inappropriate Use of the Chat Feature
When the teacher asks a specific question and directs students to answer in the chat	Chat messages that are not related to the topic we are discussing at the time
When the student has a question	When a student tells the teacher something about another student that the rest of the class should not see
When students have an encouraging response to something one of their classmates said	When a student says anything that is disrespectful toward another member of the class

Figure 4.1: Examples of appropriate and inappropriate chat.

Most online programs allow the teacher to keep a record of chat communication, which helps to hold students (and teachers!) accountable. With the chat transcript available, it's a lot harder to argue that "I never said that!" Let students know this. Some programs also allow teachers to determine who can chat with whom, publicly or privately, and when, so you can set this up in a way that best allows you to keep control of the chatting.

Taking the time to shape the culture and expectations of your class's chat area helps immensely to ensure respectful, positive interactions while you're teaching online.

TIP 33
Make Sure Your Settings Are Safe

I admit it: I was the first person I knew to ever get Zoom-bombed. I had never even heard of the term, and suddenly, my lesson on adding fractions turned into—well, I'm too horrified to give you any more details. I was so embarrassed for myself and my students, and let's just say parents had some choice words for me about my classroom management.

Zoom-bombing refers to when an uninvited guest gate-crashes your video meeting and shares their screen to bombard attendees with disturbing or distracting content. By now, we've probably all heard stories like mine, and much worse, about this disrupting practice.

Fortunately, all it takes is a few clicks in your settings to require passwords, manage screen sharing, utilize a waiting room, and prevent this from happening again. Check with whatever online platform you use for details on how to do it. And, of course, *never* share the link to your class meetings publicly.

If something like this does happen, immediately remove the intruder from your class or end the class immediately, and let parents (and your administrator) know what happened. It's better that they hear it directly from you, so that you can apologize, clearly communicate what happened, and move forward stronger (Occidental College, n.d.).

Hopefully, it's something you'll be able to laugh about (or write about in a book like this!) later down the road.

TIP 34
Use Multiple Monitors

Most of us begin teaching online with just one device that enables us to see our students, share our screen, and run our class. However, as we spend more time teaching online, we begin to see the limitations, like being unable to see all our students at once or having to fiddle with our PowerPoint presentation while trying to monitor the chat box.

Just as we build out our classroom libraries or boxes of manipulatives over the years, teaching online requires us to evolve the equipment we use so we can manage and run our class in a way that is effective and engaging.

Sharon Sanchez, a teacher in Honolulu, Hawaii, uses the setup in figure 4.2 for her virtual classroom (S. Sanchez, personal communication, April 19, 2020). On the far-right monitor, Sharon logs into class as if she's a student, so that she's able to see exactly what the students see at all times. This gives her a good overall view of the classroom.

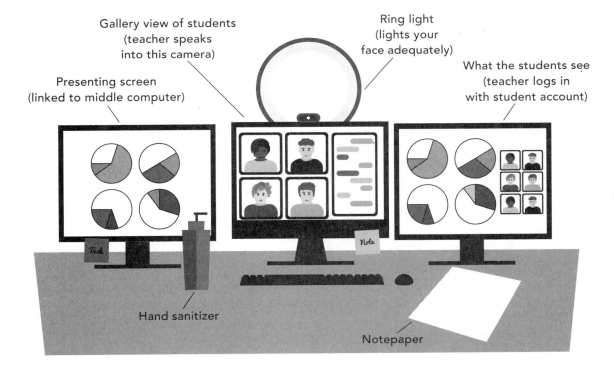

Figure 4.2: Sharon Sanchez's virtual classroom.

The middle device, her laptop, is a grid view of all her students. Like being able to look into the faces of all her students at once in the in-person classroom, she's able to look into all of her students' faces and gauge the overall "temperature" of her classroom. She also speaks directly into this device. (See chapter 1, "Looking Good on Camera," on page 5 for more on that.)

The monitor on the left is her presenting screen, from which she shows her presentations, videos, or other tools. This also enables her to tweak or change something without having to display it for the students (this monitor is hooked up to the laptop, or main device, that she presents from).

Behind the middle device, Sharon uses a ring light, which puts additional light on her face. (See tip 3, page 7, for more lighting details.) Also on her desk, she has hand sanitizer (a must for every teacher!), and some paper that she can use to make notes. When we increase our capacity to see and interact with our students online, we greatly increase our ability to keep them engaged and learning—and using multiple monitors gives it that super cool "command center" feel!

TIP 35
Be Consistent

While there are many factors that help ensure the success of your online classroom, consistency is at the top of the list!

In a world filled with constant distractions and struggles, we can help set up our students for success by structuring our classes in ways that are consistent and predictable. This leads to students feeling safe and confident.

Consistency is especially critical for our students who come from poverty or a chaotic home life. According to John F. Eller and Tom Hierck's (2022) book *Trauma-Sensitive Leadership*, the more unpredictable a student's home life is, the more they come to rely on the predictability and consistency that school offers.

For an online class, this means teachers doing the best they can to be consistent each day and week in the following areas.

- When class is held
- When new content and assignments are posted
- When assignments are due
- When students can pop in for online office hours

Of course, consistency goes beyond just how we structure our classes. It also means consistently treating our students with fairness and respect (and, at times, managing their behavior), and showing them that as teachers, we are dependable, reliable, and consistent human beings who are here to support them as a member of our online community. (More on this is in chapter 6, "Creating a Community," page 77.)

TIP 36
Turn Classroom Jobs Into Online Roles

All effective managers—from corporate leaders to sports team managers to parents running the day-to-day affairs of their families—are successful because they know that the key to management is empowering others to take on duties, responsibilities, and positions of leadership. This is especially crucial when we teach students and gives students an increased stake in the success of our online classrooms.

While students' roles might differ slightly between an in-person classroom and an online classroom, the following are four roles that your students can take on to help ensure that things run smoothly (L. Amici, personal communication, May 3, 2020).

1. **Greeter:** Before students are signing in, have a student (or more than one) sign in early and begin greeting students as they enter the online classroom. Remember that greeting and acknowledging people is an important life skill, so don't just limit this role to your most outgoing students. Greeting others online can be a safe way to do it for students who might feel intimidated in an in-person setting. Also, consider having them stay until the very end of class, bidding other students farewell.

2. **Chat monitor:** One of the best ways to make sure that the class chat area is used effectively is to give the students ownership of it. Just as it's important that they keep a physical classroom clean and clear of clutter, empowering students to make sure the chat room stays clear of inappropriate chatter will help everyone stay on task and engaged, and create a classroom culture of respect. (See tip 32, page 52, for more on monitoring the chat area.)

3. **Time monitor:** As teachers, we all know how easy it is to lose track of time—especially when taking into consideration technical issues like screens freezing up due to poor internet connections, or a student (or teacher!) who talks a bit too much on a topic. Having a student who can help monitor the time and keep the class on track can help keep the class flowing smoothly and efficiently.

4. **Announcement reader:** Remember, as the teacher, you don't have to do everything by yourself. Having a student read the announcements

at the beginning of each week or class is a great way to help students see each other "in action" in a fun way. Or, if you know what the announcements are going to be in advance of the class, consider having the students make fun videos of themselves reading the announcements and send it to you in advance. When class begins, all you need to do is roll the tape, and you could even send it out to the parents to keep them informed of what's happening. (Chapter 5, "Pulling in Parents and Guardians," on page 63 has many more ideas on connecting with families.)

TIP 37
Prerecord a Welcome Message

Online or in-person, effective teaching begins well before students enter the classroom. The most effective teachers find ways to connect with students *before* they greet them in the first class.

One way to do this as an online teacher: before the first day of school or class, create a *welcome video* where you introduce yourself, your class, what students can expect, and your expectations for them. That way, they log in already familiar with you and the culture you're creating.

Another benefit to creating this video is that you can show it to new students who transfer in midyear, saving you from having to take the time to go over all your guidelines and expectations with these new students. You can also have students watch it as they return from a break, or whenever you might need to remind or reinforce how things work in your classroom.

For maximum impact, consider creating a video specific to each situation, such as "Welcome Back From Winter Break" or "Three Things to Know Before Spring Break Ends." Get creative, have fun, and keep in mind—you only need to make the video once, and then you have it on hand to show as many times as you need!

Advice From Students

Learn how Zoom (or whatever program you're using) works, and how to control the settings. If you don't, some kids might start taking over your screen or spamming the chat. I like it when the teacher has control of the class!

—Kalla, Sixth Grade (personal communication, January 30, 2021)

Where to Go From Here

Just like in an in-person class, the effort you put into setting expectations, establishing procedures and routines, and following the other tips in this chapter will help your online classroom run smoothly and prevent problems rather than just react to them. As the old bromide says, an ounce of prevention is worth a pound of cure!

Reflect on the tips in this chapter. To what degree do you currently achieve the goal in each tip? Are there some tips you are interested in using in your classes? How would you implement them? Figure 4.3 has space for notes on your reflections.

Tips in This Chapter	To What Degree Are You Already Following the Tip?	Your Plans for Implementing the Tip
Set your expectations high.	☐ Already nailing it! ☐ Following it some but should do more. ☐ Not following it at all but should try. ☐ Not following it at all and not interested.	
Establish class procedures.	☐ Already nailing it! ☐ Following it some but should do more. ☐ Not following it at all but should try. ☐ Not following it at all and not interested.	
Establish routines.	☐ Already nailing it! ☐ Following it some but should do more. ☐ Not following it at all but should try. ☐ Not following it at all and not interested.	

Monitor the chat.	☐ Already nailing it! ☐ Following it some but should do more. ☐ Not following it at all but should try. ☐ Not following it at all and not interested.	
Make sure your settings are safe.	☐ Already nailing it! ☐ Following it some but should do more. ☐ Not following it at all but should try. ☐ Not following it at all and not interested.	
Use multiple monitors.	☐ Already nailing it! ☐ Following it some but should do more. ☐ Not following it at all but should try. ☐ Not following it at all and not interested.	
Be consistent.	☐ Already nailing it! ☐ Following it some but should do more. ☐ Not following it at all but should try. ☐ Not following it at all and not interested.	
Turn classroom jobs into online roles.	☐ Already nailing it! ☐ Following it some but should do more. ☐ Not following it at all but should try. ☐ Not following it at all and not interested.	

Figure 4.3: Reflection chart for chapter 4.

continued ▶

Tips in This Chapter	To What Degree Are You Already Following the Tip?	Your Plans for Implementing the Tip
Prerecord a welcome message.	☐ Already nailing it! ☐ Following it some but should do more. ☐ Not following it at all but should try. ☐ Not following it at all and not interested.	

Visit **go.SolutionTree.com/technology** *for a free reproducible version of this figure.*

If you want to go beyond the tips in this chapter and dig deeper into classroom management, there are many books on classroom management in the physical world that have ideas that can be applied in online teaching. The following are two to consider.

1. Start with a classic. *The First Days of School: How to Be an Effective Teacher* (Wong & Wong, 2018) is a preeminent book on classroom management and shares tips to help teachers of any level create a safe learning environment and become a more effective teacher.

2. Dale Ripley's (2022) *The Tactical Teacher: Proven Strategies to Positively Influence Student Learning and Classroom Behavior* provides research-based strategies for classroom management, including addressing disruptions and motivating students.

Pulling in Parents and Guardians

Most of the time, our students' parents and guardians* want to help. They want to be involved in their kids' learning. But oftentimes, they just don't know how. Perhaps they're very busy, or they're intimidated from their own experiences in school. However, we can empower parents and guardians to help support their children in lots of different ways, at the level they're comfortable with (Kaufman, n.d.).

When teaching online, making the shift from seeing parents and guardians as just parents and guardians to instead seeing them as our teaching partners can have a dramatic impact on student achievement (Waterford.org, 2018). (See page 76 for additional research supporting the following tips.)

---

*Note: I use the term *parents and guardians* throughout this book, and I encourage teachers to use it instead of just *parents* to be inclusive of the many students whose families don't have two parents but rather a single parent, grandparents, foster parents, older siblings, other relatives, or nonrelatives.

TIP 38
Give Parents and Guardians Questions They Can Ask

Here's a conversation that takes place almost daily:

> *Parent or Guardian: How was class today?*
> *Child: Good.*
> *Parent or Guardian: What did you do in class?*
> *Child: Not much.*

Instead of another conversation like this, consider proactively giving parents and guardians three specific questions they can ask their kids to help direct them toward a deeper conversation.

You can send these questions out daily, weekly, or whatever works best for you (and your time!). Of course, the key is to give parents and guardians questions they can ask without needing to have been in the actual class.

Figure 5.1 is an example of an email that you could send out, after reading *Wonder* by R. J. Palacio.

To: Seventh-Grade Parents and Guardians
Subject: Three Questions to Ask Your Child
Hi Parents and Guardians,
We had a great class discussion today, discussing the book *Wonder* by R. J. Palacio. The book is about a student with severe facial deformities who attends a new school.
Here are three questions you can ask your child to help continue their discussion.

1. Do you know any kids your age who look significantly different than the other kids?
2. Have you ever been in a new situation, where you had trouble making friends?
3. Can you tell me about a character in the book who you identify the most with?

Thanks again for all your support, and please let me know if you have any questions!

Figure 5.1: Sample email to parents and guardians.

Notice that in the three questions in figure 5.1, the parents and guardians do not need to have read the book to ask the questions or engage in a thoughtful discussion with their child. And you've made it very easy for them to do, by giving them the exact questions to ask.

TIP 39
Invite Them to . . .

Just as there are students who engage deeply in the content you're teaching, there are parents or guardians who might want to as well. At the same time, parents and guardians don't want to be "assigned" work.

Using the words "I'd like to invite you to . . ." is a welcoming, nonthreatening way to provide parents and guardians with an opportunity to engage with and support their children. Just make sure there aren't any penalties for parents and guardians who aren't able to accept your invitation.

The following are just a few things you can invite parents and guardians to do.

- Watch the video that the students watched
- Read the article, book, or passage that students discussed in class
- Help support another student
- Be a guest speaker (See tip 48, page 79, for details.)
- Try their skills at the online game you're having students play
- Visit the website students are using as a resource

TIP 40
Teach Parents and Guardians
Some Simple Teaching Strategies

While being a parent or guardian doesn't require a teaching credential, I sometimes watch parents and guardians interact with their kids and wish it did!

As mentioned earlier, making the shift from seeing parents and guardians as parents and guardians to seeing them as our teaching partners can have a dramatic impact on student achievement. Throughout the school year, teaching parents and guardians just a few high-leverage, easy-to-implement teaching strategies can help their student tremendously and help them feel more confident as parents, guardians, and teachers.

The following are two strategies that go a long way.

1. **Think time:** I often observe parents and guardians asking their child a question, and when the child doesn't immediately answer, the adult quickly answers for the student. They don't want to wait out the awkward silence that results while the child is thinking, or they think their child isn't quick enough.

   Take a moment to explain the importance of think time to parents and guardians and teach them to silently count to ten before they speak again. It can even be a relief for the adults to know it's OK (and preferred) to relax and give kids time to consider the question, formulate an answer, and then express that answer—and that it's perfectly normal for kids (and adults!) to take a moment to formulate a thoughtful response to a question (McCarthy, 2018).

2. **I do, we do, you do:** Whether it's a household chore, a mathematical procedure, or showing off those dance moves from high school, the *I do, we do, you do* strategy is a great way for parents and guardians to help show their child how do to something (Waddell, 2018).

   Figure 5.2 provides two examples of what this strategy might look like in action: the first example, showing a child how to tie their shoelaces, and the second, providing simple reading instruction.

	Example 1: Tying Shoelaces	Example 2: Simple Reading Instruction
I Do	The adult sits next to the child, with their feet next to each other. The adult ties and unties their own shoelaces over and over again, explaining how they're doing it, perhaps even breaking it up into smaller steps. The child is simply watching, with no pressure to start doing it themselves.	The adult sits next to the child, with the book on the table between them. The adult reads a sentence (or more than one sentence, depending on the child's reading ability). The adult reads the sentence aloud, then pauses.
We Do	The child then starts trying it with their own shoes, but with the adult helping. The adult and child both have their hands on the laces, practicing over and over again, until the child starts showing that they can do it on their own.	The adult invites the child to read the sentences aloud with them (at the same time), and the adult adjusts their reading speed to keep pace with the child.
You Do	The adult starts to separate from the child, encouraging the child to do it on their own. The child might need a reminder or help on occasion, but for the most part, they can complete the task on their own.	The adult then invites the child to read the sentences aloud on their own, and then silently until the child feels confident.

Figure 5.2: I do, we do, you do strategy examples.

Remember, if you make your own videos explaining the preceding strategies, you can send them out whenever you need, or post them on your class website so parents and guardians always have access to them. If you don't make your own videos, a quick internet search will help you easily find some that work.

TIP 41
Check In on Them

In a traditional, in-person school, students usually attend classes in a location that is not where they live (such as a physical classroom). However, when students attend class online, they are often joining the class from their own home . . . or from a yacht in the South Pacific. (OK, I'm kidding about the yacht, but how nice would that be?)

Even when this might be exactly what the parents and guardians desire for their kids' education, learning from one's home can also be very challenging. The adults are often trying to balance these classes with their priorities at home and in life, with many of them busily working at home while their children attend online classes.

It can be really tough.

Taking a moment to check in and see how your students' parents and guardians are doing with online learning can go a long way toward building powerful relationships with students and their families. Sending out a simple call, text, or online survey is all you need to do. Even if they don't answer, they'll know that you are taking the time to reach out and will appreciate it.

Now the only question that remains is, *Who is checking in on you?* (See chapter 11, "Taking Care of Yourself," on page 147 for some suggestions.)

TIP 42
Create Ways for Parents and Guardians to Help

I've seen it through the years, and I'll say it again: most parents and guardians want to help. Often, they just don't know how.

It's important to be sensitive to not place unnecessary pressure on the adults who truly do not have the time or ability to help their child. But giving them small, easy-to-complete tasks not only can lighten your own workload, but also can promote an online classroom culture where parents are involved and students are connected.

The following are just a few ways parents and guardians can help in your online classroom.

- If students are completing an activity that requires them to fill in answers (but not a test), email the parents and guardians the answers in advance, so they can go over them with their children when they finish. Not only is it one less thing you'll need to spend time on during your class, it gives the adults an opportunity to see exactly what is being covered in class.

- Ten minutes before students sign in for your online class, have parents and guardians sit with their children while they complete the anticipatory set. While teaching online, the time that you spend live with your students is a limited resource, so being intentional about when students do and don't need to be in front of you is critical. (See tip 59, page 95, for more on that.)

- Have parents and guardians make sure their child shows up. It might sound obvious, but getting every student to show up, on time, to your online class can be quite a challenge. Just like we get a reminder call and text the day before our dentist appointment, consider using a simple messaging service (like www.remind.com) to remind parents and guardians that "History class starts in thirty minutes."

TIP 43
Include Parents and Guardians in Family Projects

While it may not seem like it at first, teaching online is a fantastic opportunity to include parents, guardians, grandparents, and other family members directly with the curriculum.

Online learning allows for great family-centered video or audio projects. From interviewing a family member about their experiences during a period in history to sharing how they use (insert subject you're teaching) in their everyday lives, you can pull those involved adults in while providing a culturally relevant curriculum. (See tip 80, page 126, for more on that.)

But don't stop there with the family interviews! Students can connect further by sharing their interviews (or a shorter video with highlights from them) on the class website or on a program such as Flipgrid (https://info.flipgrid.com) and commenting on each other's videos. You could also consider starting a class podcast, with a new episode released each week.

You can also share the interviews with the person who was interviewed, further strengthening the relationship between them and the teachers, students, and even the other parents and guardians.

Teacher Feature

Leah Juelke, a high school teacher in North Dakota, has her students—who are mainly immigrants and refugees who have recently arrived in the United States—team up with their parents or other family members to produce an online cooking show. The students and their families record themselves cooking some of their favorite foods from their own cultures, in their own kitchens. Students are able to practice writing scripts while strengthening their speaking skills as well as gain valuable video production and technology skills. (L. Juelke, personal communication, June 1, 2020)

TIP 44
Promote Curiosity

Not every aspect of online teaching happens online, nor does every aspect of learning happen in perfect class-period time chunks. Teaching parents and guardians to be curious about their kids can accelerate and deepen learning . . . and inspire more.

If the adults don't feel that they're naturally curious (or their natural curiosity has been stifled by grown-up life!), we can give them some specific examples to help them get started, such as the following.

- When you're at the store, have everyone in the family guess what they think the total price of all the items will be. Or, if paying with cash, have kids estimate how much change you'll get back. (This promotes numbers sense.)

- While at home watching a movie together, take an intermission and be curious about what the child thinks is going to happen in the next part of the movie and why. (This promotes perspective, foreshadowing, and literacy.)

- Ask questions. Whenever you go somewhere or do something with your child, ask open-ended questions (like "Why do you think that . . .?" and "How do you think that . . .?"). (This promotes higher-level critical thinking and lifelong learning.)

TIP 45
Find Out Their Preferred Method of Contact

Like students, some parents and guardians are hard to reach. They never seem to pick up their phone, or our emails go unanswered. Finding out in advance their preferred method of contact can help you reduce the number of (often frustrating) outreach efforts that you make. Of course, it's always smart to have more than one method.

Simply asking parents and guardians through a quick online survey at the beginning of the year (or whenever) to rank their top two methods of being contacted can create buy-in from the adults—and as a result, some account-ability—while at the same time giving them choice. Figure 5.3 contains an example of such a survey.

What is your preferred method of being contacted (write a 1 in the box of your top preference and a 2 in the box of your second preference)?

(Important note: Only provide contact methods that you are willing to do!)

☐ Text me. (Please provide cell phone number.) _____

☐ Call me. (Please provide the best number to reach you.) _____

☐ Email me. (Please provide email address.) _____

☐ Mail me a letter. (Please provide mailing address.)

_____
_____
_____

☐ Use social media. (Please provide preferred platform and username.)

_____   _____

Figure 5.3: Sample contact preferences email.

*Visit **go.SolutionTree.com/technology** for a free reproducible version of this figure.*

Consider keeping a simple spreadsheet handy with your students' parents and guardians' contact information and their preferred method of contact. While it might seem that setting this up takes some extra work, you'll save a lot of time and frustration on the back end, when you're able to contact them on the first (or second) try!

TIP 46
Use a Translator

The language barrier that often exists between teachers and non-English-speaking parents and guardians can often create challenges for communication with those adults. Having a live translator available who can be included on a call or video meeting is very helpful, but not always something that's available.

While it might not be perfect, using an online translation program will help you get your point across, and shows the parents and guardians how hard you're trying to communicate with them. The following programs are very helpful.

- **Google Translate** (https://translate.google.com) allows you to instantly translate words, phrases, or webpages between English and over one hundred other languages.

- **TalkingPoints** (https://talkingpts.org) is an app that allows teachers to communicate with families in their home languages to build strong partnerships.

- **iTranslate** (https://itranslate.com) is another app that helps teachers communicate in over one hundred languages.

Advice From Parents

I like going into the week knowing what my child will be doing. Sending weekly updates about what students will be doing in the week ahead, along with links to videos the students will be watching, is very helpful.

—Evelyn, Parent of Third Grader (personal communication, March 6, 2021)

Where to Go From Here

Parents and guardians are their children's first teachers. Working collaboratively to involve them in your teaching can be a win-win-win for your students, their parents or guardians, and you. Pulling in parents or guardians effectively extends your classroom community into the students' larger community and helps ensure that we all learn together!

Reflect on the tips in this chapter. To what degree do you currently achieve the goal in each tip? Are there some tips you are interested in using in your classes? How would you implement them? Figure 5.4 has space for notes on your reflections.

Tips in This Chapter	To What Degree Are You Already Following the Tip?	Your Plans for Implementing the Tip
Give parents and guardians questions they can ask.	☐ Already nailing it! ☐ Following it some but should do more. ☐ Not following it at all but should try. ☐ Not following it at all and not interested.	
Invite them to	☐ Already nailing it! ☐ Following it some but should do more. ☐ Not following it at all but should try. ☐ Not following it at all and not interested.	
Teach parents and guardians some simple teaching strategies.	☐ Already nailing it! ☐ Following it some but should do more. ☐ Not following it at all but should try. ☐ Not following it at all and not interested.	

Check in on them.	☐ Already nailing it! ☐ Following it some but should do more. ☐ Not following it at all but should try. ☐ Not following it at all and not interested.	
Create ways for parents and guardians to help.	☐ Already nailing it! ☐ Following it some but should do more. ☐ Not following it at all but should try. ☐ Not following it at all and not interested.	
Include parents and guardians in family projects.	☐ Already nailing it! ☐ Following it some but should do more. ☐ Not following it at all but should try. ☐ Not following it at all and not interested.	
Promote curiosity.	☐ Already nailing it! ☐ Following it some but should do more. ☐ Not following it at all but should try. ☐ Not following it at all and not interested.	
Find out their preferred method of contact.	☐ Already nailing it! ☐ Following it some but should do more. ☐ Not following it at all but should try. ☐ Not following it at all and not interested.	

Figure 5.4: Reflection chart for chapter 5.

continued ▶

Tips in This Chapter	To What Degree Are You Already Following the Tip?	Your Plans for Implementing the Tip
Use a translator.	☐ Already nailing it! ☐ Following it some but should do more. ☐ Not following it at all but should try. ☐ Not following it at all and not interested.	

Visit **go.SolutionTree.com/technology** *for a free reproducible version of this figure.*

If you want to go beyond the tips in this chapter and dig deeper into pulling in parents and guardians, the following are a few resources to consider.

1. *Empowering Family-Teacher Partnerships: Building Connections Within Diverse Communities* by Mick Coleman (2013) is a textbook for elementary school teacher training courses, but many of the suggestions can be applied at higher levels as well. Thomas M. "Mick" Coleman is a retired professor from the University of Georgia who has published journal articles, books, and training manuals about family-teacher partnership.

2. *The Distance Learning Playbook for Parents: How to Support Your Child's Academic, Social, and Emotional Development in Any Setting* by Rosalind Wiseman, Douglas Fisher, Nancy Frey, and John Hattie (2020) is for parents of K–12 students and is an interesting way to think about collaboration from the parents' or guardians' perspectives.

CHAPTER 6

Creating a Community

There's a big difference between attending a class and being part of a community.

When you attend class, you show up, complete the work required, and usually receive some sort of evaluation (like a grade) for that work. Then you move on to the next class.

However, when you're part of a community, there is a feeling of fellowship with and accountability to others. There's a desire to be recognized by others and be around them, and a knowledge that you're part of something bigger than yourself. It feels like "we're all in this together" (Clouse, 2021).

The tips in this chapter will help you create and build an online community where your students thrive. (See page 90 for additional research supporting the following tips and to go deeper in your implementation of creating a community.)

TIP 47
Use the Word *Community*

One of the best ways to create a community is to start by calling it exactly that: a community. This is especially important when teaching online, as there isn't the shared sense of physical space or geographical similarity that occurs during an in-person class.

Figure 6.1 is a simple chart to help get you started.

Instead of Saying . . .	Consider Saying . . .
"Welcome to class!"	"Welcome to our community!"
"Class starts at 9:30 a.m. sharp."	"Our class community gathers at exactly 9:30 a.m."
"Who wants to share their answer with the class?"	"Which community member would like to share their answer?"
"Go ahead and discuss your thoughts with the person next to you."	"Go ahead and discuss your thoughts with your neighbor" (when we use the word "neighbor," community is implied).
"Thanks for coming to class today!"	"Thank you so much for being a part of this community!"

Figure 6.1: Sample phrases to build community.

TIP 48
Invite Special Guests

One of the best ways to create an online community is to help students personally connect with people, places, and ideas that are outside of your classroom bubble but related to what brings you all together. Fortunately, you don't have to look far.

Teaching online is the perfect opportunity to invite in special guest speakers to join your class and talk about the work they do. It's much easier in an online setting, as the speakers don't have to find their way to your school or check in at the front office (just make sure to check with your school's policies to make sure it's OK).

You don't need to bring in famous people, or anyone doing something considered extraordinary. Some of the best guests are from the local community and reflect your students' ethnicities interests, and experiences. It's also helpful to tell students in advance who will be speaking to them and on what topic. Then they can research the person or topic in advance and have some questions ready to go (all while they gain valuable skills about doing research on the internet!). When you book that special guest, be sure to prepare them in advance with details such as how long they'll be speaking for, what questions they can anticipate from the students (based on the questions the students prepare in advance), and anything you're currently covering in class that would be a powerful connection with what the guest is talking about.

TIP 49
Get Students (and Yourself) Out Into the Community

As mentioned previously, teaching online doesn't mean that everything in class has to happen online. You don't always have to be using the latest app or the new website you just discovered.

Getting students up and away from their screens and then coming back to share their experiences is a powerful way to build community. It can be as simple as mailing students a box of colored pencils or crayons to use for an art project. (Maybe even include the mini version of yourself that they can decorate, cut out, and share, and even take with them to snap a photo with "you" in various places.)

You might even consider having students participate in a *screen-free afternoon*, where they (perhaps along with a family member) agree to turn their screens off, and then share what they did during the next class. If an entire afternoon without screens sounds a bit daunting, try starting with a simple screen-free hour. Alternatively, teachers could challenge students to do a particular screen-free learning activity with (or without) their parents or family members, such as having everyone turn off their phones and go for a walk (as part of a physical education class), play a board game (Scrabble to help with spelling!), or cook some food together (fractions, anyone?). Sometimes, stepping away from online learning is exactly what students need to stay motivated to learn online!

Teacher Feature

Lyn Porter is a physical education teacher in the small town of Williston, Vermont. When her school closed its doors and moved to online teaching due to the COVID-19 pandemic, she wanted to make sure her students continued to get outside and move their bodies.

She collected and painted four hundred rocks bright red and placed them all around town. Any time a student found a rock, they contacted her and let her know where they found the rock. Of course, parents, grandparents, and community members all got invested in finding the rocks!

According to Lyn:

I gathered and painted about four hundred rocks that have been hidden around our community, in hopes that the families will go out for a bike ride, or a hike, or a walk; find these rocks; and then post a picture of where they found them. The rocks also have positive messages written on them, like "Tomorrow will be a better day," or something silly like a drawing of a T-shirt on a clothes hanger that says, "You wanna hang out?" It's something that makes the kids and their families smile and [is] a positive experience for them as they're out engaging in the community.

—L. Porter (personal communication, March 18, 2020)

TIP 50
Acknowledge Which Communities We're Part Of

Your students are part of your class community. But what other communities are you and your students a part of? Being able to tie in the work that you and your students do together online with other communities helps build a sense of awareness and pride.

For example, your class is most likely a part of a larger school. Acknowledging and celebrating that there are other communities like yours that exist within the same school opens up opportunities to partner with another online class or share an experience together.

Bringing in a guest speaker? Consider inviting another class community to join you.

Heading out on a virtual trip? The opportunities to partner up with another class are endless. And it could even be another community from a different school, or even in a different city or country. Finding contacts from other schools is easy: putting out a request on social media will often result in someone from your network being able to connect you with someone they know who fits what you're looking for (just make sure to screen your new contact to make sure they're legit). In addition, contacting your local, state, or national Parent-Teacher Association (PTA) or other organizations will also result in the ability to connect with other interested teachers!

Speaking of different cities and countries, one of the most exciting things you can arrange for students is to use the power of online learning to interact with students from other cultures and ways of life, to connect students with the global community we are part of—with no airplanes required! iDialogue (https://idialogue.com) is an international distance learning website that offers a variety of authentic student-to-student learning opportunities (in English). Teachers can also sign up for collaboration from one classroom to another, where students engage in live video exchanges and lessons. The site platform matches grade levels, facilitates scheduling, and even helps navigate the time zone differences. They've also hosted virtual field trips to see giraffes in Kenya, meet NASA astronomers, and explore downtown Vienna (Cohn-Vargas, 2021)!

TIP 51
Break the Class Up Into Smaller Teams That Can Work Together

Even online (sometimes especially online), being in a class with thirty or more classmates can be quite intimidating for certain students. Breaking the class up into smaller teams can help.

Having students interact in breakout rooms (many online platforms such as Zoom have built-in features that support breakout rooms), support each other in various ways, or just hang out (outside of class time, of course!) can help reduce anxiety while building community.

Determine in advance what you want the students to gain from being in smaller teams, and group them accordingly. Once grouped, how else can they communicate? Group texts, shared Google Docs, or apps such as Slack are just a few ways that students can share ideas and build relationships in an online world.

Creating teams with the intention of *learning* to work together is much different than creating teams who *already know how* to work together. In other words, if you want students to learn about other students who are different than themselves—to learn how to resolve conflict and be compassionate human beings—then it's probably best to avoid grouping "friends" together.

At the same time, you don't want to throw a struggling English learner in without someone who can support them. Make sure to be intentional about putting the teams together—and try to avoid grouping students together who are already the best of friends.

TIP 52
Connect With the Quiet Ones

As teachers, we know there are plenty of students for whom the traditional, in-person classroom simply doesn't work well. For these students, classroom culture and the social structure within it create an atmosphere where they just sit quietly most of the day, unless specifically called on.

While the class culture and social structure within an online classroom might be different, there are still those students who will sit quietly throughout the entire class. It is important to note that a quiet student is not necessarily an unengaged student—just like a loud student is not necessarily completely engaged!

While teaching online, we get to redefine what *quiet* means and acknowledge that there are a multitude of ways that students can express themselves. There are some students who love to unmute themselves and speak aloud but are very quiet in the chat room, or vice versa. Some students don't want to speak in class but will type responses into the chat or class message board.

Creating opportunities throughout your class time to connect with the quiet ones and giving them an opportunity to connect with others is a critical component to building a community where everyone feels safe, seen, and important. Use the chat feature to send a private message to a student, letting them know that you're glad they're in class and that you're hoping they will answer one of the upcoming questions. Even just an occasional "Hey Jamillah—you good?" goes a long way with helping a quiet student know that someone is looking out for them. And if you have students who might be at a loss for words, invite them to choose an emoji or GIF that communicates how they're feeling about today, or today's lesson, and post it in the chat. 😎

TIP 53
Create Ways to See and Hear Each Other

Just as students want to know "who is this person?" about their teacher, they are also asking the same question about each other. In an online environment, they're often not getting to see each other on the playground, in the halls, at lunch, at rehearsal, or in after-school sports practice.

The following are three simple ways to ensure that students have an opportunity to get to see and hear each other, without taking up too much of your valuable class time.

1. Have students send you a photo of themselves engaged in their favorite activity. Periodically (for example, each class or each week) feature these photos, and give each student an opportunity to talk a bit about why they love that activity. Depending on the number of similarities among your students, you might even create clubs within your classroom—like the reading club, the skiing club, or the animal-lovers club.

2. Using a program like Flipgrid, have students post videos of themselves talking about topics they are interested in. Have each student post a video or written response to some of the others—just make sure each student gets several responses.

3. Create *lookout partners*. Sometimes, it's nice to know that someone is looking out for you, and that you're looking out for someone else. The job of the lookout partner is simple: when your partner signs into class, say hello to them. If they haven't signed in by the time class is about to begin, just let the teacher know. It's also a great way to build accountability and communication skills among students. If a student knows in advance that they're going to miss class, they can let their teacher as well as their lookout partner know. Sometimes, all it takes is knowing one person is looking out for you to help you truly feel like you're part of the community.

TIP 54
Have Students Check in on Students

It's just a reality: there are times when students don't show up for class. And, as the teacher, you're focused on starting and running class (along with everything else you do!), not tracking down a student who isn't showing up.

Even if you do try to reach out, it's possible that a student who isn't showing up for your class may not return your call promptly. This is where you can leverage and strengthen their peer relationships.

Building on the idea of creating lookout partners in tip 53 (page 85), try having another student (preferably one who knows the student in question outside of class) try to get in contact with the no-show student. Let the second student know that you noticed their friend's absence and could use their help in making sure their friend is OK and planning to return to class.

A simple "Hey, where were you today?" from a classmate can sometimes be more effective than the teacher trying to reach out to them. And it sends that student a clear message that they are missed (by their peers as well as their teacher) and wanted back in class.

TIP 55
Plan Virtual Gatherings

Members of a community share experiences beyond the regular day-to-day happenings of a class. So, if you're going to be successful in creating a feeling of community for your online classes, you need to help create and foster experiences beyond the virtual classroom.

Scheduling virtual field trips, movie nights, class parties, and celebrations can go a long way toward building community, especially for students who might not have a lot of interaction with others outside of class.

And here's something important to remember: you don't have to plan every event, nor do you need to be at every one!

Perhaps a student can help plan a celebration or party—just make it a class expectation that *everyone* is invited. Or when planning a movie night, invite the students to select the movie from a list and plan the watch time. (For example, plan for everyone to start the movie at 7:30 p.m. on Friday night, then meet online to chat afterward!)

Get creative, have some fun, and build a community that flourishes.

Advice From Students

When you begin the class, it's really helpful to have some time to talk and say hello. Sometimes I have things that I really want to tell everyone about, and there isn't enough time once class starts!

—Noelle, First Grade (personal communication, March 10, 2021)

Where to Go From Here

Way back in 1972, renowned psychologist Rollo May stated:

> Community can be defined simply as a group in which free conversation takes place. Community is where I can share my innermost thoughts, bring out the depths of my own feelings, and know they will be understood. (p. 247)

Today, building a sense of community online is a laudable, realistic, and essential goal for online teachers.

Reflect on the tips in this chapter. To what degree do you currently achieve the goal in each tip? Are there some tips you are interested in using in your classes? How would you implement them? Figure 6.2 has space for notes on your reflections.

Tips in This Chapter	To What Degree Are You Already Following the Tip?	Your Plans for Implementing the Tip
Use the word *community*.	☐ Already nailing it! ☐ Following it some but should do more. ☐ Not following it at all but should try. ☐ Not following it at all and not interested.	
Invite special guests.	☐ Already nailing it! ☐ Following it some but should do more. ☐ Not following it at all but should try. ☐ Not following it at all and not interested.	
Get students (and yourself) out into the community.	☐ Already nailing it! ☐ Following it some but should do more. ☐ Not following it at all but should try. ☐ Not following it at all and not interested.	

Acknowledge which communities we're part of.	☐ Already nailing it! ☐ Following it some but should do more. ☐ Not following it at all but should try. ☐ Not following it at all and not interested.	
Break the class up into smaller teams that can work together.	☐ Already nailing it! ☐ Following it some but should do more. ☐ Not following it at all but should try. ☐ Not following it at all and not interested.	
Connect with the quiet ones.	☐ Already nailing it! ☐ Following it some but should do more. ☐ Not following it at all but should try. ☐ Not following it at all and not interested.	
Create ways for students to see and hear each other.	☐ Already nailing it! ☐ Following it some but should do more. ☐ Not following it at all but should try. ☐ Not following it at all and not interested.	
Have students check in on students.	☐ Already nailing it! ☐ Following it some but should do more. ☐ Not following it at all but should try. ☐ Not following it at all and not interested.	

Figure 6.2: Reflection chart for chapter 6.

continued ▶

Tips in This Chapter	To What Degree Are You Already Following the Tip?	Your Plans for Implementing the Tip
Plan virtual gatherings.	☐ Already nailing it! ☐ Following it some but should do more. ☐ Not following it at all but should try. ☐ Not following it at all and not interested.	

*Visit **go.SolutionTree.com/technology** for a free reproducible version of this figure.*

If you want to go beyond the tips in this chapter and dig deeper into creating an online learning community, there's a classic book on the topic: *Building Online Learning Communities* by Rena M. Palloff and Keith Pratt (2007). Palloff and Pratt (1999) were among the earliest educators to write about online learning, and the first edition of this book was a groundbreaker. The second edition was expanded to incorporate the burgeoning research on online learning. Case studies, vignettes, and examples throughout the book illustrate how online teachers can create communities that connect and inspire.

Organizing Your Lessons

Teaching online is a dynamic, ever-changing experience that requires constantly incorporating new ideas and strategies. There's no one-size-fits-all template for how to organize an online lesson.

However, the tips in this chapter are essential ingredients. Each can help you develop the most organized, effective lessons you can for your online teaching situation. In other words, how you bake these ingredients is up to you! (See page 103 for additional research supporting the following tips.)

TIP 56
Boil It Down, But Don't Water It Down

As teachers, there are usually standards (namely, required content) that we need to teach. Covering all those standards can be quite a challenge, especially when teaching online.

The following are two ideas on figuring out what to cover, what not to cover, and how to distinguish between the two.

1. **Focus on essential standards:** Essential standards are standards that you can guarantee *all* students will know by the end of the year. It is important to note that essential standards do not represent everything you're going to teach; rather, they're the minimum a student must learn to reach high levels of learning (AllThingsPLC, n.d.).

2. **Differentiate between *need to know* versus *nice to know*:** In conjunction with focusing on essential standards, distinguishing between what is *critical* for students to know and be able to do and what is *nice* to be able to know and do will help you plan your lessons accordingly. Here are a few questions to ask, in which *yes* answers will help you determine a definite need to know.

    a. Will this learning connect to several of the major themes we cover this year?

    b. Will this learning be critical for the students' success in the next level (namely, next year's) class?

    c. Will this learning be essential to my students' success beyond school?

TIP 57
Chunk It

Just like that full dinner plate is going to require you to cut things up into smaller pieces, the art of teaching consists of breaking a large concept, movement, or procedure down into smaller, manageable steps that can be learned in a sequential (or sometimes nonsequential) order.

Chunking information, or breaking information down into bite-sized pieces so the brain can more easily digest new information, for online learning is especially critical, as it needs to be organized in a logical and progressive way. In their book *Teaching With the Instructional Cha-Chas*, LeAnn Nickelsen and Melissa Dickson (2019) advise that:

> Chunking helps our brains see similarities, connections, and sequences between and among pieces of information. . . . While the brain naturally seeks to chunk information into meaningful segments, teachers can facilitate this memory process by planning their lessons in a way that helps students see patterns and chunks in specific content (Fonollosa et al., 2015). (pp. 49–50)

Nickelsen and Dickson (2019) recommend that each chunk last between four and eight minutes for grades K–5 students, and six to ten minutes for students in grades 6–8.

It's also important to consider aspects such as the background knowledge of the students, the relevance of the information to their lives (see tip 63, page 99, for more details), and the students' energy levels. Then, you can set out to cut your lessons into those bite-sized pieces students can digest.

TIP 58
Keep. It. Simple.

When teaching online, you don't need to have hundreds of websites, apps, teaching strategies, and activities that you think you need to use. (I know; it can be hard to stay grounded when looking at social media, which seems to be filled with celebrity teachers who always seem to be doing way more than you, in a much more stylish manner! More on that in tip 96, page 152.)

But really, it's not needed. Start with just a few tools in your toolbox, and you can build in more as you go. And of course, if something doesn't work, adjust it as needed (or ditch it if you get a better idea)!

In the spirit of keeping things simple, here are three simple ideas for doing just that.

1. **Get specific:** When having students utilize a website for the first time, avoid having them just "explore" the website. Instead, give them *one specific thing* to do on that site. This will allow them to focus on the task at hand instead of getting swept up in the multitude of possibilities that many websites offer. Of course, they can always explore more later.

2. **Limit instruction to three if you can and six if you must:** Way back in 1956, Harvard psychologist George Miller found that short-term memory could really only hold around seven pieces of information (Doorey, 2021). Of course, that was well before the internet, one-hour delivery, and YouTube videos that seem very long if they last over a few minutes! As you've probably noticed in this book, I like to limit my advice to three pieces per tip. Consider limiting each piece of instruction to three steps, three examples, or three questions at a time. If you must go over, stop at six (and pay no attention to the fact that this book is called *101 Tips for Teaching Online*!).

3. **Remember that simple doesn't mean easy:** In much of life, it takes a lot of effort to keep things simple. Teaching online is no exception. Just keep in mind that every time you make the effort to simplify, you're opening up a world of learning for your students.

TIP 59
Separate When You Need to Be There and When You Don't

Online learning comes in many forms. There are prerecorded classes, often called *asynchronous* classes; live classes, often called *synchronous*; as well as a hybrid of the two. In some cases, students attend class both online and in person, often called *blended learning*.

When teaching online and designing lessons, the time you spend live and in front of students is very valuable (and often limited). It's important to separate what you as the teacher need to be synchronously present for and what you don't.

A teacher could certainly make the case that most anything taught synchronously could also be taught asynchronously, and ultimately it is up to each individual teacher to decide what is most impactful in each situation. The key is finding the right balance between the two.

In an attempt to help you try to keep things balanced, figure 7.1 is a scale to help you make that determination. Just remember, it's ultimately up to you to decide which and how much of each goes on each side of the scale.

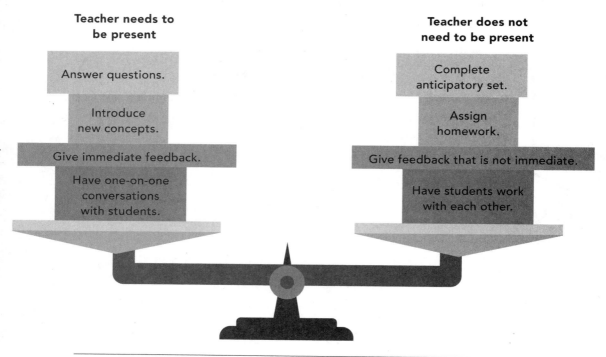

Figure 7.1: Keeping things balanced.

*Visit **go.SolutionTree.com/technology** for a free reproducible version of this figure.*

TIP 60
Provide an Agenda

Ever call a customer service line and be told by the automated voice what your estimated wait time is going to be? For many callers, knowing how long you'll be waiting is actually a relief, as it helps to eliminate uncertainty and set the expectation of what is going to happen (well, mostly).

Just as students might walk into an in-person classroom and see an agenda posted on the board, you should also give students in an online class the opportunity to know how their time will be spent.

Just taking a few moments at the beginning of class to communicate the agenda helps give students a clear picture of what to expect and what you expect of them. When posting your agenda, be sure to focus on what students will be learning and what they will be able to do (often called the *objective*) as a result of being in your class. When students clearly see that they're leaving your class smarter and more capable than when they entered, they'll see the true value of education and how to implement it in their daily lives.

You can have your agenda written on a whiteboard behind you. You can also post your objective and agenda in creative ways, such as creating a background image with your agenda on it or making a pretty file that you can put into the chat and ask students to open.

Advice From Students

I really like it when the course and lessons are well-organized and clear, and I know how my grade is going to be broken down. Also, when I take a test online, I like to know in advance whether it will be open book or closed book.

—Caleb, Eleventh Grade (personal communication, April 3, 2021)

TIP 61
Talk Less (and Listen More)

Is it just me, or do other teachers involuntarily hear the droning, incomprehensible "bwah-bwah-bwah-bwah" of the teacher from *Peanuts* cartoons in their head when we find ourselves talking too long and our students tuning out? Students can only go so long listening to their teacher talk—and this goes doubly when it's on a screen!

So, as a general rule, try not to talk for more than ten minutes without switching things up and giving students a chance to express their thinking, either verbally or in writing (or any of the other ways discussed in chapter 8, "Assessing Students," on page 105).

There's a common phrase in teaching, often credited to education researcher Jennifer York-Barr:

The one doing the talking is the one doing the learning. (Wright, 2020)

As important as it might seem that we get all our points across as teachers, much of the learning happens when we give students time to process the information. Give them a chance to talk, either to you or to each other. Then, show them that you're listening by quoting them as often as possible. For example, "I really like something that Marcella said in that last discussion. She said [repeat Marcella's quote]."

They might be on the other side of the screen, but when a student like Marcella hears herself quoted during class, she has no other option but to stay engaged and keep on learning.

TIP 62
Give Think Time

There are not many things that make a novice teacher squirm more than asking the class a question, only to hear nothing but the metaphorical crickets chirping. However, a seasoned teacher relishes in this silence, knowing that is where the magic happens. It is in this silence that higher levels of thinking are happening, opinions are forming, and true learning is taking place.

When teaching online, ten seconds of silence feels like a minute, and a minute of silence feels like ten. After five seconds of silence, students might even think that you've frozen on your screen.

The following are three suggestions to make the most of think time while teaching online.

1. After asking a question, sit comfortably in the silence. Nod your head slowly or move your hands slowly to show students that their screen is not frozen.

2. Teach students about the "uncomfortable silence" that often occurs after a question is asked. Talk about how it's a necessary part of learning—call it *think time*, even—and mention that in your class, it's going to be something that happens regularly.

3. Tell students in advance that before anyone answers (in the chat or by unmuting themselves), you're going to give them thirty seconds to think about, and maybe jot down, their answer. Then hold up a timer for students to see before you start it. Giving students a specified amount of time before they can answer can take the pressure off of them to feel like they need to answer quickly, and instead focus on answering completely.

TIP 63
Relate Lessons to Their World

Even the most well-organized lessons will fall flat if students fail to see the significance of the information and how it relates to their own lives.

Old-school teaching often tried to take academic content and force it into students' lives. Today, we know it's way more effective to *start with* the students and their lives and find places to fit them into the curriculum.

In tip 17 (page 26), I stated that one of the easiest and most effective ways to build relationships with students while teaching online is to find out their interests and hobbies and refer to them throughout the school year. This tip is the next level of that: designing lessons that reference or use your students' interests.

I learned this firsthand when I started taking my students' interest in hip-hop music and applying it to their algebra lessons, which has resulted in hundreds of thousands of views of my "Rappin' Mathematician" videos on YouTube (my first experience with teaching online!). This kind of teaching will engage students immediately and keep them interested.

With a built-in camera attached to everyone's phones these days, I always encourage students to snap a photo whenever they see something relevant to what we're covering in class and share it. The students love seeing signs around their community that have misspelled words on them and sharing them with the class (and don't even get me started on all the photos we've taken of the word *your* that should have been *you're*!).

Studying biology? Record a quick video of yourself talking to them from a zoo, the beach, or somewhere that your students have mentioned visiting, and relate it to the lesson. And remember: even if it's a bit grainy, your authentic video footage is often way cooler to your students than a professionally shot video, and you can use the same video year after year!

There's nothing better to pique student interest than students hearing their actual interests and life experiences within a lesson. Do this and, hopefully, you'll never again have to answer the question, "When am I *ever* going to use this in my life?"

TIP 64
Show What Different Levels of Success Look Like

In an in-person classroom, students might walk in and see examples of their fellow classmates' work adorning the walls. Or the teacher might pass around some completed examples, so that students can see firsthand work samples that the teacher considers ideal (and, of course, less than ideal).

You can do this in the online classroom as well, and perhaps even more effectively. By posting samples of work (perhaps you can create a Samples tab on your class website or in an online folder), students can take their time in looking them over and have a sample that they can constantly return to as they complete their assignment.

You might even consider creating a video of you holding up student work samples, and explaining how each sample did or did not meet your expectations— or perhaps exceeded them!

Where to Go From Here

Marie Kondo is a Japanese efficiency expert who has found fame and fortune teaching people how to organize their clothing, photographs, and other household possessions. For example, she teaches people how to put their clothes in a certain order in closets and drawers so they can be found and used easily. Kondo (2016) argues that an organized household not only is more efficient but also "sparks joy."

In a sense, organizing your lessons does the same thing. Students will find it easier to follow the key points in a lesson, which increases class efficiency (especially in an online environment, where every minute is critical!). A well-organized lesson also allows time for students to think deeper and reach higher levels of learning, something that surely sparks joy in every teacher.

Reflect on the tips in this chapter. To what degree do you currently achieve the goal in each tip? Are there some tips you are interested in using in your classes? How would you implement them? Figure 7.2 has space for notes on your reflections.

Tips in This Chapter	To What Degree Are You Already Following the Tip?	Your Plans for Implementing the Tip
Boil it down, but don't water it down.	☐ Already nailing it! ☐ Following it some but should do more. ☐ Not following it at all but should try. ☐ Not following it at all and not interested.	
Chunk it.	☐ Already nailing it! ☐ Following it some but should do more. ☐ Not following it at all but should try. ☐ Not following it at all and not interested.	

Figure 7.2: Reflection chart for chapter 7.

continued ▶

Tips In This Chapter	To What Degree Are You Already Following the Tip?	Your Plans for Implementing the Tip
Keep. It. Simple.	☐ Already nailing it! ☐ Following it some but should do more. ☐ Not following it at all but should try. ☐ Not following it at all and not interested.	
Separate when you need to be there and when you don't.	☐ Already nailing it! ☐ Following it some but should do more. ☐ Not following it at all but should try. ☐ Not following it at all and not interested.	
Provide an agenda.	☐ Already nailing it! ☐ Following it some but should do more. ☐ Not following it at all but should try. ☐ Not following it at all and not interested.	
Talk less (and listen more).	☐ Already nailing it! ☐ Following it some but should do more. ☐ Not following it at all but should try. ☐ Not following it at all and not interested.	
Give think time.	☐ Already nailing it! ☐ Following it some but should do more. ☐ Not following it at all but should try. ☐ Not following it at all and not interested.	

Relate lessons to their world.	☐ Already nailing it! ☐ Following it some but should do more. ☐ Not following it at all but should try. ☐ Not following it at all and not interested.	
Show what different levels of success look like.	☐ Already nailing it! ☐ Following it some but should do more. ☐ Not following it at all but should try. ☐ Not following it at all and not interested.	

*Visit **go.SolutionTree.com/technology** for a free reproducible version of this figure.*

If you want to go beyond the tips in this chapter and dig deeper into organizing your lessons, here are two resources to consider.

1. *The Together Teacher: Plan Ahead, Get Organized, and Save Time!* by Maia Heyck-Merlin (2021) provides strategies and resources for organizing lessons, classrooms, and even your own time. It was inspired by the author's personal journey as a young teacher and her later experience teaching novice teachers in the Teach for America program.

2. *The Teacher Clarity Playbook: A Hands-On Guide to Creating Learning Intentions and Success Criteria for Organized, Effective Instruction, Grades K–12* by Douglas Fisher, Nancy Frey, Olivia Amador, and Joseph Assof (2019) provides the tools teachers need to make classroom hours flow productively for students and teachers alike. As the authors say in the introduction, "When learning is organized and intentional, and when the learner knows what he or she is learning, great things can happen" (Fisher et al., 2019, p. xiv).

CHAPTER 8

Assessing Students

There's an old teacher joke that goes something like this:

Mrs. Delgado arrives at school on Monday morning, and as she walks onto campus, another teacher asks her how her weekend was.

Mrs. Delgado replies, "Great! I spent the weekend teaching my dog how to talk!"

The other teacher says, "Wow, that's amazing. When can I have a conversation with your dog?"

Mrs. Delgado replies, "I'm afraid that's not possible. I spent the weekend teaching my dog how to talk, but the dog didn't learn a thing!"

When teaching online, we can teach our students a lot, in a multitude of ways, with lots of wonderful technology. But how do we know if they've learned the information?

From very informal ways to much more formal ways of assessing our students, the tips in this chapter will help you get creative with, and perhaps even rethink, what it means to assess students in today's world. Above all, these tips will help you determine the learning that's happened. (See page 117 for additional research supporting the following tips and to improve your implementation of online student assessment.)

TIP 65
Monitor Faces and Body Language

Sometimes as teachers, we need to rely on our teacher intuition to assess whether our students are learning. It's a simple but critical tip for online teaching, too.

As I mentioned previously, a great deal of communication is nonverbal (Strain, 2020). Paying attention to our students' faces and body language helps us gauge their level of engagement on the fly. Are students:

- Slumped over in their chairs?

- Clearly distracted by their phones?

- Nodding their heads?

- Laughing at your hilarious jokes?

Keeping an eye on our students' faces and body language is our first, very informal line of defense to know when to adjust our teaching and when learning might be coming to a halt. Figure 8.1 lists a few subtle things to keep an eye out for and a possible response.

You Notice a Student Is	What You Can Say	Rationale
Looking off to the side of the screen for an extended period of time	"Hey [insert name of student], can you see the slide on the screen OK?"	Brings students' attention back to the screen, without calling them out on what might seem like they're not paying attention
Muted, but you can see their lips moving as they're clearly talking to someone off screen	"[Insert name of student], it looks like you might be talking to someone; is everything OK?"	Helps you approach this situation from a place of concern, rather than something punitive
Hunched over, sitting still in the same position, without moving (almost as if they're frozen on the screen)	"Quick tech check—everyone give me a thumbs-up if you can hear and see me clearly."	Allows you to "reset" all of the students' attention spans, and immediately connect with students who don't have their thumb up

Figure 8.1: Examples of monitoring faces and body language and what to say in response.

TIP 66
Use Hand Gestures, Emojis, and Polls

What's an effective way to know if students are learning what we're teaching?

Ask them!

A simple but important way to check for understanding and determine whether students are understanding the content is to stop and have them self-assess along the way.

While teaching online, you could have students:

- Hold up a certain number of fingers to indicate their level of understanding (one finger means they're not understanding at all; ten fingers mean they could write a book on the topic!)

- Use emojis, Bitmojis, or other graphics that communicate how they're feeling about what they're learning or their level of understanding

- Complete multiple-choice, true-or-false, or fill-in-the-blank online polls that give you and them immediate feedback on the overall level of understanding of a given topic (Interactive presentation tools such as Nearpod [www.nearpod.com] and Pear Deck [www.peardeck.com] can keep your students on topic while you check for understanding [Hooker, 2020].)

With any of these informal, in-the-moment assessment strategies, you can use the results to accelerate, slow down, or modify instruction as needed.

TIP 67
Take a Photo

If there's one thing today's students know how to do often and well, it's take photos! You can use this to your advantage with online teaching as another, more formal assessment tip.

There may be a time when you need to have students complete a more traditional pencil-and-paper quiz or test. Once completed, simply have the students take a photo of their completed work. Then they can either upload it to a class folder or just text it to you. This also works well when assessing artwork or anything that the students have built.

In addition, students can use a series of photos to show improvement over time. When appropriate, submitting a video (such as a student playing a piece of music) can be a good idea as well.

TIP 68
Use (Google) Surveys

If there's one benefit of online learning for us brick-and-mortar teachers, it's no longer having to worry about hauling that big stack of tests home, grading them late into the night, and hauling them back to class the next day. I don't miss that—do you?

The truth is, even in live classes and hybrid learning, there are now online programs that allow us to never lug those paper tests around again. Programs such as Google Forms allow you to create an assessment and receive the results in an organized spreadsheet, which enables you to view the students' responses by individual student or by individual question to help you see trends across an entire class. Programs like Poll Everywhere allow students to text in their answers, which appear in real time on the screen for immediate feedback.

So, online surveys are not only easier on the back than schlepping paper stacks home, but also easier on the environment and more efficient, too!

TIP 69
Assess Via Video

Making videos used to require a very expensive, heavy camera. Now, it just requires that little smartphone in our pockets.

We can utilize this technological advancement as an engaging way to assess our students and move them toward higher levels of thinking.

Here's how it can work.

1. Pose prompts, such as, "In a one- to two-minute video, discuss two main causes and effects of World War II." Be sure to give students a rubric of how answers will be scored.

2. Have students record themselves talking about it, either using their own video camera or using a program such as Flipgrid. (Flipgrid allows students to see each other's videos and post comments and video responses.)

Not only is this an effective way to assess learning, the process of identifying only what can be put into a one- to two-minute video is very valuable for the students to develop critical thinking. In addition, you can reuse these videos when you are reviewing student progress later in the year.

TIP 70
When Providing Feedback, Be Specific and Timely

Let's face it: today's students are used to receiving feedback very quickly. From social media to video games to ordering something online, they're not used to waiting for much of anything.

In *Feedback Revolution*, Marjorie M. Mauldin (2017) states, "Feedback is information that is shared with a person or group for the distinctive purpose of improving results or relationships" (p. i). While we might not be able to offer feedback as quickly as our students can get "likes" on their social media posts, providing it in a timely manner is critical to keeping our students engaged in their learning. Regardless of how you assess your students, provide them with timely feedback that clearly communicates whether, and to what extent, they've mastered the content.

In addition, provide feedback that's as specific as possible. This helps students understand where they've excelled, and where they can improve. Telling a student, "Good job on this story!" is nice for motivation, but it's not as effective as feedback such as, "I really like the way that you used alliteration to create imagery throughout your story."

Feedback that is specific also helps students understand exactly what they need to do to improve. Noting to a student that "This sentence feels dull and needs work" helps them much less than a more specific, "This sentence uses passive, bland verbs, and thus sounds dull. Try rewriting with active, interesting verbs, and see the difference."

In addition to being specific and timely, good feedback is ongoing and interactive, as opposed to something that is just given once. When used properly, it can be used as a powerful tool to enhance student motivation and self-esteem (McCallum, 2015)!

TIP 71
Provide Feedback Via Video or Voice Recording

We know our students generally love to make videos, but we can make videos ourselves, too, with great effect.

Try giving your students recorded (video or auditory) feedback and assessments. Then, they can watch or listen multiple times. It can also save you time, as you don't need to write or type out everything you want to say (assuming you talk faster than you type!).

If reviewing a piece of student work, utilize a program (such as Zoom) that allows you to annotate or write directly onto student work by marking up what's on the screen. You can even record a video of yourself reviewing the students' work. This is an effective way for you to point out the exact part of the students' work that you're providing feedback on, and they can see exactly what you were thinking while grading it. And bonus: they can watch it multiple times to improve for next time!

TIP 72

Have a Back Channel Where Students Can Ask for Help

One of the great challenges of assessment is catching students as they *begin* to need help, instead of after they're already lost.

Having a back channel where students can express their needs can be very helpful in preventing students from falling behind. This back channel can be as simple as students sending you a private message in the chat feature or holding weekly office hours where they can come check in with you. (See tip 83, page 134, for more information.) You might also establish a *parking lot* online discussion board where students post what they're confused about, so that you can address it during the next class.

Regardless of how you set it up, finding a way to allow students to express when they need help is a critical factor in helping to prevent them from falling behind.

TIP 73
Rethink What Counts as Cheating

For much of education's history, taking a test has meant sitting in rows, no talking allowed, and "Eyes on your own paper!" It has meant individual students' test results determine a grade for each individual student.

However, content that's been tested in the past is now only a google away. And teaching online is an opportunity to rethink *why* we give tests and *how* they benefit students.

Instead of giving tests that students might cheat on by sharing the answers, consider creating tests that students *should* collaborate on. Give them opportunities to check their answers and discuss them with others before turning them in.

Instead of giving assessments where students must select one correct answer out of four possible answers, consider giving them assessments where there might be four different conceivably correct answers, and students must justify why they chose the answer that they did.

And of course, take the time to teach them about academic honesty, avoiding plagiarism, and distinguishing between credible and non-credible sources. Back to the *why* of testing, this can help to create lifelong learners who think critically and ethically.

Advice From Students

Try to give the kids different ways to show what we know. Give us some options. Some students are artsy; some are more academic. My history teacher gives us a lot of different ways to show what we learned—we can make a song, draw a picture, or write a paragraph.

—Sophia, Seventh Grade (personal communication, April 18, 2021)

Where to Go From Here

Perhaps one of the most exciting opportunities when teaching online is the opportunity to rethink assessment. In a review of computer-based assessment literature, Kathleen Scalise (2012) argues that online students have even greater need than bricks-and-mortar students for more frequent feedback and more variety of feedback methods.

As the tips in this chapter indicate, new forms of assessment—such as video assessment—can enrich students' understanding of how well they are progressing and what they should focus on to improve their learning. Just imagine the student who exclaims, "I can't wait to log on for my class assessment!"

Reflect on the tips in this chapter. To what degree do you currently achieve the goal in each tip? Are there some tips you are interested in using in your classes? How would you implement them? Figure 8.2 has space for notes on your reflections.

Tips in This Chapter	To What Degree Are You Already Following the Tip?	Your Plans for Implementing the Tip
Monitor faces and body language.	☐ Already nailing it! ☐ Following it some but should do more. ☐ Not following it at all but should try. ☐ Not following it at all and not interested.	
Use hand gestures, emojis, and polls.	☐ Already nailing it! ☐ Following it some but should do more. ☐ Not following it at all but should try. ☐ Not following it at all and not interested.	

Figure 8.2: Reflection chart for chapter 8.

continued ▶

Tips In This Chapter	To What Degree Are You Already Following the Tip?	Your Plans for Implementing the Tip
Take a photo.	☐ Already nailing it! ☐ Following it some but should do more. ☐ Not following it at all but should try. ☐ Not following it at all and not interested.	
Use (Google) surveys.	☐ Already nailing it! ☐ Following it some but should do more. ☐ Not following it at all but should try. ☐ Not following it at all and not interested.	
Assess via video.	☐ Already nailing it! ☐ Following it some but should do more. ☐ Not following it at all but should try. ☐ Not following it at all and not interested.	
When providing feedback, be specific and timely.	☐ Already nailing it! ☐ Following it some but should do more. ☐ Not following it at all but should try. ☐ Not following it at all and not interested.	
Provide feedback via video or voice recording.	☐ Already nailing it! ☐ Following it some but should do more. ☐ Not following it at all but should try. ☐ Not following it at all and not interested.	

Have a back channel where students can express when they need help.	☐ Already nailing it! ☐ Following it some but should do more. ☐ Not following it at all but should try. ☐ Not following it at all and not interested.	
Rethink what counts as cheating.	☐ Already nailing it! ☐ Following it some but should do more. ☐ Not following it at all but should try. ☐ Not following it at all and not interested.	

*Visit **go.SolutionTree.com/technology** for a free reproducible version of this figure.*

If you want to go beyond the tips in this chapter and dig deeper into assessing students, here are two resources to consider.

1. See *Rebooting Assessment: A Practical Guide for Balancing Conversations, Performances, and Products* by Damian Cooper (2022) with Jeff Catania for a closer examination of assessing via video, with specific emphasis on the idea that products (essays, written texts, and so on) are not the only way to assess students, particularly online. Cooper makes the case that using video to assess students via conversations and performances is necessary for a balanced assessment picture.

2. *Feedback Revolution: Building Relationships and Boosting Results* by Marjorie M. Mauldin (2017) grew out of the author's experience of finding better ways to give feedback to employees in business organizations than the traditional annual performance review. She tested the tools over time, and much of the resulting model in this book is adaptable to the classroom where students need more feedback than simply a grade on a project or test.

CHAPTER 9

Ensuring Equity

When most schools shut their doors and moved to remote learning at the beginning of the COVID-19 pandemic, the inequities of our education system became even more glaringly obvious. Students with access to quality Wi-Fi, the right tech devices, and families that could oversee their schooling were at an immediate advantage. Students who did not have this access were immediately disadvantaged (Richards, Aspegren, & Mansfield, 2021; Vogels, Perrin, Rainie, & Anderson, 2020).

Luvelle Brown, superintendent of the Ithaca City School District in New York, defines equity as "reducing the predictability of who succeeds and who fails" (LaClaire, 2020). When done thoughtfully and with a determination to ensure equity, online learning can provide ALL students opportunities to learn, engage, and connect with their own community. It can also open up access to communities previously closed off to them. (See page 131 for additional research supporting the following tips on ensuring equity.)

TIP 74
Pronounce Students' Names Right
(and Learn to Say "Hello!")

In Jamilah Thompkins-Bigelow's (2020) best-selling picture book *Your Name Is a Song*, a little girl doesn't want to return to school after her teacher continually mispronounces her name. Her mother teaches her that her name is like a song. Then, the girl shows her classmates (and teacher) that *all* names are like songs, and it's a gift to each other when we learn how to sing (or say) them.

There's a reason this picture book is a bestseller. And, if it had been out when my own kids were younger, I'd have bought it for them, too. (With a last name like Kajitani, we've been called a lot of things other than our actual name!)

For students whose names might seem hard to spell or pronounce, nothing is more degrading than a teacher who constantly pronounces their name incorrectly. Especially when the teacher makes no effort to say their name correctly and mispronounces it in the presence of the other students. (Saying, "I'm no good at names!" or "That name is just too hard!" doesn't help matters.) At the same time, nothing is more empowering for such a student than a teacher who takes the time to learn to say their name correctly. This is a big, important first step in building a relationship and earning a student's trust—while being a role model for others.

Usually, it's not as hard as others think, if they just slow down and read the syllables. (For example, Kajitani is pretty straightforward: Ka-jit-ah-nee. Learn it once, and it's easy!) Often, the unfamiliar makes people nervous. See what happens if you embrace it as an opportunity to learn. An easy way to address this with a student is to say something like, "It's really important to me to pronounce your name properly. Can you say it aloud for me while I write it down?" If you feel comfortable, you could even ask the student if it's OK for you to record them saying their name a few times, so you have a firsthand recording of the proper pronunciation. Consider concluding this conversation by saying, "I want to make sure I continue pronouncing your name correctly every day, so if I ever don't get it right, just pull on your earlobe (or whatever fun sign you and the student want to go with) and I'll know I need to do better!"

You can go even further: with students who come from a different country or speak a language other than English at home, simply learn how to say "Hello!" in their native language. Show them that their language and culture is important to you, and you show them that they matter in your classroom.

These two strategies also work well to build rapport with a student's parents or guardians!

TIP 75
Be Conscious About (Camera) Backgrounds

One of the great dilemmas about online teaching is whether to require students to keep their cameras on.

While we want to be able to see the students' faces, expressions, and body language, many students don't like to see themselves on camera, and there's real concern that requiring cameras to be turned on disproportionately affects students of color or students from low-income families. Not wanting classmates or the teacher to see inside their home is most definitely a reasonable concern for a student.

There are cultural considerations. For example, students who wear hijabs might not cover their head while in the privacy of their own home; however, they would when required to turn their camera on.

There are also practical considerations. For instance, low bandwidth and unstable internet connections can also be improved when students turn their camera off.

So what can teachers do? Here are some ideas that can help.

1. Talk about it. Instead of letting students feel ashamed or embarrassed about not wanting their camera on, discuss this issue with them proactively and invite students to speak with you privately about their concerns.

2. Create a virtual background specific to your classroom, which students can use if they choose. Have fun with it—include your class colors, logo, or a picture of your class pet. You can also teach students to use stock virtual backgrounds. Many programs such as Zoom also have a blur feature, which allows students to blur their backgrounds while still showing their face clearly.

3. Design "camera on" moments. If you do have students who are going to keep their cameras off, come to an agreement with those students that maybe they check in at the beginning of class with their camera on, and once you greet them, they can turn cameras off until their "camera on" moments. You can ask them to type into the chat or answer live surveys so you know they're with you. Perhaps they also turn their camera on at the very end of class, during the send-off!

TIP 76
Know Your Students' Living Situations

Ensuring equity means knowing, whenever possible, your students' living situations and any challenges and barriers that they face.

Do they have enough food?

A roof over their head, and somewhere they can receive mail?

Reliable internet? (See tip 82, page 128.)

Are they caring for others, such as younger siblings or older grandparents, while trying to meet the demands of online learning?

Knowing at least some of the answers to these questions can help you build a relationship and get them the support they need. (See tip 82, page 128, for more on that.)

If you find that a student is in real trouble and needs help, remember that you don't have to (and probably shouldn't) take this on by yourself. Reach out to your school's counselor, administrator, or whoever is best equipped to address the situation. *The Wraparound Guide* (Colburn & Beggs, 2021) provides guidance for connecting students with services and when to make sure a school counselor or administrator needs to be involved.

Teacher Feature

When schools moved to remote learning during the pandemic, Maddie Fennell, executive director of the Nebraska State Education Association (NSEA), realized that while many students across the state didn't have access to the internet, they did have access to television.

So NSEA teamed up with News Channel Nebraska. Teachers across the state recorded lessons on a multitude of topics, which they then televised at regularly scheduled times. They also were able to show effective video lessons from outside of the state, including my California-based "Wacky Math Hour" pandemic show! (M. Fennell, personal communication, April 8, 2020)

TIP 77
Find the Reason Behind the Reason

For every struggling student, there is a reason. For every student who doesn't show up for an online class, there is a reason. For every student . . . you get the picture.

As teachers, it's very difficult to find solutions when we don't know the reasons behind student issues. When finding out the reasons, try taking it one step further, and find out the "reason behind the reason."

For example, a student in your class hasn't turned in their essay that was due last week. You make contact with that student, who tells you that they haven't had time to do it.

It's easy to dismiss this student as disorganized or lazy; however, dig a bit deeper with the student and you might find that they are required to watch their younger siblings during the day while their parents are at work. Now you know the reason behind the reason, and you can now work with that student. Perhaps the student agrees to turn in one paragraph at a time until the draft of the essay is done.

Only when we know the true reasons behind the reasons can we begin to help students remove the barriers they face and obtain the equitable education that they are entitled to.

TIP 78
Embrace Race and Diversity

Tolerance is a word often used when talking about diversity. The old paradigm told us to tolerate differences, from race to religion to so much more. But how does it feel to have someone be asked to "tolerate" who you are, your race, your culture? Not great, right?

The new paradigm, which better serves all our students, is to *embrace* differences. This means seeing diversity as a truly added benefit to our classrooms and celebrating it.

Embracing differences can look like the following.

- Openly and compassionately discussing race as a social construct and issue

- Allowing space in discussions for students' experiences with their differences from the mainstream

- Inviting students to showcase their culture, holidays, language, and so on in class events or presentations

- Encouraging students to respectfully write about race in their work

This may feel uncomfortable at first, particularly if your experience fits the mainstream. But it gets easier the more you do it. And remember, demographics are shifting everywhere, so the mainstream may shift, too. It's to *everyone's* advantage to embrace and celebrate the diversity among us.

TIP 79
Commit to Culturally Responsive Teaching

Culturally responsive teaching means using knowledge of our students' cultures, prior (and current) experiences, and the communities they live in to guide why, how, and what we teach. It means, as UCLA Distinguished Professor of Education Pedro Noguera puts it, teaching the way they learn, rather than expecting them to learn the way we teach (ChaseLearning.org, n.d.). At the same time, it's important to note, according to Zaretta Hammond (2020), that "culturally responsive instruction doesn't mean you're only mentioning issues of race and implicit bias"; rather, "you're also focused on building brainpower by helping students leverage and grow their existing funds of knowledge."

The following are two ideas Hammond (2020) recommends that teachers use to implement culturally responsive online teaching.

1. Deepen students' background knowledge by building reading lists and Netflix-style playlists of movies, shows, and documentaries that explore and address issues of cultural importance to your students. Not sure where to start? Ask the students for their recommendations! Then, take it a step further by having students reflect, discuss, debate, and dive deeper by conducting online research and using some of the online apps and programs discussed throughout this book (see also Major, 2020).

2. Remember that *responsiveness* means you need to respond. With so much of our lives (especially our students' lives) playing out online these days, as teachers we need to be ready to respond as quickly as possible, and help our students respond, to the rapidly changing world that we live in. When Black Lives Matter protests took hold of the United States during the summer of 2020, many of our students were watching the protests play out both in their own cities as well as on popular social media sites such as TikTok, and many of our older students were participating. Being conscious of what is happening in our students' lives and communities and responding thoughtfully is a critical component to committing to culturally responsive teaching.

TIP 80
Be Diverse in Your Video and Photo Selections

Videos and photos are a terrific way for you, the online teacher, to make learning come to life and deepen learning in an engaging and interactive way. It won't take long for you to build up a library of fantastic video clips that connect to the content you're teaching.

However, making that learning real, authentic, and culturally relevant for our students means intentionally selecting videos and photos that include ethnically diverse representations.

Rudine Sims Bishop (as cited in Chenoweth, 2019) coined the concept of *windows and mirrors*: students need to see people of other ethnicities than their own (windows) *and* to see people who look like themselves (mirrors) to be well-rounded learners and citizens. Particularly when it comes to minority students, mirrors are of utmost importance. When students see themselves in your lessons, they will feel more seen and understood, and in turn be more engaged in learning with you (Chenoweth, 2019).

When searching for photos for your presentations (on royalty-free sites such as www.pexels.com or www.unsplash.com), include the ethnicity of your students at the beginning of your search term. For example, if you have Latinx students in your class, when looking for a photo of "kids playing in a park," include the word *Latinx* at the beginning of your search, so it says "Latinx kids playing in a park."

You might have to sort through a few more photos, but taking just a bit of extra time to ensure that your students' ethnicities, and other ethnicities, are well-represented in your curriculum benefits everyone.

TIP 81
Create Teams With Equity in Mind

I once keynoted a conference for five hundred human resources (HR) directors from across the United States. After my speech, I asked them, "What is your biggest challenge with managing people who were once students in our schools?"

One of the most prevalent answers was that many of their employees had trouble working in teams with people who were "not like them." All too often, they would come to the HR director and ask to switch to another team, citing "not being able to get along" as the reason for their desired switch.

While I didn't specifically ask (although I should have) what "not like them" meant, I knew what they were referring to: people who were from different cultures, races, and life experiences. I began thinking about how we often group students in schools based on who we know they will get along with so a task or project gets done with minimal conflict. Inevitably, this often means we group high-performing students with each other and low-performing students with each other, which further divides them and moves us *away* from equitable practices.

Teaching online is an opportunity to move beyond the traditional ways of grouping students. The students don't necessarily see each other in the cafeteria or on the playground, and much of the social dynamic (usually created in between classes) that exists in in-person schools is not present online.

When grouping students, be conscious and intentional about how you group them, and remember that the key to creating compassionate students who can work well together is to *incorporate*, not eliminate, racial, cultural, ability, and gender-identity differences so they become more familiar and comfortable to all students.

TIP 82
Ensure Access to the Internet and a Reliable Device

This tip might seem obvious, but it wouldn't be right to leave it out. One of the most important steps we can take to ensure equity is to make sure that *all* our students have good internet access and a reliable device.

The following are a few ideas to make this happen for all your students.

- Some internet providers offer a sliding scale monthly service charge, based on income. Find those providers in your area and make a list for your students and their families.

- Provide mobile hotspots that can be distributed to families. Or, if getting internet in the home is not possible, encourage (or help) your students to identify places in their community where they can take advantage of free Wi-Fi, such as a library, community center, or perhaps a neighbor's house (Hayat, 2020).

- Make sure providing devices for *all* students (or whatever words will get it done) is included in your school's budget.

You might also need to raise the issue of providing internet access and devices with your school's or district's leadership and technology department. It's always a good idea to ask questions and gather information first (like finding out if any surveys have been done to determine how many students have or need access, or if there are any teams that are already working on this issue) before insisting that immediate action be taken!

Advice From Students

I don't think teachers should always call on the people who always know the answers. They should call on them less and give more help to the students who really need it.

—Owen, Second Grade (personal communication, April 18, 2021)

Where to Go From Here

Striving for equity in our educational system has been a long road, with much still left to achieve. In the early days of the COVID-19 epidemic, the move to widespread online education highlighted another source of inequity: the *digital divide*, unequal access to computers, tablets or smartphones, and the internet. According to Bill Gates (1995), if countries can provide the infrastructure to support online education, there is great opportunity to increase equity:

> One of the wonderful things about the information highway is that virtual equity is far easier to achieve than real-world equity. We are all created equal in the virtual world, and we can use this equality to help address some of the sociological problems that society has yet to solve in the physical world. (p. 258)

As online teachers, we have the opportunity, *every day*, to work toward this equity.

Reflect on the tips in this chapter. To what degree do you currently achieve the goal in each tip? Are there some tips you are interested in using in your classes? How would you implement them? Figure 9.1 has space for notes on your reflections.

Tips in This Chapter	To What Degree Are You Already Following the Tip?	Your Plans for Implementing the Tip
Pronounce students' names correctly (and learn to say "hello").	☐ Already nailing it! ☐ Following it some but should do more. ☐ Not following it at all but should try. ☐ Not following it at all and not interested.	
Be conscious about (camera) backgrounds.	☐ Already nailing it! ☐ Following it some but should do more. ☐ Not following it at all but should try. ☐ Not following it at all and not interested.	

Figure 9.1: Reflection chart for chapter 9.

continued ▶

Tips in This Chapter	To What Degree Are You Already Following the Tip?	Your Plans for Implementing the Tip
Know your students' living situations.	☐ Already nailing it! ☐ Following it some but should do more. ☐ Not following it at all but should try. ☐ Not following it at all and not interested.	
Find the reason behind the reason.	☐ Already nailing it! ☐ Following it some but should do more. ☐ Not following it at all but should try. ☐ Not following it at all and not interested.	
Embrace race and diversity.	☐ Already nailing it! ☐ Following it some but should do more. ☐ Not following it at all but should try. ☐ Not following it at all and not interested.	
Commit to culturally responsive teaching.	☐ Already nailing it! ☐ Following it some but should do more. ☐ Not following it at all but should try. ☐ Not following it at all and not interested.	
Be diverse in your video and photo selections.	☐ Already nailing it! ☐ Following it some but should do more. ☐ Not following it at all but should try. ☐ Not following it at all and not interested.	

Create teams with equity in mind.	☐ Already nailing it! ☐ Following it some but should do more. ☐ Not following it at all but should try. ☐ Not following it at all and not interested.	
Ensure access to the internet and a reliable device.	☐ Already nailing it! ☐ Following it some but should do more. ☐ Not following it at all but should try. ☐ Not following it at all and not interested.	

*Visit **go.SolutionTree.com/technology** for a free reproducible version of this figure.*

If you want to go beyond the tips in this chapter and dig deeper into ensuring equity, you could begin your exploration by imagining how our educational system could be different. Two resources to consider are as follows.

1. *Humanizing Distance Learning: Centering Equity and Humanity in Times of Crisis* by Paul Emerich France (2021) is a deeply thoughtful book about how to take advantage of the recent large-scale movement to online education to reduce structural inequities in our educational systems. France illustrates what a more equitable, humanized system would look like and encourages teachers to explore the possibilities in their own distance learning environment.

2. Now in its third edition, *Reclaiming Youth at Risk: Futures of Promise* by Larry K. Brendtro, Martin Brokenleg, and Steve Van Bockern (2019) merges Native American knowledge and Western science to provide an alternative approach to reaching disconnected or troubled youth.

If you want additional tips for dealing with specific equity issues, there are a number of books you can consult, including the following two.

1. *Beyond Conversations About Race: A Guide for Discussions With Students, Teachers, and Communities* by Washington Collado, Sharroky Hollie, Rosa Isiah, Yvette Jackson, Anthony Muhammad, Douglas Reeves, and Kenneth C. Williams (2021) explains how to use scenarios and

discussion questions to broach challenging topics, such as, "How can something be my responsibility when it's not my fault?"

2. In *Disrupting Poverty: Five Powerful Classroom Practices* by Kathleen Budge and William H. Parrett (2018), each chapter begins with "Voices From Poverty" telling the story of how education affected a particular impoverished student. The book's premise is that teachers can help break the cycle of poverty by implementing five practices, including having high expectations for impoverished students while providing needed support.

Differentiating Learning

Differentiation means tailoring instruction to meet the students' individual needs (Fogarty & Pete, 2011). This can be done in a multitude of ways, including how we tailor the content we're teaching, the learning environment, the processes we use, and the products we ask our students to produce (Kise, 2021).

In short: each student is different, and so are their needs. The following tips will help you differentiate your instruction while teaching online. (See page 145 for additional research supporting the following tips on differentiation.)

TIP 83
Hold Online Office Hours

As hard as you try, as well as you explain things, and as engaging as you are, sometimes (OK, more than sometimes) you just can't get every student to learn everything you want them to from your lesson. By scheduling online office hours, students can pop in virtually and get their questions answered while they get some individual attention.

You can also assign certain individuals, or small groups, to join you at a specified time to provide extra support, or perhaps complete an activity that extends the learning from the regular class.

Furthermore, knowing that they can always come to you at a specified time each week for assistance helps teach students to advocate for themselves, while building trust between them and their teacher (that's you!). (See figure 10.1.)

Figure 10.1: Hold online office hours.

TIP 84
Make and Take Appointments

Of course, there are times when students might need help but don't show up to online office hours. If you find that your office hours result in you sitting at your desk by yourself, hoping someone might show up, consider instead making appointments with your students. They can use these appointments to go over their mistakes on that last test, get help with their reading fluency, or whatever is needed.

Whatever you schedule, keep the appointments short and focused (twenty minutes is usually a good amount of time).

You might consider having a calendar link (like Calendly.com) that students can use to schedule a time that you've specified you're available. This helps avoid the back-and-forth that often results from trying to find a time that works for both of you.

TIP 85
Send Care Packages

One part of differentiating learning means making sure students have all the tools and supplies they need to be successful. In an in-person classroom, the teacher can easily provide items like rulers and paper and keep Bunsen burners on hand for the day's science lab.

When teaching online, this can be more of a challenge. Sending care packages home to students is a great way to make sure they have what will be needed to complete their work. You can also include fun stuff in the care packages, which can be a wonderful way to build relationships with students. (Who doesn't love getting a cool surprise in the mail?)

You could also send items that are specific to students' needs, such as sensory tools for special education students, sticky notes for students who need frequent reminders, or a small alarm clock for the student who struggles with making that morning class on time. Perhaps you might even be able to include a few healthy snacks for studying and make food equity something that is important as well.

TIP 86
Teach Students to Pause and Go Back

One of the biggest detriments to learning in a traditional, in-person classroom is that students' minds might wander, or they might get confused for a bit, only to find themselves completely lost a few minutes later. At that point, it can be pretty intimidating to admit what happened, and even more intimidating to ask the teacher to go back and reteach the past several minutes. In addition, a student who is absent essentially misses the experience of everything that happened that day.

However, with online teaching, we have the ability to record and post our lessons, so individual students who miss a class, or a portion of the class, can rewatch the video or just the portion that they need.

Teaching students to pause and go back is a useful tip that helps differentiate the learning, helps students meet their individual needs, and at the same time, teaches them a useful approach for lifelong learning.

TIP 87
Understand Depth of Knowledge

When teaching online, it can be quite challenging to create rich environments where all students learn at a high level. What might seem a simple question or task to one student might require quite a lot of thought for another.

Instead of trying to come up with one magic question or task that challenges all students, learn and understand Norman Webb's Depth of Knowledge (DOK) levels. These levels help us categorize questions and tasks according to the complexity of thinking required to answer and complete them. (See tip 88, page 139, for more on questions and tasks.)

According to Webb (1997), the four levels are as follows.

1. **Recall and production:** Questions and tasks require recall of facts or rote application of simple procedures.

2. **Skills and concepts:** Questions and tasks require students to engage in mental processing (beyond recall) and decision making.

3. **Strategic thinking:** Questions and tasks at this level require students to explain or justify their thinking and provide evidence. Or, they might require students to design or analyze something.

4. **Extended thinking:** Questions and tasks at this level require complex reasoning and time to research, plan, problem solve, think, and analyze, as well as make connections and applications to the real world.

Take some time to really understand the DOK levels to lay a foundation for your online question-asking. (*Deconstructing Depth of Knowledge: A Method and Model for Deeper Teaching and Learning* by Erik M. Francis (2022) is an excellent resource to help you not only understand DOK but gain a method and model for creating lessons that are rigorous, socially and emotionally supportive, and student responsive.) It's important to note that DOK levels are not necessarily sequential or developmental. Even the youngest students like preschoolers are capable of strategic and extended thinking. And as adults, we've all been in situations where we couldn't recall something!

TIP 88
Ask Three Questions

This tip uses knowledge of DOK levels from tip 87 (page 138)—so read that one now, if you haven't, and then head back here!

One effective way to differentiate learning is to ask three questions at different DOK levels. For example, when discussing the story your class is reading, you could ask:

- Who are the main characters in this story? (Level 1)

- What causes the character to flee, and what do you think will be the effect on her family? (Level 2)

- How does the author's voice change as the story progresses past the third chapter? (Level 3)

In an online classroom, you could assign or have students select which question they would like to answer, and then put them into breakout rooms to discuss. Or, you could put them into smaller breakout rooms to discuss all three, which will expose them to all three DOK levels.

There are a multitude of directions you can take with students and DOK levels, but intentionally designing our questions to include the different levels is a great way to help all our students learn (Francis, 2022).

TIP 89
Surround Students With Visuals

Since differentiation means tailoring instruction to meet our students' individual needs, one of the best ways we can promote and reinforce learning is to surround them with visuals.

This is especially helpful for our English learners and our students with special needs. Visuals give them an example of exactly what we're talking about to clarify and reinforce the concepts, which is especially important when we're teaching online.

I once told my mathematics class that I was going to show them how to use a protractor, and at the end of class, each student would get to take the protractor home to use. One of my EL students nervously exclaimed, "I don't have room at my house for a tractor!" Imagine their relief when I held up a small protractor before launching into my lesson.

Fortunately, with royalty-free sites like Pexels (www.pexels.com) or Unsplash (https://unsplash.com), finding and using high-quality images for your presentations and classroom discussions is very easy. However, sometimes the best images you can use are images from the students' own community, or photos that you have taken yourself. This way, students can directly relate to the content you're teaching. With all of us walking around with a camera in our pockets these days, always be on the lookout for photo (and video) opportunities.

Surrounding your online students with these kinds of visuals can make their learning more effective and their experience feel more meaningful, authentic, and real.

TIP 90
Add Subtitles to Your Videos

Taking the time to add subtitles to your videos is a highly effective and important way to help students grasp the videos' content (Albright, 2018). It's especially necessary for our English learners and deaf students or hard of hearing students, but all kinds of students can benefit from seeing the words along with hearing them.

One benefit to using subtitles is that students can watch the videos without the sound on, whenever they need to—an option especially important in small, crowded homes. Another benefit is reaching different kinds of learners and processors.

If you teach English learners and are especially subtitle-savvy, consider including subtitles in your students' native language.

There are plenty of programs that allow you to easily add subtitles to your videos, which range from video editing software (such as iMovie and Adobe Spark) to programs such as Zubtitle (and several others). Websites such as YouTube and Vimeo also allow you to add subtitles.

TIP 91
Give Them Tomorrow, Today!

It's hard for anyone to take in all the information a teacher gives us the first time around. For an English learner or a student with learning challenges, online class can be especially daunting as it's hard to pick up on the teacher's mannerisms and posture. In addition, nobody wants to miss a cultural reference or the joke in the video and have to fake smile while the rest of the class is laughing along.

Thus, it helps to preload students with information they'll need in the next class. Here are some ideas to do this.

- Give your students (or some of them) the link to the video you're planning to show in the next class. Then, they can preview it in advance as many times as they need to.

- If students are going to be taking notes during the next class, consider giving those who need help the notes, or part of the notes, in advance. Then, they can focus on understanding the content, rather than just trying to keep up with everyone while writing.

- When appropriate, you can even give students the questions that you are planning on asking the class during the discussion. Then, they can have time to process the questions, consider their answers, and be ready for the class discussion.

When we give our students tomorrow in advance, we help to set them up for success when today comes around!

Advice From Students

I really like having online office hours to go to—my teacher had a Google Doc where we sign up to meet with her for fifteen-minute meetings. Every time I sign up, she starts by saying, "What can I do for you?" and she often asks me to come in the following week to check in.

—Kaya, Tenth Grade (personal communication, April 8, 2021)

Where to Go From Here

Tailoring instruction to meet students' needs can make information accessible and more engaging, and lead to deeper learning—a goal we all want our students to reach! While the thought of customization in an online class can seem overwhelming, this chapter focused on tips to differentiate learning without overcomplicating your classes and lesson plans.

Reflect on the tips in this chapter. To what degree do you currently achieve the goal in each tip? Are there some tips you are interested in using in your classes? How would you implement them? Figure 10.2 has space for notes on your reflections.

Tips in This Chapter	To What Degree Are You Already Following the Tip?	Your Plans for Implementing the Tip
Hold online office hours.	☐ Already nailing it! ☐ Following it some but should do more. ☐ Not following it at all but should try. ☐ Not following it at all and not interested.	
Make and take appointments.	☐ Already nailing it! ☐ Following it some but should do more. ☐ Not following it at all but should try. ☐ Not following it at all and not interested.	
Send care packages.	☐ Already nailing it! ☐ Following it some but should do more. ☐ Not following it at all but should try. ☐ Not following it at all and not interested.	

Figure 10.2: Reflection chart for chapter 10.   continued ▶

Tips in This Chapter	To What Degree Are You Already Following the Tip?	Your Plans for Implementing the Tip
Teach students to pause and go back.	☐ Already nailing it! ☐ Following it some but should do more. ☐ Not following it at all but should try. ☐ Not following it at all and not interested.	
Understand Depth of Knowledge.	☐ Already nailing it! ☐ Following it some but should do more. ☐ Not following it at all but should try. ☐ Not following it at all and not interested.	
Ask three questions.	☐ Already nailing it! ☐ Following it some but should do more. ☐ Not following it at all but should try. ☐ Not following it at all and not interested.	
Surround students with visuals.	☐ Already nailing it! ☐ Following it some but should do more. ☐ Not following it at all but should try. ☐ Not following it at all and not interested.	
Add subtitles to your videos.	☐ Already nailing it! ☐ Following it some but should do more. ☐ Not following it at all but should try. ☐ Not following it at all and not interested.	

| Give them tomorrow, today! | ☐ Already nailing it!

☐ Following it some but should do more.

☐ Not following it at all but should try.

☐ Not following it at all and not interested. | |

*Visit **go.SolutionTree.com/technology** for a free reproducible version of this figure.*

If you want to go beyond the tips in this chapter and dig deeper into differentiating learning, you could begin your exploration by considering two resources.

1. *Doable Differentiation: Twelve Strategies to Meet the Needs of All Learners* by Jane A. G. Kise (2021) is targeted to teachers who initially may feel that differentiation is too complex and too time-consuming. The author demonstrates that there are simple, *doable* ways to differentiate to accommodate different learning styles.

2. *Deconstructing Depth of Knowledge: A Method and Model for Deeper Teaching and Learning* by Erik M. Francis (2022) begins with four chapters that explain the theory of DOK, followed by five chapters focused on the application of the DOK model. The application chapters each end with a professional development activity that helps you focus on how you could develop learning experiences that help your students achieve deeper learning.

CHAPTER 11

Taking Care of Yourself

Teaching is a tough job. *Very* tough.

In the physical classroom, it requires the physical strength to be constantly on our feet and moving. In the virtual classroom, it often requires the physical strength to be constantly sitting and not moving. Whether it's sore feet or a sore back at the end of the day, taking care of ourselves is often pushed aside to take care of all our students' needs (Boogren, 2020; Romano-Arrabito, 2019). Add in all that we have going on in our personal lives, and we can quickly find ourselves feeling physically and emotionally deflated.

The good news is that being an effective online teacher doesn't require that you run marathons, eat perfectly, or have the ability to sit in a lotus position for hours on end. It just means that you take some steps that can help you stay active, balanced, and excited about the work you do each day. (See page 159 for additional research supporting the following tips on taking care of yourself.)

TIP 92
Stand Up!

When James Levine first coined the statement, "Sitting is the new smoking" (Tri-City Medical Center, n.d.), it seemed pretty dramatic. But many medical experts now believe it to be accurate. The amount of time we spend sitting down each day at desks, in cars, or in front of screens creates health risks comparable to those caused by smoking (Tri-City Medical Center, n.d.).

Teachers who teach in in-person classrooms spend most of their day on their feet, buzzing around the classroom and across campus. It often takes us needing to use the restroom, or attending a staff meeting, just to get us to sit down!

However, when teaching online, the opposite can happen. We spend most of our time sitting down, and it takes needing to use the restroom just to get us to stand up!

Making sure you stand up regularly can have a profound impact on your overall health. The following are simple ways to make it happen.

- **Set a timer:** It's pretty easy to sit down to do "one quick thing"—and the next thing we know, a few hours have passed. Setting a timer (like the one on your phone) to go off every twenty to thirty minutes forces us to remember to stand up. Consider putting your timer across the room from you, so you have to stand up to turn it off (and when you stand up, see the next tip).

- **Have a few go-to stretches:** A few simple stretches you can do both in and out of your chair can help keep your body moving and loose.

- **Make it social:** For many people, any form of exercise is more fun when doing it with other people. Get together with your colleagues (or maybe even your entire school) and agree to set your timers at a certain time. That way you know when you're stretching, you're not alone!

- **Make it a part of class:** By making standing up a part of class, you're not only ensuring that you'll stand up from time to time, but also demonstrating the good habit to your own students. (And it gives those squirrely students some much-needed movement.)

TIP 93
Lean on Others for Help

We all know that while *teacher* might be our job title, as teachers, we often take on the roles of parent, counselor, coach, and so many more.

It can seem like there is always a student who is struggling, or one we could be doing something extra for. It can become so consuming that we often forget to step back and think of others who can help us help our students.

When needed, refer a student to your school's counselor, specialist, or administrator. There might be community resources that you can utilize as well. They're there to help (and many of them are *really* good at their jobs!), and they can help take the burden of feeling like you have to "do everything" off you.

Just because you're teaching alone in a room doesn't mean you're alone in the work you are doing to teach students. As educators, we're part of communities, and we're all in this together!

TIP 94
Set Time Boundaries

It can be very tempting to answer that parent's email at 9:30 p.m. before you go to bed. But be careful.

When you do that, you're indirectly sending the message that you're the type of teacher who answers emails at 9:30 p.m. (And maybe you are, but you don't have to be!) You might also find yourself answering emails throughout the day, which can be distracting and time-consuming. Martin Reisert, a sixth-grade social studies teacher and California Teacher of the Year, has found much success having a dedicated time each day where he answers all his emails (a practice referred to as *batching*), which frees him up to enjoy his evenings (M. Reisert, personal communication, January 26, 2021).

Also, when setting appointments, make sure to include the end time for your appointment. A meeting set for 10 a.m. might give the person you're meeting with the impression that they have an hour or more with you, but setting the meeting for 10 to 10:30 a.m. (or even 10:25 a.m.) sets the tone that it can't drag on.

Setting time boundaries helps keep you organized and focused, and frees you up to do your best online teaching.

TIP 95
Picture Your Happy Place
(and Put a Frame Around It)

As an online teacher, you spend a lot of time at your desk and in front of your computer. But there are moments (probably several moments each day) when you get stressed.

Dedicate an 8 × 10-inch space on the wall behind your computer to hang a photo of a place that makes you happy. Maybe it's somewhere you've been, or somewhere you dream of going. (See figure 11.1.)

When the stress starts to creep in, or class starts to go off the rails a bit, take a deep breath, look at the photo, and picture yourself there. It only takes a moment, but it can be a welcome reset to your mind and soul.

And feel free to switch up the photo from time to time!

Figure 11.1: Picture your happy place (and put a frame around it).

TIP 96
Don't Compare Your Insides
to Someone Else's Outsides

Teaching online means you spend a lot of time, well, online. It also means you probably spend time on social media, which is filled with regular people who are constantly touting the amazing things they're doing.

Perhaps it's the amazing teacher who seems like they're always posting about the over-the-top cool things they do with their students. Or maybe it's the parent you know whose photos always seem to be free of clutter in the background, mostly because they are constantly going to such amazing places (and wow, they're looking so thin and fit these days!).

Stop.

Stop comparing the moments when you're stressed out to someone else's carefully curated "I took twenty photos just to get the one that I could post" lifestyle. Stop comparing that project you just started (because you're passionate about it) to someone else's beautiful website that they've spent months or years on.

Everyone on social media is totally normal, just like you. And everyone is totally amazing, just like you. So, stop comparing, and go back to being your amazing self.

TIP 97
Ditch the Guilt

Somewhere, there's a piece of DNA that seems to be embedded in every teacher that makes them think, "I could and should be doing *more*."

More to help that student.

More to plan that lesson.

More to learn that new program.

It's true—there's always more we could be doing. But, at what expense?

Perhaps it's time to ask a new question. Instead of asking yourself, "What else could I be doing to accomplish more as a teacher?" consider asking, "What else could I be doing to pursue a balanced life as a person?"

By shifting this question away from constantly fulfilling the needs of others to focusing on what you need to do to be a happy, healthy person, you will actually be a more effective teacher. When we ditch the guilt of feeling like we're never doing enough, we can embrace the idea that we're all truly doing the best we can.

Advice From Students

Be patient. Be patient with yourself, with the tech, and with us. Sometimes it takes a few minutes to get on the apps that we're using, or to get into the activity. Also, let us go outside and run around so we can reset our brains!

—Simon, Fourth Grade (personal communication, March 6, 2021)

TIP 98
Share the Work

You don't have to create every online lesson, every video, or every assessment by yourself. Team up with your department or other teachers at your school (or any teaching community you are a part of), and split up the work.

The following are three straightforward and effective ways to share the work.

1. **Split the work up by weeks:** If each teacher takes just one week, then four of you will have the entire month covered!

2. **Split the work up by task:** If one person is especially good at making videos, maybe that person makes all the videos while another teacher creates the assessments, and another creates the slide presentations.

3. **Split the work up by topic:** Teaching online is an opportunity to move away from the traditional model where every teacher teaches every subject (or every topic within their subject). It's also an opportunity to move away from the idea that students should have the same teacher all year long. Consider splitting a fifteen-week semester into five three-week workshops, where students focus on one topic with one teacher and then rotate to another. This helps expose students to several different teachers and perspectives. And it allows the teachers to become experts in teaching a specific topic that they can constantly test, refine, and improve for the next rotation of students.

TIP 99
Understand What Burnout Is (and Isn't)

Teaching is a tough gig, and burnout among teachers is a real and serious issue. As teachers, we get tired. We get frustrated. And some days are really, really hard. But that doesn't necessarily mean we're burned out.

According to psychologist Herbert Freudenberger (as cited in Brown, 2020), *burnout* can include any of the following components.

- **Emotional exhaustion:** The fatigue that comes from caring too much for too long

- **Decreased sense of accomplishment:** Feeling like nothing you do makes any difference

- **Depersonalization:** Depletion of empathy, caring, or compassion

Do any of the preceding components sound familiar to you as a teacher? If you're struggling with burnout, find a therapist or someone else knowledgeable regarding burnout who you can talk to or who can point you in the right direction. Burnout is real, and there are real solutions that can help. You're not alone!

TIP 100
Surround Yourself With Good People

There's nothing better you can do for your day-to-day teaching, and your career, than to surround yourself with good people. As Adam Grant (2013) states, "Three decades of research shows that receiving support from colleagues is a robust antidote to burnout. Having a support network of teachers is huge" (p. 177).

Surround yourself with people you can learn from. People you can share stories with. People you can go to when you need to laugh, cry, vent, or scream. People who lift you up and cheer you on. People who feed your soul. (See figure 11.2.)

With our kids, my wife and I talk about choosing to be with and listen to the people who "fill your bucket" (and letting go of and not listening to the ones who empty it). Know your "bucket-filling" people, turn to them, and feed those relationships.

And remember: to another teacher, that person is *you*.

Figure 11.2: Surround yourself with good people.

Where to Go From Here

As someone who travels to work with educators at all levels, I've flown on enough airplanes to know by heart the advice about what to do if oxygen masks are ever needed. Adults traveling with children should put their oxygen masks on first, and then take care of their children. The logic is clear: if you don't take care of yourself, you may not be in the best position to help a child who needs you.

Life as a teacher involves a lot of stress. There's our own stress because of all the tasks we must complete to deliver our classes, and there's the stress we often take on for our students and their families. To be highly effective, we must remember to take care of ourselves—physically, mentally, and emotionally. We have to put on our oxygen masks first.

Reflect on the tips in this chapter. To what degree do you currently achieve the goal in each tip? Are there some tips you are interested in using in your classes? How would you implement them? Figure 11.3 has space for notes on your reflections.

Tips in This Chapter	To What Degree Are You Already Following the Tip?	Your Plans for Implementing the Tip
Stand up!	☐ Already nailing it! ☐ Following it some but should do more. ☐ Not following it at all but should try. ☐ Not following it at all and not interested.	
Lean on others for help.	☐ Already nailing it! ☐ Following it some but should do more. ☐ Not following it at all but should try. ☐ Not following it at all and not interested.	

Figure 11.3: Reflection chart for chapter 11. continued ▶

Tips In This Chapter	To What Degree Are You Already Following the Tip?	Your Plans for Implementing the Tip
Set time boundaries.	☐ Already nailing it! ☐ Following it some but should do more. ☐ Not following it at all but should try. ☐ Not following it at all and not interested.	
Picture your happy place (and put a frame around it).	☐ Already nailing it! ☐ Following it some but should do more. ☐ Not following it at all but should try. ☐ Not following it at all and not interested.	
Don't compare your insides to someone else's outsides.	☐ Already nailing it! ☐ Following it some but should do more. ☐ Not following it at all but should try. ☐ Not following it at all and not interested.	
Ditch the guilt.	☐ Already nailing it! ☐ Following it some but should do more. ☐ Not following it at all but should try. ☐ Not following it at all and not interested.	
Share the work.	☐ Already nailing it! ☐ Following it some but should do more. ☐ Not following it at all but should try. ☐ Not following it at all and not interested.	

Understand what burnout is (and isn't).	☐ Already nailing it! ☐ Following it some but should do more. ☐ Not following it at all but should try. ☐ Not following it at all and not interested.	
Surround yourself with good people.	☐ Already nailing it! ☐ Following it some but should do more. ☐ Not following it at all but should try. ☐ Not following it at all and not interested.	

*Visit **go.SolutionTree.com/technology** for a free reproducible version of this figure.*

If you want to go beyond the tips in this chapter and dig deeper into taking care of yourself, you could begin your exploration by considering these two resources.

1. Try any of Tina Boogren's books on self-care for educators. One good place to start is *180 Days of Self-Care for Busy Educators* (Boogren, 2020). Each week, there are a small (manageable) number of self-care activities to implement.

2. In *For All You Do: Self-Care and Encouragement for Teachers,* Peter Mishler (2021) draws on his own teaching life (his current record is two weeks of "teaching bliss" at the beginning of a new class before the stress kicks in) to reflect on why he so loves teaching. His stories and reflections take self-care seriously and can motivate you to do the same.

On the topic of sharing the work, there are many resources on how to collaborate successfully, including *Teacher Teamwork: How Do We Make It Work?* by Margaret Searle and Marilyn Swartz (2015).

Final Thoughts

With much of our days and nights spent online, there is no shortage of opportunities to connect, learn, and grow in the virtual space. As teachers, the challenge is not how to get students online and learning but how to get and keep them engaged, build strong relationships with them, and ensure that they master the academic content necessary to pursue happy, productive lives.

I hope that this book has given you several ideas and strategies that you can use tomorrow, next week, and throughout your career. Perhaps you've felt validated by some of the ideas in this book, as they are in line with what you are already doing. And, hopefully, you've been inspired by some of the ideas in this book and now have a plethora of strategies that you can implement *immediately* to be a highly effective online teacher who (as the title suggests) helps students think, learn, and grow—no matter where they are!

Which leads us to . . . the last tip!

TIP 101
Create the World as It Can Be

I hope you have found this book to be both practical and inspiring, and a helpful step in becoming a highly effective online teacher. Moreover, I hope it helps us on our journey that helps us move beyond, "How do we take the traditional ways of teaching and put them online?" to instead build a new reality to educate students in a multitude of ways that work for them.

As you envision the future, and your students' lives and existence in it, imagine the world not as it is, but *as it can be*. A world where students log on and instantly feel like they are part of an important community of learners. A world where students feel safe to take risks, receive feedback, and grow alongside other students and their teacher (that's you!), separated only by a thin screen. A world that no longer requires students to sit together in rows in the same location, but where they can come from all over the world, celebrate and learn from their unique differences, and bring that learning back to their communities—all while led by a teacher who connects with them, validates them, and shows them a world that they can help make better.

Together, let's go create it.

References and Resources

Advaney, M. (2017, May 6). *To talk or not to talk that is the question.* Accessed at https://youth-time.eu/to-talk-or-not-to-talk-that-is-the-question-at-least-70-percent-of -communication-is-non-verbal/ on December 14, 2021.

Albright, D. (2018, March 7). 7 reasons your videos need subtitles [Blog post]. *Uscreen.* Accessed at www.uscreen.tv/blog/7-reasons-videos-need-subtitles-infographic on April 21, 2021.

AllThingsPLC. (n.d.). *Identifying essential standards.* Accessed at www.allthingsplc.info/files /uploads/identifying-essential-standards-presentation.pdf on April 13, 2021.

Aungst, G. (2014, September 4). Using Webb's depth of knowledge to increase rigor [Blog post]. *Edutopia.* Accessed at www.edutopia.org/blog/webbs-depth-knowledge-increase -rigor-gerald-aungst on April 19, 2021.

Baer, D. (2015). *Google's genius futurist has one theory that he says will rule the future—and it's a little terrifying.* Accessed at www.businessinsider.com/ray-kurzweil-law-of-accelerating -returns-2015-5 on December 23, 2021.

Boogren, T. H. (2020). 180 days of self-care for busy educators. Bloomington, IN: Solution Tree Press.

Brendtro, L. K., Brokenleg, M., & Van Bockern, S. (2019). Reclaiming youth at risk: Futures of promise (3rd ed.). Bloomington, IN: Solution Tree Press.

Brown, B. (Host). (2020, October 14). Brené with Emily and Amelia Nagoski on burnout and how to complete the stress cycle [Audio podcast episode]. In Unlocking Us. Accessed at https://brenebrown.com/podcast /brene-with-emily-and-amelia-nagoski-on-burnout-and-how-to-complete-the-stress-cycle on April 13, 2021.

Budge, K. M., & Parrett, W. H. (2018). Disrupting poverty: Five powerful classroom practices. Alexandria, VA: Association for Supervision and Curriculum Development.

Burgess, C. (2016, September 21). How to frame your webcam video like a pro [Blog post]. *envatotuts+.* Accessed at https://photography.tutsplus.com/tutorials/how-to-frame-your -webcam-video-like-a-pro--cms-27228 on April 13, 2021.

ChaseLearning.org. (n.d.). *5 ways to move toward culturally responsive learning for students.* Accessed at https://www.chaselearning.org/single-post/2018/01/11/5-ways-to-move -toward-culturally-responsive-learning-for-students on September 20, 2021.

Chenoweth, R. (2019). *Rudine Sims Bishop: 'Mother' of multicultural children's literature.* Accessed at https://ehe.osu.edu/news/listing/rudine-sims-bishop-diverse-childrens-books on April 14, 2021.

Clouse, J. (2021, May 9). How to build an online community (and why I'm all in on Circle) [Blog post]. *JayClouse.com.* Accessed at https://jayclouse.com/how-to-build-an-online-community/ on February 17, 2022.

Cohn-Vargas, B. (2021). *How students can meet their peers all over the world.* Accessed at www.edutopia.org/article/how-students-can-meet-their-peers-all-over-world on December 23, 2021.

Colburn, L., & Beggs, L. (2021). *The wraparound guide*: How to gather student voice, build community partnerships, and cultivate hope. Bloomington, IN: Solution Tree Press.

Coleman, M. (2013). Empowering family-teacher partnerships: Building connections within diverse communities. Los Angeles: SAGE.

Collado, W., Hollie, S., Isiah, R., Jackson, Y., Muhammad, A., Reeves, D., & Williams, K. C. (2021). Beyond conversations about race: A guide for discussions with students, teachers, and communities. Bloomington, IN: Solution Tree Press.

Cooper, D. (2022). Rebooting assessment: A practical guide for balancing conversations, performances, and products. Bloomington, IN: Solution Tree Press.

DeVito, M. (2016). *Factors influencing student engagement* [Thesis, Sacred Heart University]. EDL Sixth Year Theses. https://digitalcommons.sacredheart.edu/edl/11/

Ditch That Textbook. (2020, April 17). Remote learning tips from an online teacher [Video file]. Accessed at https://www.youtube.com/watch?v=NsVQpsL0s4g on February 17, 2022.

Doorey, M. (2021). *George A. Miller: American psychologist.* Accessed at www.britannica.com /biography/George-A-Miller on April 13, 2021.

Eller, J. F., & Hierck, T. (2022). *Trauma-sensitive leadership: Creating a safe and predictable school environment.* Bloomington, IN: Solution Tree Press.

Fisher, D., Frey, N., Amador, O., & Assof, J. (2019). The teacher clarity playbook: A hands-on guide to creating learning intentions and success criteria for organized, effective instruction, grades K–12. Thousand Oaks, CA: Corwin.

Fisher, D., Frey, N., & Hattie, J. (2020). *The distance learning playbook, grades K–12: Teaching for engagement and impact in any setting.* Thousand Oaks, CA: Corwin.

Flynn, M. (2020, October 12). Improve your laptop camera mobility for remote teaching [Video file]. Accessed at www.youtube.com/watch?v=5JPVEa0Lq_E on April 13, 2021.

Fogarty, R. J., & Pete, B. M. (2011). *Supporting differentiated instruction: A professional learning communities approach.* Bloomington, IN: Solution Tree Press.

France, P. E. (2021). Humanizing distance learning: Centering equity and humanity in times of crisis. Thousand Oaks, CA: Corwin.

Francis, E. M. (2022). Deconstructing depth of knowledge: A method and model for deeper teaching and learning. Bloomington, IN: Solution Tree Press.

Gates, B. (1995). *The road ahead.* New York: Viking.

Graham, J. (2020, April 11). Six tips for looking great in a Zoom meeting. *USA Today.* Accessed at https://www.usatoday.com/story/tech/2020/04/11/zoom-meetings-go-better -these-6-tips-look-your-best/5125980002/ on February 16, 2022.

Grant, A. M. (2013). *Give and take: A revolutionary approach to success.* New York: Viking.

Hammond, Z. (2020, April 3). *Moving beyond the packet: Creating more culturally responsive distance learning experiences* [Webinar]. Culturally Responsive Teaching and the Brain. Accessed at https://crtandthebrain.com/about/ on October 3, 2021.

Hayat, M. U. (2020). *Remote learning for students who don't have internet access in 2020.* Accessed at https://elearningindustry.com/remote-learning-students-dont-have-internet -access-2020 on April 14, 2021.

Hellerich, K. (2020, August 20). 3 ways to build relationships—in person or virtually. *Edutopia.* Accessed at https://www.edutopia.org/article/3-ways-build-relationships-person -or-virtually on February 17, 2022.

Heyck-Merlin, M. (2021). The together teacher: Plan ahead, get organized, and save time! (2nd ed.). Hoboken, NJ: Jossey-Bass.

Hooker, C. (2020). *Strategies for assessing students remotely.* Accessed at www.techlearning.com /how-to/strategies-for-assessing-students-remotely on April 14, 2021.

Jarzabek, B. (2020, October 5). 4 tricks for building relationships during remote learning. *We Are Teachers.* Accessed at https://www.weareteachers.com/building-relationships -remote-learning/ on February 16, 2022.

Jung, C. (1981). *Collected works of C. G. Jung, Vol. 17: The development of personality.* Princeton, NJ: Princeton University Press.

Kaufman, T. (n.d.). Family engagement and student success: What the research says. *Understood.* Accessed at https://www.understood.org/articles/en/family-engagement-and -student-success on February 17, 2022.

Kennedy, G. (2020, May). *What is student engagement in online learning . . . and how do I know when it is there? Parkville, Victoria, Australia:* Melbourne Centre for the Study of Higher Education. Accessed at https://melbourne-cshe.unimelb.edu.au/__data/assets/pdf_ file/0004/3362125/student -engagement-online-learning_final.pdf on February 16, 2022.

Kise, J. A. G. (2021). *Doable differentiation: Twelve strategies to meet the needs of all learners.* Bloomington, IN: Solution Tree Press.

Kondo, M. (2016). *Spark joy: An illustrated master class on the art of organizing and tidying up.* Berkeley, CA: Ten Speed Press.

Kurzweil, R. (2001, March 7). The law of accelerating returns. *Kurzweil*. Accessed at www.kurzweilai.net/the-law-of-accelerating-returns on April 13, 2021.

LaClaire, H. (2020). *Brunswick schools launch equity initiative*. Accessed at www.pressherald.com/2020/11/01/brunswick-schools-launch-equity-initiative/ on December 17, 2021.

Levy, D. (2020). Teaching effectively with Zoom: A practical guide to engage your students and help them learn. Cambridge, MA: Author.

Lufkin, B. (2020, April 8). *Five tips to look your best on video calls*. Accessed at https://www.bbc.com/worklife/article/20200407-zoom-five-tips-to-look-your-best-on-video-calls on February 17, 2022.

Major, A. (2020). *How to develop culturally responsive teaching for distance learning*. Accessed at www.kqed.org/mindshift/55941/how-to-develop-culturally-responsive-teaching-for-distance-learning on April 14, 2021.

Mauldin, M. M. (2017). *Feedback revolution: Building relationships and boosting results*. Denver, CO: Fillmore Press.

May, R. (1972). *Power and innocence: A search for the sources of violence*. New York: Norton.

McCallum, D. (2015). *The feedback-friendly classroom*. Markham, Ontario, Canada: Pembroke.

McCarthy, J. (2018). *Extending the silence*. Accessed at www.edutopia.org/article/extending-silence on April 13, 2021.

McCombs School of Business. (2020, March 25). *7 ways to look your best online | McCombs School of Business* [Video file]. Accessed at https://www.youtube.com/watch?v=9Tj8NTHpkOs on February 17, 2022.

Mening, R. (2016). *A story from a dinner party Winston Churchill's mother attended over a century ago illustrates what it means to be a charismatic leader*. Accessed at www.businessinsider.com/charismatic-leadership-tips-from-history-2016-10 on April 13, 2021.

Mishler, P. (2021). For all you do: Self-care and encouragement for teachers. Kansas City, MO: McMeel.

Morris, W. (2020, July 25). How to look good on Zoom: What to wear and where to sit [Blog post]. *Elegant Themes*. Accessed at https://www.elegantthemes.com/blog/business/how-to-look-good-on-zoom-what-to-wear-and-where-to-sit on February 16, 2022.

Nickelsen, L., & Dickson, M. (2019). *Teaching with the instructional cha-chas: 4 steps to make learning stick*. Bloomington, IN: Solution Tree Press.

O'Block, T. (2020, July 27). How to build relationships with your students virtually & in the classroom [Blog post]. *Lessons for Little Ones*. Accessed at https://lessons4littleones.com/2020/07/27/how-to-build-relationships-with-your-students-virtually-in-the-classroom/ on February 17, 2022.

O'Donnell, W. (2020, June 18). Tips from a filmmaker about looking great on Zoom [Blog post]. *Wes O'Donnell*. Accessed at https://medium.com/the-innovation/tips-from-a-filmmaker-about-looking-great-on-zoom-95afaedcf56e on April 13, 2021.

Occidental College. (n.d.). *Settings to prevent Zoom-bombing.* Accessed at www.oxy.edu /offices-services/its/services/video-conferencing/settings-prevent-zoom-bombing on April 13, 2021.

Palloff, R. M., & Pratt, K. (1999). Building learning communities in cyberspace: Effective strategies for the online classroom. San Francisco: Jossey-Bass.

Palloff, R. M., & Pratt, K. (2007). Building online learning communities: Effective strategies for the virtual classroom (2nd ed.). San Francisco: Jossey-Bass.

Parker, D. (2019). Building bridges: Engaging students at risk through the power of relationships. Bloomington, IN: Solution Tree Press.

Pica, R. (2015). *What if everybody understood child development?* Thousand Oaks, CA: Corwin.

Rawls, J. D., & Robinson, J. (2019). Youth culture power: A #HipHopEd guide to building teacher-student relationships and increasing student engagement. New York: Lang.

Reed, K. M. (2017). On-camera coach: Tools and techniques for business professionals in a video-driven world. Hoboken, NJ: Wiley.

Richards, E., Aspegren, E., & Mansfield, E. (2021, February 4). A year into the pandemic, thousands of students still can't get reliable WiFi for school. The digital divide remains worse than ever. *USA Today.* Accessed at https://www.usatoday.com/story/news/education /2021/02/04/covid-online-school-broadband-internet-laptops/3930744001/ on February 17, 2022.

Ripley, D. (2022). The tactical teacher: Proven strategies to positively influence student learning and classroom behavior. Bloomington, IN: Solution Tree Press.

Romano-Arrabito, C. (2019). To manage stress, teachers need to prioritize themselves. Start with self-care. EdSurge. Accessed at www.edsurge.com/news/2019-12-18-to-manage-stress-teachers-need-to-prioritize-themselves-start-with-self-care on March 8, 2022.

Scalise, K. (2012). *Creating innovative assessment items and test forms.* In R. W. Lissitz & H. Jiao (Eds.), *Computers and their impact on state assessments: Recent history and predictions for the future* (pp. 133–156). Charlotte, NC: Information Age.

Searle, M., & Swartz, M. (2015). Teacher teamwork: How do we make it work? Alexandria, VA: Association for Supervision and Curriculum Development.

Serravallo, J. (2020). Connecting with students online. Portsmouth, NH: Heinemann.

Smith, D. (2020, February 18). Nonverbal communication: How body language & nonverbal cues are key [Blog post]. *Lifesize.* Accessed at www.lifesize.com/en/blog /speaking-without-words on April 13, 2021.

Smith, D., Fisher, D., & Frey, N. (2019). The on-your-feet guide to building authentic student-teacher relationships. Thousand Oaks, CA: Corwin.

Sprecher, M. (n.d.). 6 ways to look *really* good on Zoom [Blog post]. *Remote Bliss.* Accessed at https://remotebliss.com/how-to-look-good-on-zoom/ on February 17, 2022.

Strain, K. (2020). *How much of communication is really nonverbal?* Accessed at www.pgi.com /blog/2020/03/how-much-of-communication-is-really-nonverbal/ on December 22, 2021.

Teach and GO. (n.d.). *10 must have classroom props for online teaching.* Accessed at https:// teach
andgo.com/blog/props-online-teaching on April 13, 2021.

Thompkins-Bigelow, J. (2020). *Your name is a song.* Seattle, WA: The Innovation Press.

Tri-City Medical Center. (n.d.). *Why everyone keeps saying "sitting is the new smoking."* Accessed at www.tricitymed.org/2017/07/everyone-keeps-saying-sitting-new-smoking on April 21, 2021.

Vogels, E. A., Perrin, A., Rainie, L., & Anderson, M. (2020, April 30). 53% of Americans say the internet has been essential during the COVID-19 outbreak. *Pew Research Center.* Accessed at https://www.pewresearch.org /internet/2020/04/30/53-of-americans-say-the-internet-has-been-essential-during-the -covid-19-outbreak/ on February 17, 2022.

Vulpo, M. (2021). *20 teachers who went above and beyond for their students during the Coronavirus pandemic.* Accessed at www.eonline.com/news/1146382/17-teachers-going -above-and-beyond-during-the-coronavirus on April 13, 2021.

Waddell, K. J. (2018). *You do, we do, I do: A strategy for productive struggle.* Accessed at www.ascd.org/ascd-express/vol14/num11/you-do-we-do-i-do-a-strategy-for-productive -struggle.aspx on April 13, 2021.

Wagner, J. (1995). *Edith Ann: My life, so far.* New York: Hyperion.

Walden, J. (2021, July 7). Best practice tips for using Zoom [Blog post]. *Generation Digital.* Accessed at https://www.gend.co/blog/best-practice-tips-for-using-zoom on February 17, 2022.

Walden University. (n.d.). *The importance of emotional engagement in elementary education.* Accessed at https://www.waldenu.edu/online-bachelors-programs/bs-in-elementary -education/resource/the-importance-of-emotional-engagement-in-elementary-education #:~:text=Simply%20put%2C%20emotional%20engagement%20is,they%20enjoy%20 that%20participation%20more on February 17, 2022.

Waterford.org. (2018, November 1). *How parent involvement leads to student success.* Accessed at https://www.waterford.org/education/how-parent-involvment-leads-to-student-success on February 17, 2022.

Webb, N. L. (1997). *Criteria for alignment of expectations and assessments in mathematics and science education* [Research Monograph No. 6]. Madison, WI: National Institute for Science Education. Accessed at https://files.eric.ed.gov/fulltext/ED414305.pdf on March 6, 2021.

Wiseman, R., Fisher, D., Frey, N., & Hattie, J. (2020). The distance learning playbook for parents: How to support your child's academic, social, and emotional development in any setting. Thousand Oaks, CA: Corwin.

Wright, J. (2020). *Should your students be talking in class? (The answer is yes!).* Accessed at https://ctlonline.org/should-your-students-be-talking-in-class-the-answer-is-yes/ on December 17, 2021.

Wong, H. K., & Wong, R. T. (2018). *The first days of school: How to be an effective teacher* (5th ed.). Mountain View, CA: Wong.

Index

A

agendas, 96
American Sign Language (ASL), 39
announcement reader, 57–58
appointments, making and taking, 135
assessing students
    about, 105
    advice from students, 114
    assessing via video, 110
    channels for asking for help, 113
    feedback, specific and timely, 111
    feedback via video or voice
        recording, 112
    monitoring faces and body
        language, 106
    reflection chart for, 115–117
    rethinking cheating, 114
    taking a photo, 108
    using hand gestures, emojis, and
        polls, 107
    using surveys, 109
    where to go from here, 115, 117
assigning versus inviting, 65

B

backgrounds
    being conscious about camera
        backgrounds, 121
    looking good on camera, 11
    surroundings, help students get to
        know your, 24
batching, 150
Bishop, R., 126
blended learning, 95
boundaries, setting time boundaries,
    150

Brown, L., 119
building relationships with students.
    See relationships
burnout, 155

C

"camera on" moments, 121
cameras. *See also* looking good on
    camera
    considering a mic and a good
        camera, 13
    lighting and, 7–8
    positioning, 9, 10
    props, 11, 12, 25, 39, 140
    using multiple monitors, 54–55
care packages, 136
chair yoga, 41
channels for asking for help, 113
chat areas
    classroom jobs, 57
    monitoring, 52
cheating, rethinking, 114
checking in
    on parents and guardians, 68
    on students, 86
chunking, 40, 93
class procedures, establishing, 50
classroom jobs, 57–58
classroom management
    about, 47
    advice from students, 59
    being consistent, 56
    classroom jobs, turning into
        online roles, 57–58
    definition of, 47
    establishing class procedures, 50
    establishing routines, 51

monitoring the chat, 52
prerecorded welcome
    messages, 59
reason behind the reason, 123
reflection chart for, 60–62
safety settings, 53
setting high expectations, 48–49
stand up, 148
using multiple monitors, 54–55
where to go from here, 60, 62
clothing and jewelry, 14
cohosts, 27
collaboration, 114, 154
community. *See also* creating a
    community
    definition of, 88
    sample phrases to build
        community, 78
comparisons, 152
consistency, 56
COVID-19 pandemic and teaching
    online, 2
creating a community
    about, 77
    acknowledge which communities
        we're a part of, 82
    advice from students, 87
    breaking the class up into
        smaller teams that can work
        together, 83
    connecting with the quiet
        ones, 84
    create ways to see and hear each
        other, 85
    getting students and yourself out
        into the community, 80

have students check in on
    students, 86
inviting special guests, 79
planning virtual gatherings, 87
reflection chart for, 88–90
teacher feature, 80–81
use of the word community, 78
where to go from here, 88, 90
creating the world as it can be, 162
culturally responsive teaching, 125
curiosity, promoting, 71

D

Dickson, M., 93
differentiating learning
    about, 133
    advice from students, 142
    appointments, making and
        taking, 135
    asking three questions, 139
    online office hours, holding, 134
    pause and go back strategy, 137
    preloading students with
        information, 142
    reflection chart for, 143–145
    sending care packages, 136
    subtitles, adding, 141
    understanding depth of
        knowledge, 138
    visuals, surrounding students
        with, 140
    where to go from here, 143, 145
Digital Divide, 129
diversity
    embracing race and diversity, 124
    in videos and photo selections,
        126
do not disturb signs, 15

E

emails
    sample contact preferences
        email, 72
    sample email to parents and
        guardians, 64
emotional exhaustion, 155
engaging students
    about, 33
    advice from students, 42
    greeting students, 34
    increasing your enthusiasm, 37
    interactive videos, 38
    keeping 'em moving, 41
    mixing it up, 40
    phone calls home, 42

reflection chart for, 43–45
students' names, 35
using cards and hand signals, 39
waving your arms, 36
where to go from here, 43, 45
English learners (ELs)
    and adding subtitles, 141
    and breaking the class into smaller
        teams, 83
    and preloading students with
        information, 142
    and using a translator, 73
    and using props, 12
    and using visuals, 140
    and video backgrounds, 11
ensuring equity
    about, 119
    access to internet and reliable
        devices, 128
    advice from students, 128
    camera backgrounds, 121
    creating teams with equity in
        mind, 127
    culturally responsive teaching,
        125
    diversity in video and photo
        selections, 126
    embracing race and diversity, 124
    finding the reason behind the
        reason, 123
    knowing your students' living
        situations, 122
    pronouncing students' names
        right and learning to say "hello,"
        120
    reflection chart for, 129–131
    teacher feature, 122
    where to go from here, 129,
        131–132
enthusiasm, increasing, 37
equity. *See* ensuring equity
essential standards, 92
expectations, 48–49

F

family projects, 70
fast fingers, 51
feedback
    assessing students, 111, 115
    via video or voice recording, 112
Feedback Revolution (Mauldin), 111
filling your bucket, 156
First Days of School, The (Wong and
    Wong), 48

Fisher, D., 103

G

Gates, B., 129
Grant, A., 156
greeting students
    classroom jobs, 57
    engaging students, 34
    pronouncing students' names
        right and learning to say "hello,"
        120
guardians. *See* parents and guardians
guilt, ditching, 153

H

Hammond, Z., 125
hand signals, 39
headphones, 11
help
    appointments, making and
        taking, 135
    channels for asking for help, 113
    creating ways for parents and
        guardians to help, 69
    online office hours, holding, 134

I

I do, we do, you do, 66, 67
interactive videos, 38
internet access, 128
introduction
    about this book, 3–4
    power of online teaching, 1–3
    remembering what teachers do, 4
inviting versus assigning, 65
"Itty-Bitty Dot, The," 1

J

Jerome, J., 21
Jung, C., 30

K

Kondo, M., 101

L

lessons. *See* organizing your lessons
Levine, J., 148
lighting
    looking good on camera, 7–8
    using multiple monitors, 55
listening, talking less and listening
    more, 97
live classes, 95
looking directly into your camera, 6
looking good on camera
    about, 5
    advice from students, 15

camera at eye level, 9
considering a mic and a good camera, 13
distance to camera, 10
do not disturb signs, 15
let the light shine on you, 7–8
looking directly into your camera, 6
mixing up your background, 11
professional image for, 14
reflection chart for, 16–17
teacher feature, 11
using props, 12
where to go from here, 16, 18
lookout partners, 85, 86

M
managing your classroom. *See* classroom management
Mauldin, M., 111
May, R., 88
micro-chunking, 40
microphones, 11, 13
movement
keeping 'em moving, 41
stand up, 148
using hand gestures/signals, 39, 107
waving your arms, 36
"mystery locations," 11

N
names
saying students' names, 35
students' names and learning to say "hello," pronouncing, 120
need to know and nice to know standards, 92
new reality, 162
Nickelsen, L., 93
nonverbal communication
engaging students, 36
monitoring faces and body language, 106
using cards and hand signals, 39
using hand gestures, emojis, and polls, 107

O
office hours, 134
organizing your lessons
about, 91
advice from students, 96
boil it down, but don't water it down, 92
chunking it, 93

keeping it simple/simplicity, 94
providing an agenda, 96
reflection chart for, 101–103
relating lessons to their world, 99
separating when you need to be there and when you don't, 95
showing what different levels of success look like, 100
talking less and listening more, 97
think time, 98
where to go from here, 101, 103

P
parents and guardians
about, 63
advice from parents, 73
checking in on parents and guardians, 68
creating ways for parents and guardians to help, 69
giving parents and guardians questions they can ask, 64
including parents and guardians in family projects, 70
inviting versus assigning, 65
preferred method of contact, 72
promoting curiosity, 71
reflection chart for, 74–76
sample email to parents and guardians, 64
teacher feature, 70
teaching parents and guardians simple teaching strategies, 66–67
use of term, 63
using a translator, 73
where to go from here, 74, 76
parking lots, 113
pause and go back strategy, 38, 137
phone calls home
checking in on parents and guardians, 68
engaging students, 42
preferred method of contact, 72
photographs
assessing students, 108
diversity in video and photo selections, 126
picture your happy place, 151
preloading students with information, 142
pre-recorded classes, 95
props
differentiating learning, 140
mixing up your background, 11

stuff, help students get to know your, 25
using cards and hand signals, 39
using props, 12
pulling in parents and guardians. *See* parents and guardians

Q
questions for parents and guardians to ask, 64

R
race and diversity, embracing, 124
"Rappin' Mathematician, The," 1–2
realia, 12
reason behind the reason, finding, 123
recorded messages
feedback via video or voice recording, 112
prerecorded welcome messages, 59
relationships
about, 19
advice from students, 29
being interested and interesting, 21
connecting with the quiet ones, 84
definition of, 19
reflection chart for, 30–32
showing up, 28–29
stories, help students get to know your, 23
student cohosts, 27
students' interests, 26
stuff, help students get to know your, 25
surroundings, help students to know your, 24
taking the time, 20
teacher feature, 25
three types of relationships in a class, 22
where to go from here, 30, 32
remembering what teachers do, 4
ring lights, 55
routines, establishing, 51

S
Sackman-Ebuwa, D., 11
safety settings, 53
Sanchez, S., 54–55
screen-free afternoons, 80
self-care. *See* taking care of yourself
sharing the work, 154

sign language, 39
simplicity, 94
special guests, 79, 82
standards, 92
stories, help students get to know your, 23
students. *See also* engaging students
  checking in on, 86
  cohosting duties, 27
  connecting with the quiet ones, 84
  consistency and, 56
  greeting students, 34
  knowing your students' interests, 26
  knowing your students' living situations, 122
  relating lessons to their world, 99
  students' names and learning to say "hello," pronouncing, 120
  students' names, saying, 35
  three types of relationships in a class, 22
stuff, help students get to know your, 25
success, showing different levels of, 100
surround yourself with good people, 156
surroundings, help students get to know your, 24
surveys/polls
  using hand gestures, emojis, and polls, 107
  using surveys, 109
swivel trays, 12

T

taking care of yourself
  about, 147
  advice from students, 153
  comparisons, don't compare your insides to someone else's outsides, 152
  ditching the guilt, 153
  leaning on others, 149
  picturing your happy place, 151
  reflection chart for, 157–159
  setting time boundaries, 150
  sharing the work, 154
  standing up, 148
  surrounding yourself with good people, 156
  understanding what burnout is and isn't, 155
  where to go from here, 157, 159
talking head syndrome, 36
teaching strategies, 66–67. *See also* organizing your lessons
Teaching with the Instructional Cha-Chas (Nickelsen and Dickson), 93
teams
  breaking the class into smaller teams, 83
  equity and, 127
  sharing the work, 154
technology/devices
  access to internet and reliable devices, 128
  laptop camera at eye level, 9
  using multiple monitors, 54–55
think time, 66, 98
time monitor, 57
tips
  for assessing students, 106–114
  for building relationships with students, 20–29
  for creating community, 78–87
  for creating the world as it can be, 162
  for differentiating learning, 134–142
  for engaging students, 34–42
  for ensuring equity, 120–128
  for looking good on camera, 6–15
  for managing your classroom, 48–59
  for organizing your lessons, 92–100
  for pulling in parents and guardians, 64–73
  for remembering what teachers do, 4
  for taking care of yourself, 148–156
Tomlin, L., 30
translators, 73

V

videos
  assessing students, 110
  diversity in video and phot selections, 126
  feedback via video or voice recording, 112
  pause and go back strategy, 38, 137
  prerecorded welcome messages, 59
  pre-recorded classes, 95
  subtitles, 141
virtual gatherings, 87
visuals
  differentiating learning, 140
  picture your happy place, 151

W

"Wacky Math Hour," 2
waving your arms, 36
Webb's Depth of Knowledge (DOK), 138, 139
welcome videos/messages, 59
windows and looking food on camera, 7–8
windows and mirrors, concept of, 126
Wong, H., 47, 48
Wong, R., 47, 48

Y

York-Barr, J., 97

Z

Zoom
  COVID-19 pandemic and, 2
  design guides, 18
  Zoom-bombing, 53

Owning It
Alex Kajitani

Today's fast-changing culture presents a great challenge—and a great opportunity—in schools and in the teaching profession. With *Owning It*, you will discover an array of easy-to-implement strategies designed to help you excel in your classroom, at your school, and in your community.
BKF835

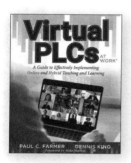

Virtual PLCs at Work®
Paul C. Farmer and Dennis King

As the educational landscape continues to evolve, ensure your PLC evolves right along with it. With this resource you'll acquire an abundance of tools and tips for maintaining your PLC in a virtual environment along with proven best practices to help your team thrive beyond the four walls of your school.
BKG028

Capturing the Classroom
Ellen I. Linnihan

Harness the power of video to cultivate equity, create stability, and reach students any time. With *Capturing the Classroom*, you will learn concrete and doable ways to record lectures, classroom discussions, tutorials, review sessions, and more to support any content area or curriculum.
BKF998

Shifting to Digital
James A. Bellanca, Gwendolyn Battle Lavert, and Kate Bellanca

Rely on *Shifting to Digital* to give you clear, concise, and helpful answers to all of your remote teaching questions. This comprehensive guide provides specific strategies for planning high-engagement instruction, handling technology, assessing collaboration and assignments, and more.
BKG006

Solution Tree | Press
a division of
Solution Tree

Visit SolutionTree.com or call 800.733.6786 to order.

GL⬤BAL PD

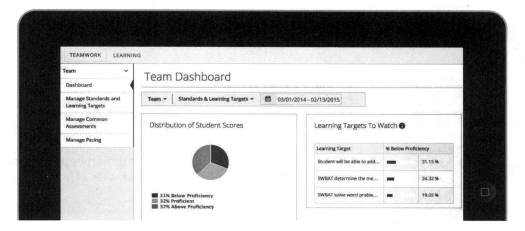

The **Power to Improve**
Is in Your Hands

Global PD gives educators focused and goals-oriented training from top experts. You can rely on this innovative online tool to improve instruction in every classroom.

- Get unlimited, on-demand access to guided video and book content from top Solution Tree authors.

- Improve practices with personalized virtual coaching from PLC-certified trainers.

- Customize learning based on skill level and time commitments.